W9-BAP-569

THE CATHOLIC PASSION

THE CATHOLIC PASSION

REDISCOVERING THE POWER AND BEAUTY OF THE FAITH

DAVID SCOTT

LOYOLAPRESS.
CHICAGO

LOYOLAPRESS.
3441 N. ASHLAND AVENUE
CHICAGO, ILLINOIS 60657
(800) 621-1008
WWW.LOYOLABOOKS.ORG

Nihil Obstat
Reverend John G. Lodge, S.S.L., S.T.D.
Censor Deputatus
May 18, 2005

Imprimatur
Reverend George J. Rassas
Vicar General
Archdiocese of Chicago
May 23, 2005

The *Nihil Obstat* and *Imprimatur* are official declarations that a book is free of doctrinal and moral error. No implication is contained therein that those who have granted the *Nihil Obstat* and *Imprimatur* agree with the content, opinions, or statements expressed. Nor do they assume any legal responsibility associated with publication.

Ex Nihilo, Working Model, intermediate-scale model for the full-scale plaster for the final stone sculpture of *Ex Nihilo,* commissioned as part of *The Creation Sculptures* at Washington National Cathedral. The clay was executed circa 1975-76. Cast marble edition authorized by Washington National Cathedral.

Cover and interior design by Michael Karter
Art direction by Adam Moroschan

Library of Congress Cataloging-in-Publication Data
Scott, David, 1961–
The Catholic passion : rediscovering the power and beauty of the faith / David Scott.
p. cm.
Includes bibliographical references.
ISBN 0-8294-1479-7
1. Catholic Church. I. Title.
BX1751.3.S29 2005
282—dc22

2005014276

Printed in the United States of America
06 07 08 09 10 M-V 10 9 8 7 6 5 4 3 2

For Sarah

CONTENTS

PREFACE

This is a book about Catholics—who we are, what we believe, and why we believe and do the things we do. It is not really intended as a book about Catholicism—that set of dogmas, doctrines, rules, and rituals that makes it one of the great world religions.

Maybe this is a distinction without a difference. It is true that what Catholics do is not easily separated from what Catholicism teaches. But what the faith looks like and how we understand and live that faith depend on where we allow the stress to fall. If the accent is on dogmas and doctrines, the faith will come across one way. Put the accent on the lives and works of flesh-and-blood Catholics, and we will see things differently. The one is not wrong and the other right. They are two ways of trying to understand the same complex reality.

For example, we can quote the Baltimore Catechism: God is an infinitely perfect supreme being who made us to show forth his goodness and to share with us his everlasting happiness in heaven. Or we can talk about Paul Claudel.

One of the nineteenth century's finest poets and playwrights, Claudel also spent forty years as a French diplomat, serving as ambassador to Tokyo, Brussels, and Washington, DC. Early in his life, Claudel fell away from the church, convinced that God was a figment of the imagination of a prescientific world. Nonetheless, out of nostalgia or habit, he went to Mass on Christmas Eve at Notre Dame Cathedral in Paris in 1886. During the service he heard a voice from on high say, "There is a God." It changed his life.

In describing his experience of God's love for him, Claudel once wrote: "Overcome with wonder, I can only say it is madness, it is too much. . . . Look, see God striding across the earth like a sower; he takes his heart in both hands and scatters it over the face of the earth!" Now, Claudel is saying nothing different from what the Baltimore Catechism says. Both statements are beautiful. Both statements are true.

In this book I chose to go with Claudel, to explain Catholicism by way of the experience and faith expressions of real Catholics—saints, composers, poets, playwrights, missionaries, ordinary believers. This approach seems appropriate to Catholicism, which is not a philosophy of life so much as a personal encounter and relationship with a divine person, Jesus. The church's creeds, dogmas, and doctrines are indispensable—they ensure that this encounter with Jesus is true—but if this neat order of rules and laws is the theorem, then Catholicism's proof will always be found in what Catholics think and hope for, how they pray, and what they do with their lives.

That said, this is not a gathering of various personal visions or idiosyncratic approaches to Catholicism. The Catholics you will meet in these pages—and the works of art, literature, and music that are discussed—have been selected to reflect the ancient and authentic faith of Catholic orthodoxy. This book is not about what individual Catholics might wish the church to believe. Instead it is about what the church actually does believe—as that faith is expressed in its Scriptures, prayers, and authoritative teachings.

If this is a book about Catholics, it is also a book for Catholics. It is unfortunate that many of us receive our entire education in the faith at a relatively young age. Often we discover, as did Claudel, that the explanations of Catholic beliefs and practices we learned in Sunday school are inadequate or irrelevant to the cares and demands of our adult lives. On many of the most important questions, the Catholic answers we were given in our youth seem less compelling than the answers offered by scientists, philosophers, politicians, and the mass media. As a consequence, many of us end up drifting away from the faith, finding other things to believe in, other passions to occupy our days.

But the faith was never meant to be something we "graduate" from as we do high school. Our knowledge and understanding of what we believe is meant to deepen as our relationship with Jesus deepens. The early Christians spoke of mystagogy, a kind of lifelong immersion in the mysteries of the faith. This book is a small exercise in twenty-first-century mystagogy.

Whether or not you are Catholic, this book invites you to take another look at the Catholic faith. In this book you have the chance to enter into a conversation with Catholics from every continent and walk of life from the last two thousand years. It is a conversation about the biggest questions—the only ones that matter, really: Who is Jesus? Who is God? Why do we need a church? Who are we, where do we come from, where are we going, and how do we get there?

→ I ←

SON OF MARY, MAN OF HEAVEN

On a chill evening in March 1897, an ex-monk named Charles de Foucauld entered Nazareth, a village in the hill country of Galilee. He had walked about 125 miles in little more than a week since climbing off a steamer in the Mediterranean port of Jaffa. He made his way to Bethlehem and then to Jerusalem, sleeping in fields and begging bread along the way. Charles had come to Nazareth to breathe the same air and to live the same obscure life of poverty and manual labor that Jesus Christ had nineteen centuries before.

Charles was thirty-nine years old and had already led a colorful life. Of French aristocratic blood, he scandalized his family by washing out of the military academy and squandering his inheritance on feeding his extravagant appetites for food, wine, and love. Then, to everyone's surprise, he enlisted in the French army to fight in the deserts of North Africa. Later, he embarked alone on a dangerous and groundbreaking geographical expedition to Morocco.

In the deserts of the Sahara, Charles found God. Coming home, he slowly rededicated himself to the Catholic faith he had been born into and had fallen away from. He went off to live in a monastery in Syria for seven years. He quit that to become a hermit in Nazareth—"to be one with Jesus, to reproduce his life . . . to imitate as perfectly as possible our Lord's hidden life," as he wrote to a friend at the time.

Charles's search for Jesus of Nazareth was the most Catholic of impulses. All Catholics are natives of Nazareth, though most of us will never see the place. In Nazareth, we believe, the creator of the universe took flesh in a woman's womb and became one of us. For thirty years God lived in that village, made his home with a mother and a father, held down a job, and answered to a common name, Jesus. We believe that God came to Nazareth to share his life with the human family he had created, that he came to reveal a plan of love that includes you and me and every person ever born or yet to be born. Here, God came to live a man's life so that we could live God's life.

This is an audacious claim, unique among the world's religions and philosophies. The history of religion is the history of the human search for inner peace, prosperity, and transcendence—in a word, for God. Singular in that history is the Catholic confession that the tables have been turned, that God has come in search of us.

Nazareth is where he came to start looking for us, and from there the name Jesus has gone forth to the ends of the earth. In Guatemala, the people revere him as el Señor Cristo Negro—the Black Christ who suffers with a suffering people. In Mindanao, one of the isles of the Philippines, he is Manluluwas-Kauban, two words that mean every good thing: "He who cares, who gives aid to the hungry, who travels with his people, who protects the persecuted, who pardons sinners; the liberator." In Papua New Guinea, Catholics pray to him simply as Kamungo—"The Big Man."

In every culture and language, the name *Jesus* has brought strong men to their knees, raised up the weak, changed lives, saved people from ruin, made sinners into saints. Jesus of Nazareth has inspired the most exalted achievements of human art and science and formed the spiritual, intellectual, and moral foundation of Western civilization.

The deepest longings of the human heart, Catholics believe, have a single name: Jesus. On his knees in prayer, St. Francis of Assisi once asked: "Who are you, O Lord? And who am I?" The two questions can never be pried apart. Who you are and who I am, and what our respective destinies are, depend on our answer to the question Jesus first put to his disciples and continues to ask men and women in every age: "Who do you say that I am?"

As Charles de Foucauld knew, the answer takes us back to Nazareth—a place so obscure that until Jesus arrived, it had never been mentioned in a single book or included on any map.

"Salvation Is from the Jews"

It was no accident of history that caused Jesus to be born in that time and place. Jesus was born a Jew, of the elect race to whom God first chose to reveal himself, nineteen hundred years before Foucauld's time somewhere in present-day Iraq. Why was Jesus born of this people? Because, as he would later say, "salvation is from the Jews." To know Jesus we must know the history of this special people. For it was in the history of the Jews that God disclosed the purpose and destiny of the world. In its broadest outline, that history reads like this:

The father of the Jewish people was Abraham. God made a covenant with Abraham, vowing to give him a vast land and to make his descendants more numerous than the stars in the sky. God swore he would bestow his blessings, his salvation, on all the nations of the earth through Abraham's children. Abraham's beloved son Isaac bore a child named Jacob. God renewed his covenant with Jacob and changed Jacob's name to Israel. Ten of Jacob's twelve sons and two of Jacob's grandsons in turn became fathers of twelve tribes, which together formed the great nation known as Israel.

The story of God's relationship with the people of Israel reads like an account of a stormy love affair, and indeed it was. Through it all, even when his chosen people wandered astray, God remained true to his promises. But his people's infidelity had terrible consequences. They suffered devastating defeats at the hands of their enemies and saw their kingdom shattered, the twelve tribes scattered in exile, their promised land carved up and overrun by a succession of invaders and occupation forces. Still, they hoped in the Messiah, the Christ ("anointed one") promised by God. The Messiah, they believed, was to ascend the throne of their long-dead king David and reign forever, reuniting the scattered tribes into a single family, a holy kingdom through which God would fulfill his promise to Abraham and bring salvation, God's blessing, to the world.

But the Jews hoped for far more than political restoration. Speaking through his prophets, God had foretold a deeper, more intimate union with his people. He revealed that his love for his people was like the nuptial love of a man for a woman. He promised a new covenant—the coming of a day when he would take the people Israel to himself as a groom cleaves to his bride. "On that day," he said through the prophet Hosea, ". . . you will call me, 'My husband.' . . . . I will take you for my wife forever."

All this history and anticipation formed the backdrop to the drama that unfolded in Nazareth. An angel, a messenger of God, appeared to Mary, a Jewish maiden engaged to a carpenter named Joseph. Catholics remember this moment as the Annunciation, the "announcement." What the angel announced was nothing short of a miracle—that God desired to send his Holy Spirit to "overshadow" Mary and make her pregnant with his Son. The angel later told Joseph to call the boy Jesus—a name that means "God saves." *God saves* is at once his name, his identity, and his mission.

The prophets had referred to Israel as "daughter Zion" and promised that she would one day rejoice to see the coming of her Messiah. In the Annunciation, Mary played that role, representing her people as the virgin daughter who awaits the arrival of her divine groom. Mary even responded with a bridal vow of self-dedication and love: "Here am I, the servant of the Lord; let it be with me according your word."

Catholics call Mary's vow her great *fiat* (Latin for "let it be done"). By her fiat Mary opened herself to God, allowing his plan, his Word, to unfold within her life—within her own body. The child conceived in her by the power of the Holy Spirit would be the Word of God, the Son of God, and the Christ, the long-anticipated Messiah.

From Eden to Nazareth

The Annunciation was more than an episode in the history of Israel. The encounter at Nazareth marked a new chapter in the story of God's relationship with the human race, a story that actually began before the foundation of the world. What Mary assented to was nothing less than the fulfillment of God's eternal design—what the apostle Paul called "the mystery hidden for ages."

All of history led up to that moment at Nazareth. As St. Maximus the Confessor, a monk of seventh-century Constantinople, once sang:

> This is the blessed destiny for which the cosmos was brought into existence. This is the ultimate design which God had in mind before the beginning of anything created—the end foreknown, by reason of which all things exist . . . that everything created by God would finally be in him recollected into the original unity. This is the great mystery that embraces all the aeons . . . that revealed the heart of hearts of the Father's loving kindness, so that he might show to us, in his own person, the ultimate destiny toward which has been created everything that arose and came into being.

The son born of Mary of Nazareth will reveal the blessed destiny of the cosmos, the heart of God, and the purpose of creation. He will reveal that God is not simply a first cause or prime mover of the universe, but rather a loving Father who seeks to wrap all creation in his loving embrace.

That was God's original intent in creating the world, and, indeed, humankind once enjoyed this intimacy with its Father. God created the first man and woman, Adam and Eve, in a garden called Eden, to be the glory of his creation. He made them in his image, as his children, to share in his freedom, holiness, and life. They were to grow in friendship with him, to serve as guardians and ministers of the world he created—to become parents of a worldwide family of God.

At the prompting of the devil, a rebellious angel who disguised himself as a serpent, Adam and Eve lost their nerve. They stopped believing in God's promise of divine life, stopped returning the love the Father had lavished upon them. Instead, they believed the serpent's lie—that they could live without God, that they could be like "gods" themselves.

By rejecting God, our first parents separated themselves and all future generations from the Father. Down through the centuries, the children of Adam and Eve groped in darkness for the love they once had but lost. The empty spaces that God once filled they sought to fill with false idols—wealth, accomplishment, power, and pleasure. But the Father pursued them as a shepherd pursues his lost sheep. He disclosed his marvels in the splendors of creation. He scattered seeds of the truth about him in their philosophies, arts, and religions.

Finally, God made himself known to Abraham and the Jewish people. God gave them a divine law to live by, sent prophets to inspire them, and made them a "light to the nations"—a beacon of hope in a fallen world. His covenant with Abraham was meant to be the first step in the rehabilitation of the human race. Through Israel, God would teach the nations to walk in his ways.

Yet even his chosen people continued to fall. When their prophet Isaiah cried out, "O that you would tear open the heavens and come down," he was confessing the anguish of his people, who knew how desperately they needed God but also the futility of all their efforts to keep his covenant.

At Nazareth, the Father finally tore open the heavens and came down. His children were like the man in Jesus' parable of the good Samaritan—beaten and left for dead on the side of the road, sick unto death, unable to go any farther. St. Gregory of Nyssa, a mystic in fourth-century Asia Minor, described it this way:

> Sick, our nature demanded to be healed; fallen, to be raised up; dead, to rise again. . . . Closed in the darkness, it was necessary to bring us the light; captives, we awaited a Savior. . . . Are these things minor or insignificant? Did they not move God to descend to human nature and visit it, since humanity was in so miserable and unhappy a state?

The angel's visit to Mary announced a new beginning for the world. That is why the scene seems to revisit the fall from grace in Eden. At Nazareth, however, the story had a different ending. At Eden, a fallen angel came to a woman and convinced her to disobey and disbelieve God. At Nazareth, an angel of God appeared and asked a woman to believe in God's promise and put herself in the service of his will. In both places—Nazareth and Eden—the fate of the race depended on the woman's response.

In God's plan, the anguish caused at Eden was a prelude to the glory revealed at Nazareth. In the wake of Adam and Eve's sin, God cursed the serpent and declared that one day a child born of a woman would crush the serpent's head, stamping out the Evil One and reversing his legacy of sin and death. Mary was that woman promised by God. Jesus was "born of a woman" as God had promised.

The early followers of Jesus called Mary the "new Eve," as they called Jesus the "new Adam." The first Eve orphaned her descendants by her sin—making alienation, fear, and death endemic to the human race. By her fiat, Mary turned things around. She became the "first woman" of a new creation, the mother of a people who live by faith as children of God.

"The knot of Eve's disobedience was untied by Mary's obedience," St. Irenaeus wrote in the second century. "What the virgin Eve bound through her unbelief, the Virgin Mary loosened by her faith." St. Ambrose of Milan preached that because Mary believed and gave herself in faith to the word of God, she became "the mother of reconciliation and of the reconciled, the mother of salvation and of the saved."

Mary's son was the "last Adam," the firstborn of a born-again humanity, the apostle Paul said. As Mary reversed Eve's sin, Jesus reversed Adam's failure to believe and to love. Jesus would be tempted by the devil, as Adam was—first in the wilderness and later in the Garden of Gethsemane. But he would not fall, as Adam did, and by his love and obedience to God's will Jesus would reverse the death sentence humanity had lived under since Eden.

This is the divine drama that was played out at Nazareth. Mary stood at the crossroads of human history. The French monk St. Bernard wrote in the twelfth century:

> The angel awaits an answer. . . . We too are waiting, O Lady, for your word of compassion. The sentence of condemnation weighs heavily upon us. The price of our salvation is offered to you. We shall be set free at once if you consent. . . . This is what the whole earth waits for. . . . For on your word depends comfort for the wretched, ransom for the captive, freedom for the condemned—salvation for all the sons of Adam, the whole of your race. Answer

> quickly, O Virgin. . . . Speak your own word, conceive the divine Word.

Little Child, Eternal God

The one who took human form in Mary was not just a special man, the new Adam. Jesus was at the same time God incarnate—literally, God "in the flesh." By his incarnation, Jesus became the presence of the Almighty dwelling among us.

Mary was the virgin Isaiah had prophesied, and she was to conceive and bear a son, Emmanuel, a name that means "God is with us."

From all eternity, God had prepared the womb of Mary to be the immaculate soil, the fertile ground for this new creation. As Adam had been fashioned from the earth and infused with the Spirit of God, the new Adam was to be formed in the immaculate flesh of Mary's womb and quickened by that same Holy Spirit.

That is why the early followers of Jesus called Mary the Theotokos—the "God bearer," or mother of God. St. Cyril, a fifth-century Egyptian, used the common Greek term for a fetus to express the astonishing reality: God, he marveled, had become a *brephos*! "A little child is the eternal God!" exclaimed St. Romanus, a priest in sixth-century Constantinople whose beautiful poetry earned him the nickname "the Melodist."

In opening her womb to her creator, Mary gave God a human body. The flesh of Mary became the flesh of God. As does every other baby, the infant God looked like his mother. A hymn that Byzantine Catholics sing on Christmas night imagines Mary cradling the child in her arms and praying:

> How were You sown as a seed in me?
> And how have You grown within me,
> O my Deliverer and my God?

Our Deliverer and God came by the quietest of signs, in the everyday miracle of a baby being born—the same way that you and I came into the world. He was born amid tears of joy, swaddled in a blanket, and held in the gentle arms of his father. On the first night of his life, he likely fell asleep nursing, his head nestled against his mother's warm breast—like countless babies before him and countless babies since.

Why this way? Why not in power and glory, in fire that swept down from the mountaintops, in the upheaval of nations, or in bloodred stars falling from the sky? Because in coming to us as a child, God was making what amounts to an "autobiographical" statement. The Incarnation was God's confession, his full disclosure of who he is. In the baby conceived at Nazareth and later born in a stable in Bethlehem, God revealed himself as a God of love and mercy—a Father who seeks us in the wilderness of our fallen world. This is how St. Bernard explained it nine centuries ago:

> God's Son came in the flesh so that mortal men could see and recognize God's kindness. . . . To show his kindness, what more could he do beyond taking my human form? . . . How could he have shown his mercy more clearly than by taking on himself our condition? . . . The incarnation teaches us how much God cares for us and what he thinks and feels about us.

True love requires that lovers be free. Love is a preference, a decision to give oneself wholly to another. "Love" that has no other choice is no love at all. It is servitude. To create beings to love and be loved, God had to make us "a little lower than God," as the psalmist said, and he had to give us the freedom to love—or not to love.

There was a divine risk in all this, of course; namely, that the people he made would freely choose not to love him in return. And indeed that is what happened. The original sin of Adam and Eve separated the race from the love of God, and only God could save us from this fate. Only God could make it possible for us to live and love again.

He could have chosen to save us from sin any way he wanted. He did not have to humble himself by dwelling for nine months in the confines of a human womb. He could have set us free by decree—speaking a saving word that would lift us from the dunghill of sin and death and plant us again in paradise. Instead he chose to come by way of compassion, as one like us, to fight alongside us against temptation and the devil. St. Hippolytus said in early third-century Rome:

> God wished to win man back from disobedience, not by using force to reduce him to slavery, but by addressing to his free will a call to liberty. . . . We know that his manhood was of the same clay as our own. If this were not so, he would hardly have been a teacher who could expect to be imitated. . . . No, he wanted us to consider him as no different from ourselves—and so he worked, he was hungry and thirsty, he slept.

We are saved by Jesus because while being the Son of God he was also, as his neighbors perceived him to be, "the son of Mary." He came among us fully human and fully divine. He had a human body and a human soul, a human mind and a human will, and he loved with a human heart. And yet in all these things, he expressed perfectly the divine life of God. In his divine-human person, Jesus showed us the depths of the communion that God desires with the human family.

The Imitation of Christ

By humbling himself to share in our humanity, Jesus made it possible for us to share in his divinity. "God became man so that we might become God," according to the bold expression of St. Athanasius, the heroic fourth-century Egyptian bishop and defender of the faith. This is the Catholic claim, that the Son of God became the Son of Man so that every son and daughter of man could be made a child of God. In the language of the early church, we are to be "deified," or "divinized"—made godlike, divine.

This is the promise that has changed so many lives down through the centuries. Take the case of Johannes Scheffler, a royal physician in seventeenth-century Poland. Stirred by wonder at the Incarnation, he renounced his fortune, gave everything he had to the poor, and changed his name to Angelus, the name of the church's prayer recalling the Annunciation and in honor of the Incarnation. Angelus wrote a beautiful poem that captures the glory the Incarnation makes possible for each of us:

Look! God becomes I,
Comes down to misery on earth.
I enter thus his kingdom and be he!

Because God *becomes I,* each one of us can become him. We do this by following the way of Jesus—not necessarily in the literal fashion, as Charles de Foucauld did at Nazareth, but in a daily effort to understand his gospel and be faithful to it.

"There is nothing little in the life of Jesus," said Blessed Columba Marmion, the Irish monk who was one of the spiritual masters of the twentieth century. "Christ is God appearing amongst men, conversing with them under the skies of Judea, and sharing with them by his human life how a God lives among men, in order that men may know how they ought to live so as to be pleasing to God."

Every day in our reading of the Scriptures we stand with Jesus under the Judean skies. We see the face of God and the ideal of human life disclosed in his every breath and gesture, in his every act and word. We read because we want to walk in the footsteps of he who said, "Follow me." We read because we want to model our lives on he who said, "Learn from me" and "I have set you an example."

St. Augustine, the fifth-century African who was the church's seminal teacher, penned a striking phrase to describe the example of Jesus: *Caro quasi vox* ("Christ's flesh is like a voice"). What he meant is that at every stage of Jesus' earthly life—his life in the flesh—he is calling to us, inviting us personally to live in the mystery of divine love that he reveals.

The flesh of Jesus calls to us from the womb of Mary, showing us that God's love for us begins long before we are born. The flesh of Jesus calls to us from the crude nursery in Bethlehem, telling us of God's love for the poor, for the homeless, for all who have no place in this world. His flesh calls to us again from his infancy in exile in Egypt, telling us of God's solidarity with the refugee, with the dispossessed, with all who are persecuted for God's sake.

The flesh of Jesus calls to us from the poverty and obscurity of his thirty years in Nazareth, what Charles de Foucauld called his "hidden life." In one of Foucauld's meditations, he imagines Jesus speaking:

> It was for your sake I went there, *for love of you*. . . . I instructed you continually for thirty years, not in words, but by my silence and example. . . . I was teaching you primarily that it is possible to do good to men—great good, infinite good, divine good—without using words, without preaching, without fuss, but by silence and by giving them a good example. . . . The example of devotion of duty toward God lovingly fulfilled, and goodness toward all men, loving kindness to those about one, and domestic duties fulfilled in holiness. The example of poverty, lowliness . . . the obscurity of a life hidden in God. . . . I was teaching you to live by the labor of your own hands, so as to be a burden on no one and to have something to give to the poor. And I was giving this way of life an incomparable beauty—the beauty of being a copy of mine.

When Jesus began to preach and teach—after thirty years of life as a poor man, an ordinary worker, a neighbor and son—his message was constant with the unspoken lessons of Nazareth. He lived a life devoted simply to the love of God. He taught by way of story and parable, drawing many of his images from the domestic life he knew so well—grinding meal, mixing yeast and dough, mending a tear in a cloak. He drew examples too from the marketplace and the world of work—day laborers seeking a just wage, merchants investing money, farmers sowing seed.

He was especially fond of children, and the intimacies of family life became vivid symbols of his promised kingdom—mothers in labor and nursing their young, a father forgiving a wayward son, the preparing of a wedding feast. His most revolutionary teaching—that God is a tender Father who calls us to be his beloved children—resonates with the warmth he must have felt as the child of his earthly father, Joseph.

Jesus went so far as to say that the goal of our lives is to become "little children" of God: we have to have the faith of a child, the unquestioning trust that we will receive what we ask for from our Father in heaven. And we have to love as a child does, with a love unsoiled by selfish motives or thirst for gain.

The flesh of Jesus calls out a single word: *love.* To unveil the love of God, Jesus supped with prostitutes, thieves, and cheats; embraced women, lepers, and Samaritans. For the cause of love, he healed them and forgave their sins. For love's sake he denounced the false-hearted teachers making people feel afraid and unworthy of the love of God.

When Jesus laid down a "new commandment," it was a law of love: "Love one another as I have loved you." He preached a way of love so radical that it calls us to forgive every trespass against us, to love even our enemies, to extend to others the mercy we expect God to extend to us. The revelation of love was the "will of God" that Jesus said he had come into the world to do. In the flesh of Christ we see God's loving will that all men and women be saved from sin and death and be gathered into his family, his kingdom of love.

The Italian mystic St. Catherine of Siena wrote to a friend in the 1370s:

> You must, then, *become love,* looking at God's love, who loved you so much not because he had any obligation towards you but out of pure gift, urged only by his ineffable love.

The gospel of Jesus is both an announcement of God's love for us and a *vocation*—a calling from God to "become love." We are to follow his call by listening to the voice of his flesh, by loving the way Jesus loved. We are, in Jesus' words, to take up our personal cross and follow him, to lose our lives in order to find new life in his.

His Love Is No Hoax

The flesh of Jesus spoke most eloquently when it was battered and bloodied, nailed to the executioner's tree. "Even the insults, even the spitting, the buffeting, even the cross and the tomb, were nothing but You speaking in the Son, appealing to us by Your love, stirring up our love for You," said William of Saint-Thierry, a monk in twelfth-century France.

To know how much God loves you, look at any crucifix, with its image of Jesus pierced, broken, and dead. "No one has greater love than this, to lay down one's life for one's friends," Jesus said.

Catholic devotion and art are so vivid because they reflect our faith that his suffering was an act of self-sacrifice for our sake. He knew you and loved you, as he loved me—even as they whipped his back and drove a crown of thorns into his head, as the taunts of the crowd filled his ears, as they hammered spikes through his hands and feet, as he breathed his last, abandoned to loneliness and pain.

With our eyes raised to the crucified, we can say with St. Paul: "The Son of God . . . loved me and gave himself for me." That is why we reenact his death in Passion plays, meditate on his "sorrowful mysteries," retrace the "stations of the cross," listen again and again to his seven last words. Our devotions express the awe of St. Bonaventure, who once cried: "Who am I, O Lord? Why have you loved me so much?"

We recognize his passion as a personal drama in which each of us is implicated. But we do not forget that his suffering and his death, like his birth and his life, are embedded in human history. The Crucifixion was an event that even non-Christian historians documented. Jesus was tortured and killed because Israel's religious leaders came to regard him as a heretic and a blasphemer. Quite legitimately, they feared that the passions he aroused would incite the Jewish masses to revolt, and that the Romans would use putting down the uprising as a pretext to destroy their temple and the Jewish nation. So the religious leaders had Jesus arrested, and they convinced Roman authorities to execute him as an enemy of Caesar, a would-be rebel "king of the Jews."

But the Jewish people are not to blame for killing Jesus. Individual Jews and Romans freely pursued their own motives in the affair, and there is no collective guilt that attaches to the peoples involved. Something more epic was taking place beneath the machinations of high priests and political functionaries. Unknown to them, they were delivering up Jesus "according to the definite plan and foreknowledge of God," as Peter would later preach.

The final hours of Jesus of Nazareth's life show the human race at its darkest—betrayal and cowardice; conspiracy, bribery, and deceit; backroom deal making and crowd manipulation; torture and sham legal proceedings. All the injustice and cruelty that sinful humanity can muster is brought to bear against history's one sinless man, and it all culminates in the execution of this man everybody knew was innocent all along.

"Which of you convicts me of sin?" Jesus challenged his accusers. He knew he was the only person since Adam to be completely blameless before God, to have lived his whole life in conformity to God's will, to have loved God with his whole heart and strength, and to have loved his neighbor as himself. Even as he prayed at Gethsemane to be spared from suffering, he was offering himself humbly to God: "Father, if you are willing, remove this cup from me; yet, not my will but yours be done."

The Father's will is that we be liberated from our enslavement to sin. Otherwise, we would all have to perish for our sins—because sin is separation from God, and no one can live apart from the giver and sustainer of life. To free us from sin and death, Jesus traded places with us. To do the Father's will, he paid with his life the penalty for our sin. He died instead of us.

In his last days, Jesus was revealed as the "suffering servant" foretold by the prophet Isaiah. He is the "man of suffering" who Isaiah said would be "wounded for our transgressions," going silently as a lamb to the slaughter to make himself "an offering for sin." He freely took upon himself all the sins ever committed and all the sins that ever will be committed—the sin of Adam and Eve, my sins and your sins, the sins of our grandchildren's children, all sins until the end of the age. Innocent, he died for the guilty.

This truth about Jesus' death is illustrated dramatically in the studies of the crucifix done in the 1960s and 1970s by William Congdon, an abstract-expressionist painter and Catholic convert. In his *Crocefisso no. 2,* Congdon renders the human figure of Jesus as a flattened shaft of dull light scraped hard against a sky of umber and black. His body is no longer distinguishable from the cross he hangs on. Where you look for human features, you find only marks of suggestion—a narrow twist forms a rib cage, a thorny scrawl his sunken head. Raising his eyes to the crucified, Congdon saw this:

> The body I met is my own body hurting from sin, a body soaked with pain to the point of being unable to distinguish the body from the pain, as if the pain had become a body and not the body become pain. . . . The Christ on the cross is myself, that is my sin that is nailed to the cross!

This identification with the suffering Christ is characteristically Catholic. It is a solemn recognition of just how much we are loved. In the fourteenth century, Blessed Angela of Foligno was praying when she heard Jesus speak: "My love for you has not been a hoax!"

What Paul called the "foolishness" of the cross is the final display of God's foolish love, a love willing to suffer even for those who do not care about his love. Jesus' offering of his life to the Father was an *atonement;* it literally makes us again "at one" with God. In his sacrifice God made a new and final covenant with his people. That is how Jesus explained his approaching passion and death to his twelve apostles at their last meal together. He told them to remember his life as poured out from beginning to end for us, his body given up once for all, his blood spilled for the forgiveness of the sin of the world.

Passing Over from Death to Life

Jesus died during Passover, the holy season when the Israelites solemnly recalled their ancestors' liberation from Egypt. At Passover, the temple priests offered sacrifices of unblemished lambs, and families gathered to eat a ritual meal of lamb and unleavened bread, as was commanded by Moses centuries before.

Celebrating his last Passover with the Twelve the night before he died, Jesus instituted a new and living memorial of *his* passing over from death to life, which liberated Israel and all nations from sin and death. Jesus called the feast of his passing over the Eucharist (literally, "thanksgiving") and said that it would be a divine sign, a sacrament, of his love that would last throughout the ages. Every day the Eucharist brings us into the real presence of his body and blood offered for us on the cross.

Jesus died a lonely death—in utter failure, so it seemed—crucified between two thieves in a place called Golgotha, or "Place of the Skull" (*Calvary* in Latin). In a final indignity, a soldier thrust a spear into his side, stabbing his heart; blood and water flowed out. But even this cruel and unnecessary act had meaning in God's plan.

The piercing of Jesus' side is the final parallel between the life of Jesus—the new man—and the life of Adam, the first man. In the beginning, God put Adam into a deep sleep and drew out from his side the woman Eve, the mother of the human race. To announce the start of a new world, the new Adam hung in the sleep of death on the cross. From his side, God drew out water and blood to symbolize the church, the bride of Christ and the mother of a new race, giving life through the water of baptism and the blood of the Eucharist. St. Gregory of Elvira, writing in the late fourth century, described it this way:

> Who does not know that our Lord when he hung on the wood of the cross, did not only shed blood from the wound in his side, but also a stream of living water, showing that his bride, that is, the Church, like our first parents, is formed from his side, as Eve was formed from the side of Adam.

On the ground at Calvary, only Jesus' mother was with him at the end, along with his beloved apostle John and a handful of other women disciples. The rest had denied him and fled, fearing they too would be arrested and tortured. From the cross, Jesus looked into the tearstained face of Mary and entrusted her to John. Jesus was a dutiful Jewish son to the end, making sure Mary would be provided and cared for after he was gone. "Woman, here is your son," he said. To John he said: "Here is your mother."

Even in this moving scene of human anguish, the flesh of Jesus speaks. He is giving his church a visible face—the face of his mother. We are to behold Mary as he did—as *our* mother. We are to love her as he did, to learn from her pure trust in the will of God. We are to hold fast to him as Mary did—in times of joy and in times of anguish.

On Calvary, the bloody posterity of original sin reached its logical conclusion. Cain, Adam and Eve's firstborn, committed history's first homicide, killing his brother Abel in cold blood. On Calvary, the children of Adam and Eve finally rose up and committed deicide—killing God himself. "No event is so sublime as this—the blood of God has been poured out for us," said St. John Chrysostom, fourth-century bishop of Constantinople. From a Friday afternoon until the early hours of a Sunday morning, it could be declared that God was dead on earth, his voice silent in the land.

Jesus died as true God. And he died as a true man. His solidarity with every aspect of our humanity, begun in the womb, continues to the tomb. Because death is our lot in life, death became his. The early creeds stress this by professing that Jesus "descended into hell," meaning the netherworld, the abode of the dead.

Raising Adam

Jesus went among the dead to offer salvation to those who died before Jesus came into the world. He preached the gospel to the souls in the prison of death, Peter said. According to Paul he descended into the abode of the dead to lead the dead out. Jesus himself had foretold an hour when the dead would hear the voice of the Son of God and would live.

A fourth-century homily attributed to the monk Epiphanius envisions the dramatic encounter beyond the grave between Adam ("our first parent") and Jesus ("he who is both God and the son of Eve"). Jesus calls out to Adam:

> Rise up, work of my hands! You who were created in my image. . . . For your sake I, your God, became your son. . . . For the sake of you who left a garden, I was betrayed . . . in a garden. . . . See on my face the spit I received in order to restore to you the life I once breathed into you. See there

> the marks of the blows I received in order to refashion your warped nature in my image. On my back see the marks of the scourging I endured to remove the burden of sin that weighs upon your back. See my hands, nailed firmly to a tree, for you who once wickedly stretched out your hand to a tree. . . . I slept on a cross and a sword pierced my side for you who slept in paradise and brought forth Eve from your side. . . . Rise, let us leave this place. The enemy led you out of the earthly paradise. I will not restore you to that paradise but I will enthrone you in heaven. . . . The bridal chamber is adorned, the banquet is ready, the eternal dwelling places. . . . . The kingdom of heaven has been prepared for you from all eternity.

On the third day, Jesus rose from the abyss of death. The Easter icons of Byzantine Catholics depict a scene of triumphant joy—Jesus stepping out of darkness and flames, trailed by a multitude, with Adam at the head of the pack. For them and for us, Jesus' rising from the dead means that the human condition has passed over from death to life. By his dying he destroyed our death, and by his rising he won us life. "For as all die in Adam, so all will be made alive in Christ," Paul said.

His resurrection, like his birth, was an event shrouded in silence, simplicity, and humility. He did not come as a conquering hero to lord himself over those who doubted him, mocked him, and killed him. An ancient tradition holds that he appeared first to his mother and to his earthly father, who was among the dead who were raised: "After his resurrection they came out of the tombs . . . and appeared to many," St. Matthew's Gospel says.

Then he went among his friends. He appeared first to Mary Magdalene and other women disciples who discovered his empty tomb just after daybreak. Later that first Sunday, he appeared to two disciples making their way to Emmaus, outside Jerusalem. They did not recognize him until he explained the Scriptures to them and blessed and broke the bread as he had during his last supper. Then their eyes were opened. Still later that night he walked through the walls of the upper room and appeared to Peter and the other apostles. In the weeks that followed he appeared to many, once to a gathering of more than five hundred, many of whom were still alive when Paul wrote his first letter to the Christians of Corinth around the year 56.

The risen Jesus was no ghost. He ate and drank with his apostles. They probed the wounds in his hands and side. Jesus had passed from death to a new order of existence. His was a transfigured, glorified body, filled with the Spirit of God, no longer bound by earthly limits of time and space. He can come among us now in any way he desires and at any time—in our neighbor, in the poor, in the pages of Scripture, and in the breaking of the bread. Raised from the dead, the son of Mary is now, in the words of Paul, "the man of heaven."

The man of heaven is also, as Paul said, "the firstborn from the dead." If we believe he is the risen Son of God, we can share in his inheritance and have new life as children of God. Because God raised him up, we can trust that we who believe in him will one day rise to live forever in new, glorified bodies.

The Mission of the Resurrection

For forty days Jesus stayed among the people, until he was taken up to heaven in a cloud. During this time, he laid the foundations for his church to continue his presence and work on earth.

He gave final instructions to his twelve handpicked apostles, the patriarchs of this new extended family of God.

He had instructed them privately throughout his ministry and given them powers to heal and cast out demons in his name. In those last forty days, he taught them how to interpret the Scriptures and preach. He breathed his Spirit into them, confirmed their authority to forgive sins in his name. He gave them a mission—to preach the good news of his salvation to the ends of the earth, to celebrate the breaking of the bread in his memory, to teach what he had taught them, to baptize all nations and make them one family in God. He promised he would remain on earth through his church—present in the sacraments, living signs that truly bring people into contact with his saving presence.

Jesus ascended to heaven in his glorified, risen body. He took his place in heaven in all the fullness of his humanity, bearing for all time the marks where the nails had been, the signs of his passion carved forever into his precious skin. From that day forward, we could never think of God without thinking of humankind. The very being of God—the Trinity of Father, Son, and Spirit—now contains One who is one of us.

Jesus is now "seated in glory at the right hand of the Father." He is "King of kings and Lord of lords." He will come again one day to render a final judgment on the living and the dead and to usher in the never-ending kingdom that Israel's prophets proclaimed, the new Jerusalem that will come down from heaven. Until that day, Jesus will remain our high priest in the precincts of heaven, hearing our prayers and sending us his Spirit. He is the one mediator between our Father and us, the only one who can save us from the sin of the world.

Until Christ comes again, Catholics live as the first apostles did—as witnesses to his resurrection, trying by his grace to testify with our entire being to the salvation he won for us. We live by faith in all that he revealed about God. We experience our lives as people born of the water and blood that flows from his sacred heart. We call God our Father and love all men and women as our brothers and sisters. We live by hope in the promise that the kingdom is coming, growing and spreading under the Father's watchful eye in the church of his Son, empowered by his Spirit. And we live by love, in imitation of Jesus, with the love of God in our hearts giving meaning to everything we do. By his grace, we live as he did, as living "Eucharists," as offerings of praise and thanksgiving.

And we see miracles every day, not only at the altar where bread and wine become his body and blood. We see lives changed by the encounter with the risen Jesus, and we believe that no person stands beyond the pale of his love. We have seen with our own eyes the truth of what he said, that with God all things are possible. We have seen hateful persecutors like Paul become the greatest of evangelists, and wasted lives like Charles de Foucauld's turned into offerings of extraordinary holiness and love.

Foucauld was living the Catholic life when he answered a knock at his door in December 1916 and found himself staring down the barrel of a gun. He had long since left Nazareth, realizing that, as he put it, "the life of Nazareth can be lived everywhere." He had chosen to live "his" Nazareth in the remote Sahara in Algeria, to imitate Jesus by a life of quiet goodness and friendship among the desert nomads and Muslims.

But to a rebel band of Muslim nationalists, Charles was just another agent of French imperialism. On that December morning they beat him and bound him like an animal, pulling his hands behind his back and tying them with coarse rope to his ankles. Witnesses say they held him like that for almost a day. Through it all he remained quiet, prayers moving silently across his bloodied lips. He was finally shot through the temple, in the fading light of day. He went to his death as he had lived, in imitation of Jesus of Nazareth, and he died knowing that he would see that Man in heaven, face-to-face.

→ II ←

GOD, THE HOUND OF HEAVEN

"I fled Him, down the nights and down the days; / I fled Him, down the arches of the years . . ." The words fell out in a dour sigh, all booze and smoke. Long after hours in the back room of a Greenwich Village bar called the Hell Hole, the man who would become America's most celebrated playwright seemed to be straining in a hell all his own. He was reciting from memory "The Hound of Heaven," a long poem about the ways of God and the evasive maneuvers of the human soul:

> . . . I fled Him, down the labyrinthine ways
> Of my own mind; and in the mist of tears
> I hid from Him . . .

On that cold winter night in 1917, Eugene O'Neill's audience was a crowd of self-styled freethinkers and artists, free-love bohemians and hangers-on. At his side was Dorothy Day, a twentysomething reporter for the nation's largest socialist daily newspaper, the *New York Call.* Like O'Neill, she was a lonely idealist with a taste for rye whiskey and lover-done-me-wrong songs. They used to walk pressed together on the late-night streets, lost in conversation about the mystic lyrics of Baudelaire and the "God is dead" philosophy of Nietzsche. She had never heard O'Neill speak of this poem before.

> I stand amid the dust o' the mounded years—
> My mangled youth lies dead beneath the heap.
> My days have crackled and gone up in smoke,
> Have puffed and burst as sun-starts on a stream.
> Yea, faileth now even dream. . . .
> And now my heart is as a broken fount,
> Wherein tear-drippings stagnate . . .

Published in 1893 by a former opium addict turned Catholic named Francis Thompson, "The Hound of Heaven" could have been O'Neill's spiritual autobiography. Reared Catholic and educated in Catholic schools, O'Neill had forsaken his parents' faith in a disillusionment that spiraled down a back alley of reckless excess. He professed a morose and anguished atheism, refusing homage to a God who could allow so much suffering in the world.

Dorothy Day parted company with him not long after that night in the Hell Hole. O'Neill went on to fame—winning four Pulitzers and the Nobel Prize in Literature—but not quite happiness. His plays were studies in loss: he wrote of a God who failed to deliver, of sin and guilt and the burden of memory, of the search for satisfaction and the terror of death.

At first, Day continued along the downward path she and O'Neill had been on. She was wounded in action in the Jazz Age's sexual revolution—knocked up and then abandoned by a hard-drinking journalist. She had an abortion, married a man on the rebound, and lived for a time as an expatriate in Paris and Capri. Her marriage broke up, and she bore a daughter out of wedlock with another man.

In December 1927, a decade after that winter with O'Neill, she surrendered to the relentless "Hound of Heaven" and entered the Catholic Church. The long days until her death in 1980 were spent not far from the Hell Hole. She lived without income or security while sheltering the homeless, speaking out against injustice and war, and spreading through her writings and her life's witness a radical belief in the merciful kingdom of God. Many believe she will one day be declared a saint.

She never stopped praying for Eugene O'Neill, who had opened her eyes with that poem. "It is one of those poems that awakens the soul, recalls to it the fact that God is its destiny," she wrote in her first autobiography, *From Union Square to Rome.* "The idea of this pursuit fascinated me; the inevitableness of it, the recurrence of it, made me feel that inevitably I would have to pause in the mad rush of living to remember my first beginning and last end."

A God in Epic Pursuit

Our destiny. Our first beginning and last end. Inevitable pursuit. That is about as succinct a definition of God as you are going to find. God is "our Father in heaven," as Jesus taught us to pray to him. He is the origin and goal of our lives, and the loving sustainer of all points in between. He put us here. He knows where we came from, where we have been, and where we are now. And he knows where we should be heading—always on the road back to him.

In his poem, Thompson calls God "this tremendous Lover." He is out to get us. He hounds our days and hounds our nights. He knows what we need even before we ask, and he knows that he alone is what each of us is searching for. This is the God Dorothy Day knew. This is the God revealed in the pages of the Scripture.

The whole Bible can be read as an epic chase—an adventure of divine pursuit. The drama begins with God making the first man and woman in his own image to share his life. Quickly his children spurn his love. He pursues them, calls to them with words that will resound through the pages of biblical history, and in every human heart today—"Where are you?"

The Bible shows God pleading with every generation to return to him. Finally God sends his only Son. Jesus reveals that God is like a mother hen gathering her brood, like a shepherd seeking a lost sheep, like a father longing for his wayward son to come home. Jesus gave his church the job of continuing his work. Through his church, the Father still seeks out the lost and works to bring his children home. He wants every man and woman to turn back to him in love. He wants each of us to feel the divine love that caused the apostle John to cry: "See what love the Father has given us, that we should be called children of God; and that is what we are."

God wants us to discover what Dorothy Day found out on the road one night:

> I was traveling and far from home and lonely, and I awoke in the night almost on the verge of weeping with a sense

> of futility, of being unloved and unwanted. And suddenly the thought came to me of my importance as a daughter of God, daughter of a King, and I felt a sureness of God's love. And I felt a sureness of God's love and at the same time a conviction that one of the greatest injustices, if one can put it that way, which one can do to God is to distrust his love, not realize his love. God so loved me that he gave his only begotten son. "If a mother shall forget her children, never will I forget thee." Such tenderness, and with such complete ingratitude we forget the Father and his love!

The Capacity for God

The divine drama of God's pursuit is also the story of our hiding from him, our failure to realize his love. Try as we might, however, we can never elude him. The best we can do is delude ourselves that we have given him the slip. Like it or not, we are made for God. The ancient Christian teachers used to say that we are created *capax Dei*—"capable of God."

We have an inborn capacity to know him and love him. Through our reason and creativity, our sensitivity to beauty, we can know the Maker by the world he has made. "The whole visible world is like a book, as it were, written by the hand of God . . . created by divine power. Each of its creatures are like forms . . . established by the divine will in order to make manifest the wisdom of the invisible things of God," Hugh of Saint-Victor wrote in the twelfth century. We sense God, too, in our longings for love and union, for what is true and beautiful. As the yearning for God is written into our very natures, so is the ability to find him.

St. Augustine said that if he knew himself, he would know God. There has always been this mystical strain of devotion in the church—Catholics who seek God not only in the wonders of nature but in the interior mansions of their own souls. In the depths of our being, the mystics say, we can make contact with a dazzling darkness or a cloud of unknowing. Origen, the third-century martyr, called this place "the Paternal Abyss." Pseudo-Dionysius the Areopagite, the great sixth-century mystic, said:

> It is in the silence, in fact, that we learn the secrets of this darkness . . . that shines with the most dazzling light. It, even remaining perfectly intangible and invisible, fills with splendors more beautiful than beauty, the intelligences that know to close their eyes.

God grants the mystic an exalted intelligence, but he does not leave the rest of us in the dark. We can come to him with eyes wide open, because in his love he has revealed himself to us personally in Jesus. In fact, throughout Scripture, we find God in gentle kindness stooping down to our level, speaking to us in words and deeds we can understand. Origen said that God talks "baby talk . . . like a father caring for his own children." St. Gregory of Nazianzus saw God as more like "a tender mother, who joins in the inarticulate utterances of her babe, giving to our human nature what it is capable of receiving."

In Jesus, the Father finally came to speak to his children man-to-man, as it were. In sending his Son, God has told us everything. It may take us an eternity to fully understand this revelation, but all that we need to know about God we can learn by fixing our gaze on Jesus and giving our hearts to him.

One Love, Three Lovers

Jesus revealed to us a God who is a Trinity, a communion of three divine persons in love—the Father, the Son, and the Holy Spirit.

We see this Trinity everywhere in Jesus' life, beginning with his conception. At Nazareth, the Father overshadowed Mary, and the Son of God was conceived by the power of the Holy Spirit. When Jesus was baptized in the River Jordan, the Holy Spirit descended upon him, and the Father declared, "You are my Son, the Beloved." When the Son died on the cross, he offered himself totally to the Father, into his hands commending his Spirit. And when he rose from the dead, he sent his apostles out as his Father had sent him, breathing into them the Spirit of God.

Jesus taught that God was truly the one Lord who had revealed himself to the children of Israel. He called God his Father and identified himself as God's Son. He said, "The Father and I are one." He promised that he and the Father would send "the Spirit of truth" to bear witness in his church. Finally, in his last instructions, he gave the church the mission to baptize—literally, to immerse the world "in the name of the Father and of the Son and of the Holy Spirit."

The proper name of God is Father, Son, and Holy Spirit. To say that God is a Trinity does not mean that we believe in three gods. It does not mean that there are three "modes" or ways that God expresses himself. To say that God is a Trinity is to say that there are three real, distinct Persons within the unity of the one God. It is a mystery best described by a word, as the apostle John did—"God is *love*." Augustine would later say, "In truth, to see the Trinity is to see love."

What does that mean? That in the heart of the Trinity is an endless circuit of love uniting Father, Son, and Spirit. This is not idle speculation. Our understanding of the Trinity flows directly from what we have seen in the mission of Jesus, the image of the invisible God. He told us that love was to offer your life for another. An early Catholic hymn, found in Paul's letter to the Philippians, sings of how Jesus "emptied himself" to be born in our likeness and to offer himself on the cross. In emptying himself to become man, and again in offering himself on the cross, Jesus revealed the love of God—not only God's love for us, but also the nature of the love that is God, the inner workings of the Trinity.

Within the Trinity, the very life of God, the Father pours himself out in love, eternally fathering the Son. The Son eternally receives himself as a gift of the Father's love and offers himself back completely to the Father in love. The Holy Spirit is that love that gives life, proceeding from the total gift of Father to Son and Son to Father. The love in the Trinity is like the love we experience on earth. Love is always a triad involving the lover, the beloved, and the nexus of love, the bond that unites lover and beloved. In the Trinity, the Father is always lover, the Son the beloved, and the Spirit the tie that binds the lovers' knot.

These are words of worship and wonder, more poetry than precise schematic. And yet these words reflect not only the teaching and example of Jesus, but also the history of humankind's experience of God. Though we do not often think of it this way, we know God in our lives as a Trinity—as the Father who made us, as the Son who saved us, and as the Holy Spirit who gives us new life as God's children.

The hound of heaven. This tremendous lover. These are simply different poetic ways of talking about the Trinity. The Trinity is *love*—love on a mission to make us his own. All creation and all history flow out of this love. And all creation and all history flow on toward this love, back into the Trinity. Synesius of Cyrene expressed this faith in a fifth-century hymn to the triune God:

> A single font and a single root,
> a single form filled with the triple splendor.
> There, where the profundity of the Father shines,
> breaks forth the power of the Son,
> wise Creator of the entire universe,
> fruit generated from the Fatherly heart!
> And there shines out
> the unifying light of the Holy Spirit.

A Universe Seen and Unseen

All creation flows from the single font of the Trinity. All creation is the fruit of the love in the Father's heart, breaking forth in the power of the Son, filling everything with the radiant light of the Holy Spirit.

The very first words of Scripture catch the Trinity in the act of creating. God the Father is there speaking his word ("Let there be"). So is the Spirit, brooding over the face of the deep. We even overhear a conversation that seems to take place in the depths of the Trinity—"Let *us* make humankind in *our* image." The Father made all things through his Word, the beloved Son of God, by the creative action of the Holy Spirit.

He created for love, to share the glory that is the inner splendor of the divine life. He created everything *ex nihilo* ("out of nothing"), the heavens and the earth. His creation includes a world that is invisible to us, in which the Trinity dwells in the company of spirit beings known as angels, who have intelligence and free will, as we do, and are created by God to be his servants and messengers.

From the angels to the stars in the night sky to the face we behold in the mirror—all that is seen and unseen owes its existence to the Trinity. Catholic poetry and preaching have always celebrated the majesty of the Creator, the beauty and diversity of his creation, the glories revealed in earth and sky, water and fire, trees and mountains, rivers and seas.

St. Gregory of Nazianzus earned the title "the Theologian" for his eloquent defense of the Trinity against heretics while serving as a bishop in fourth-century Constantinople. In this poem, he dwells on the Trinity's artistry:

> The Trinity is one God
> who created and filled all things:
> the heavens with heavenly beings,
> the earth with creatures of earth,
> the sea, the rivers and springs,
> with creatures of the waters,
> giving life to all things by his Spirit,
> that all creatures
> might sing the praises of their wise Creator,
> who alone gives life and sustains
> all life in being.
> Above all others, let the creature who reasons
> celebrate him always
> as the great King and good Father.

We are the creatures who reason, made to stand in adoration and worship before the creation of this great King and Father. Listen to the swells and silences, the rapturous sonorities of Franz Joseph Haydn's choral masterpiece, *The Creation*. In it you hear the majestic heights to which Catholic contemplation of God's handiwork can transport us. Indeed, Haydn wrote the piece, he later said, to put the listener "in a frame of mind where he is most susceptible to the kindness and omnipotence of the Creator."

The Catholic believes that the Trinity has left marks of his kindness and omnipotence in creation, like a divine tattoo. "The world is charged with the grandeur of God," said the nineteenth-century Jesuit priest Gerard Manley Hopkins, perhaps the finest Catholic poet. Another poet of the divine, the sixteenth-century Spanish monk St. John of the Cross, saw vestiges of the Trinity everywhere:

> Scattering a thousand graces,
> He passed through these groves in haste,
> And looking upon them as He went,
> Left them, by His grace alone,
> Clothed in beauty.

All this beauty, all this power and glory, is meant to lift us up, to lead us deeper into the weft of the Father. We know with Augustine that "heaven and earth and all that is in the universe cries out to me from all directions, that I, O God, must love you."

From the first "Let there be," creation is a deliberate act of the Father, Son, and Holy Spirit. It has a purpose and a plan—what Paul called "the plan of the mystery hidden for ages."

Everything was oriented to the new creation that would come with Jesus. In Jesus, all things in heaven and on earth, including your life and mine, are destined to be united with God in love.

In the Father's Eyes

Jesus came into the world to show us the fatherly face of our Creator. He revealed the meaning of all of God's covenants with our biblical ancestors. The apostle Paul brought together a series of quotes from the prophets to describe the personal, filial relationship that God offers to each of us in Jesus:

> I will live in them and walk among them,
> and I will be their God,
> and they shall be my people. . . .
> I will be your father,
> and you shall be my sons and daughters,
> says the Lord Almighty.

The almighty creator of heaven and earth wants each of us to be his son or daughter, his kin. That promise was on Jesus' lips in the garden on that Sunday morning when he rose from the dead. He told Mary Magdalene: "Go to my brothers and say to them, 'I am ascending *to my Father and your Father, to my God and your God.*'"

That is the good news his church still preaches. Where Jesus has gone, we can go—to the Father, by way of the Son, led by the Spirit. Through the gift of the Holy Spirit we can speak to God in the same intimate way that Jesus did. Jesus called his Father "Abba," an Aramaic term of endearment best translated as "papa" or "daddy." That is how we should think of God—as our papa, our daddy. St. Cyprian, the third-century African martyr, said the prayer that Jesus taught his followers was a "family prayer." When we pray the Our Father, Cyprian said, the Father should hear on our lips the words of his Son.

To call God our Father does not mean that we think of God as a man.

God does not have a body to which we can attribute "masculine" or "feminine" characteristics. "God is spirit," Jesus told the woman at the well of Jacob, and Scripture describes the "image of God" as male and female. God is our Father, but with the prophet Isaiah we can speak of God's motherly love, how he bears us like a mother bears an infant in the womb, how he nurses and comforts us. Numerous saints and mystics have shown us a "motherly" side of God. St. Mechtild of Hackeborn, a thirteenth-century German mystic, heard this in a vision:

> Thou shalt call none other thy mother, and My love shall be thy mother. And as children suck their mothers' breasts, even so shalt thou suck from My love inward consolation and unutterable health, and My love shall also feed thee, and clothe thee, and provide for thee in all thy wants, like a mother who provideth for her only daughter.

Though we may feel and describe God's maternal comfort and consolation, we can never rightly address God as "our mother." None of the saints, not even those who explained the "feminine" qualities of the Godhead, ever prayed to God by any other name but Father. Neither Jesus nor any of the prophets before him ever called God "Mother." In the mystery of his revelation to us, God is Abba, our Father.

The words that survive from Jesus' childhood are words that describe his special filiation with God. When Mary and Joseph found him in the temple teaching, he told them, "Did you not know that I must be in my Father's house?"

When Jesus began preaching, the Father was his only message. In his most famous sermon, he tells us to live as "children of your Father in heaven. . . . Be perfect, therefore, as your heavenly Father is perfect." Many of his parables were stories of fathers and sons. The most prophetic of these is also the most graphic—a father sends his son to reason with the wicked tenants of a vineyard he owns, but the tenants rise up in jealousy and rage and kill the son.

And this is what happened to Jesus. Sent to reveal the Father, he spoke so much about him and in such intimate terms that the religious leaders of his day deemed him a heretic and a blasphemer. The Gospel of John reports: "For this reason the Jews were seeking all the more to kill him, because he was . . . calling God his own Father, thereby making himself equal to God."

The name of the Father was on his lips in the lonely garden on the night he was arrested, and again as he breathed his last—"Father, into your hands I commend my spirit." After he rose from the dead, he gave his apostles the gift of the Holy Spirit, which he called "what my Father promised," and commissioned them to continue the mission of God's only Son: "As the Father has sent me, so I send you." It was a mission of family building, to make all nations children of God our Father through baptism in his name.

So what does it mean to have God as our Father? Before we can understand this, we must throw out any ideas or images we have of human fathers, especially any bad experiences we might have had with our own fathers. The French poet Charles Péguy, killed in World War I, said that God looks on us with "fatherly eyes." The way God sees it, Péguy said, we are "sweet children, inimitable children, Jesus' brothers," and he loves each of us as he loves his Son:

> They remind me of my Son
> And he was like them. . . .
> That is why I love them, says God.

The Problem of Evil

Jesus taught that our Father holds each of us in his loving gaze. It is not as if, in creating the universe, God set a timer and then sat back, paring his nails, waiting for the clock to run out. Our Father is in the details—he knows when a sparrow falls from a rooftop; he feeds the birds and grows the flowers. There is nothing so small that he does not see it. The Father has numbered every hair on our heads and appointed an angel to watch over each one of us, posted before the very face of our Father in heaven.

We are always on God's mind. He loves each of us as if there were nobody else in the world. To each of us, he speaks the words he spoke to Blessed Angela of Foligno:

> My daughter who is sweet to me,
> my daughter who is my temple:
> My beloved daughter. . . .
> Love me, for I greatly love you
> and much more than you love me.

There are no accidents in our lives. “Everything comes from love,” St. Catherine of Siena reminds us. “All is ordained for the salvation of man. God does nothing without this goal in mind.” Everything that happens—our sorrows and joys, our expectations and anxieties, even our most unspeakable sufferings—is somehow part of his loving plan for the world.

This is the great paradox of our Father’s love. In a world filled with evil and innocent suffering, how can we believe in God’s love? How could a God who supposedly cares personally about each and every one of his children permit them to suffer? These questions gnawed away at Eugene O’Neill. “His whole life” was consumed with “the problem of evil and God’s permissive will,” Dorothy Day said.

His anguish was hardly original. The scandal of evil haunts the Catholic imagination and is the theme of some of our greatest art, literature, and philosophy. The painful refrain of *Silence,* Shusaku Endo’s novel about the persecution of missionaries in seventeenth-century Japan, hangs over all Catholic meditations on the Father: “Why is God continually silent while those groaning voices go on?”

Any answer is bound to sound smug and pious when compared to the fate of the suffering. As Augustine realized before his conversion, “I sought whence evil comes and there was no solution.” What the Catholic believes, however, is that God in his wisdom chose to create a world that is *in statu viae*—“in a state of journeying”—toward the perfection that will not come until the end of time. Until that last day, the world will be scarred by physical evil—earthquakes, floods, famines, tsunamis, babies born with horrible deformities. Things will arise and things will disappear. Natural forces of destruction and creativity will exist alongside each other, as will the perfect and the less perfect.

And because he has created men and women with free will, God has allowed the possibility that we will freely choose to work evil against ourselves and others. From our free will come the seemingly unlimited varieties of man's inhumanity to man. God does not in any way cause us to do evil, nor does he inflict evil on us as a punishment. But he permits it.

He also permits the "personified evil" at work in the world, the devil. Scripture tells us that the devil leads a band of rebellious angels who prowl about the world tempting us to do evil. "The Son of God was revealed for this purpose, to destroy the works of the devil," the apostle John said. By his cross and resurrection, Jesus proclaimed God's victory over the devil and over evil.

The cross, which on Good Friday was the symbol of God's apparent powerlessness against evil and injustice, was transformed on Easter Sunday into a pledge of triumph to all who suffer: God will bring a greater good out of even the most evil circumstances. Faith in Jesus means faith that those who suffer in Christ will also be raised to new life with him. Because the Father delivered his Son from death, we can be confident that our Father will deliver us too from evil and lead us into everlasting life.

In faith we can find God working even in the midst of tragedy. This does not mean that we are to remain passive in the face of innocent suffering. Quite the opposite: suffering marks the hour of Christian witness. Blessed Mother Teresa of Calcutta used to remind people that the innocent suffer often because of our failures to love and sacrifice: "If sometimes our poor people have to die of starvation, it is not because God didn't care for them, but because you and I didn't give, were not instruments of love in the hands of God."

In faith we respond to suffering with works of mercy. And though we discern God's will only dimly, we trust with Paul that "all things work together for good for those who love God," and that all the "sufferings of this present time are not worth comparing with the glory about to be revealed to us." We trust that, as Jesus told Dame Julian of Norwich in a vision in 1375, "sin is necessary, but all shall be well, and all shall be well, and all manner of things shall be well."

A Crucified God

Our faith in the victory of God over evil also stems from the witness of twenty centuries of Christian martyrs. The martyrs testify to the real presence of God in a world that claims he is dead or indifferent.

The first Christian martyrs approached the cruelty of their fates with the faith that they were joining their sufferings to the sufferings of Christ. "The pangs of birth are upon me," St. Ignatius of Antioch said before being fed to the lions in Rome in 107. "Leave me to imitate the passion of my God." In the face of his imminent torture and death, he spoke of the new life given to him in baptism and nurtured in him by the Eucharist:

> There is within me a water that lives and speaks, saying to me inwardly, "Come to the Father." I have no delight in perishable food, nor in the pleasures of this life. I desire the bread of God, the heavenly bread, the bread of life, which is the flesh of Jesus Christ, the Son of God.

We see this same faith in the Carmelite nuns of Compiègne, martyred on the guillotine at the height of the French Revolution. Branded enemies of the "progress of public spirit," they were killed as part of the Revolution's systematic effort to efface all trace of the living God from France.

Priests and nuns were jailed and killed by the score, churches confiscated, seminaries and religious houses closed. Notre Dame Cathedral was desecrated and refashioned as a pagan "Temple of Reason." During the height of the Terror in Paris, wild mobs would gather each day to cheer the executioners on, the air thick with the stench of their victims decomposing in open mass graves.

But witnesses say something remarkable happened on July 17, 1794. As sixteen Carmelites filed up the scaffold singing hymns, the feverish crowd fell silent for no apparent reason. All that could be heard were the strains of the nuns singing the Salve Regina, a hymn to the Blessed Mother, and the Te Deum, the ancient Catholic hymn to the Trinity. That, and the sound of the blade lopping off their heads, one by one. Ten days later, the Reign of Terror abruptly ended as Robespierre and his revolutionary government collapsed.

The nuns offered their lives as sacrifices for the truth about God and his reign of love. "We are victims of the age, and we must sacrifice ourselves for its reconciliation with God," said one, Sister Julie-Louise of Jesus. In prison awaiting death, she composed a song to brace them for the guillotine. She sang of her faith in a God who sacrificed himself for our sakes:

> Our bodies belong to the Lord:
> Let us climb, let us climb the scaffold
> And make him victorious! . . .

> Let us adore the justice of God;
> May the fervent priest,
> The faithful believer
> Seal, seal with every drop of their blood,
> Faith in a crucified God.

Our God is a crucified God, a Father who groans in compassion for his suffering humanity. In his love, the Father sent his only Son, from out of the heart of the Trinity, to take a body like our own, to walk in our shoes, to suffer in his broken flesh the wages of sin, the most unfathomable depths of evil.

Mission of Mercy

The mission of the Son is a mission of mercy. He reveals the merciful face of God. Jesus comes to those who are weighed down by the sin of the world and those who have drifted too far from shore. He comes to seek us out and bring us back to the Father. To every generation lost in sin, to each of us without a map and far from him, he promises, "Your Father is merciful."

This was the meaning of the Incarnation, as the Virgin Mary sang in her great canticle, the Magnificat. The child born of her womb was proof that God's "mercy is . . . from generation to generation," she said. Mary herself was known in the early church as the "mother of mercy." Before the Romans cut out his tongue in 662, the holy monk St. Maximus explained:

> She was truly the mother of mercy, the mother of the merciful one . . . the mother of the one who became incarnate

> and was crucified for us in order to pour out upon us, his rebellious enemies, his mercy.

No matter how grievously we have rebelled against his love, the Father is "rich in mercy," as the apostle Paul said. The mercy of the Father is the theme of perhaps Jesus' most famous story, the parable of the prodigal son. The prodigal son represents the entire human race, which has squandered its birthright and degraded the image of God in which all were created. Like the prodigal son in the story, the children of Adam and Eve are slaves to sin, no longer worthy to be called sons and daughters of the Father. Yet God in his mercy reaches out to the lost sons and daughters and welcomes them back.

Jesus intended each of us to hear this story as our own. We are to make our way back to the Father's house. We go by way of conversion, sorrow, and repentance, saying with the prodigal son, "I will get up and go to my father, and I will say to him, 'Father, I have sinned against heaven and before you; I am no longer worthy to be called your son.'" The parable's promise is Jesus' promise to each of us—that we will see our Father running out to embrace us, to cover us in kisses, to exult in his joy: "This son of mine was dead and is alive again; he was lost and is found!"

Living River of Divine Light

On the road to the Father, the Holy Spirit is our guide and advocate. In Jesus' farewell talk to his apostles, he said that he would not leave them orphans but would send his Spirit to comfort and guide them. True to his word, the Father and the Son poured out the Spirit of God on his church, and through the church the Spirit still flows as a gift of love given to a world of orphan souls.

The mission of the Spirit is to complete the saving plan of God. In the Spirit, we can know ourselves no longer as orphans but as sons and daughters of the living God. The Spirit comes to us in baptism, making us what Paul called a "new creation" and what Peter called "participants of the divine nature." By our baptism in the name of the Father, the Son, and the Holy Spirit, John said, we can call ourselves "children of God."

These words of St. Paulinus of Nola, written in the early fifth century to be inscribed on a baptismal font, describe the marriage of the earthly and the divine, the spiritual and the material worlds, brought about by the Holy Spirit:

> This font, generator of souls in need of salvation, emits a living river of divine light. The Holy Spirit descends from heaven into this river and unites the sacred waters with the heavenly source. The wave becomes impregnated with God and from the eternal seed generates a holy progeny with its fertile waters.

As we grow, the Spirit shows us the love of the Father and teaches us his name. "Because you are children, God has sent the Spirit of his Son into our hearts, crying, 'Abba! Father!'" Paul said. The Spirit teaches us to pray, to know that we can speak to the Father and hear his words in our hearts. Through the Spirit we are able to look upon the world with the eyes of a child of God, to see his gifts and marvels all around us.

By the Spirit, we are taught to walk in the ways of the Son and are guided along the path to our Father. As we walk by the

Spirit, we daily become more like the "little children" that Jesus said we should be—children who look up to their Father in love, who want to be just like him when we grow up. We are "transformed into the same image," as Paul described this spiritual process, becoming more deeply "conformed to the image of his Son," who is the "image of God."

God's Love Dwelling in Our Hearts

As we grow in the Catholic life, we find the Trinity living in our very hearts. That is our destiny. That is why the Father revealed himself in the Son and poured out his Spirit of love upon us.

Mary is the prototype for what every human person is to become. The early church called her *sanctae trinitatis domicilium*—"dwelling place of the Most Holy Trinity." Mary was the first to experience what Jesus promised to all of us—that if we come to the Father through faith in Jesus, he and the Father will come to dwell in each of us. "On that day" he added, "you will know that I am in my Father, and you in me, and I in you."

That day is what we are made for—and the Trinity is *whom* we are made for. On that day we enter into the most intimate personal communion with God. We become secret sharers in the life of the Trinity, and the Trinity takes up residence in each of us. That is why St. Augustine called the Holy Spirit "the gift made in love." Through the Spirit, he said, "God's love spreads in our hearts by making the Trinity dwell in us."

Russian Catholics call the Spirit "the Crimson Dove, the God of love." The Spirit wings us into the very heart of love and brings the very heart of love to beat in our breasts. Not in some symbolic way, not as a "feeling"—but as a true and real presence.

The Catholic promise is that if we open the doors of our hearts, we will experience on earth the heavenly joy of Blessed Elizabeth of the Trinity:

> I confide to you what has made my life an anticipated Heaven—believing that a Being called Love dwells in us at every moment of the day and night and that he asks us to live in communion with him, to receive every joy, like every suffering, equally as coming directly from his love.

Elizabeth was one of the quiet prophets of early twentieth-century Catholicism. As a young girl reared in a well-to-do family, she was a promising classical pianist with a fiery temper and a feisty attitude. She set it all aside to enter the cloistered life of the Carmelites at the age of twenty-one. Five years later she was dead of Addison's disease. But in hundreds of letters and poems she taught us the joy of living in communion with the Trinity. "There is a wholly adorable intimacy," she said. "You are never alone again!"

His Unhurrying Chase

To bring us out of the solitude of a life lived without God, to bring us into a life of adorable intimacy with the Trinity—that is why the "Hound of Heaven" keeps after each of us "with unhurrying chase, / And unperturbèd pace," as Thompson puts it in his poem.

If we pause in the mad rush of our living, as Dorothy Day did, we will hear the insistent voice of the Father, promising to

fill us with the love we long for. He pleads with us in t] of Thompson's poem:

> Whom wilt thou find to love ignoble thee,
> Save Me, save only Me?

Only God knows if Eugene O'Neill ever felt that sa We do know that while he lay on his deathbed in Bosto Dorothy Day was still praying fervently for him and as priest be sent to him. She hoped that in his last momen would cease his futile wrestling with God and reall words he recited in that barroom on that cold winter's

> All which thy child's mistake
> Fancies as lost, I have stored for thee at home:
> Rise, clasp My hand, and come!

⇢ III ⇠

LIVING AS THE IMAGE OF GOD

Harry Wu would be the first to admit it: he was a fairly lukewarm Catholic in 1960 when Mao Zedong's police threw him into a forced labor camp for protesting the Chinese Communist regime's human rights abuses. But Wu believed what the good Jesuit missionaries had taught him, and he bristled at the taunting of his interrogator, an officer named Yang.

"Catholics say that a human being is made by God," Yang said. "How did he do it? Did he just take some dirt in his hand and blow on it like some kind of magic?"

Wu replied: "You are a Party member—*you* tell *me* where humans came from."

"Men evolved from apes," Yang pronounced.

"So when I go to the zoo, I can see your forefathers?" Wu mused. Yang's face clouded, but he returned to his attack: "Anyway, your God is of no help to you here—I guess sooner or later you'll give him up."

Wu's voice was calm and determined: "Someday I'll give up my body's life, but not my spiritual life."

Harry Wu survived two decades in captivity, suffering unspeakable indignities. He lived to tell his story and to become one of the last century's most visible advocates for human rights and religious freedom.

The twentieth century was a strange and conflicted century. Human liberation movements like communism flourished, everywhere proclaiming deliverance from every conceivable kind of bondage—political, economic, psychological, and moral. Millions like Wu were sacrificed to seductive new ideas about the meaning and destiny of human life. Some became victims of race wars, class wars, and "holy wars"; others were killed in their mothers' wombs; others still, deemed unfit to live because of old age or disability, were offered euthanasia, or a "good death."

For the Catholic it is no surprise that the century's utopian dreams turned into nightmares. The promise of a world without God is always a false one. To try to solve human problems without reference to God's plan is to embark down a blind alley. The last century was the proof: without God we become a mystery to ourselves and monsters to one another.

Original Sin, Happy Fault

For all their differences, the ideologies of the modern age are almost unanimous in believing that the notion of human sinfulness is a religious fiction. But for the Catholic, sin explains a lot, maybe even everything, about why the world is the way it is. Indeed, sin is written into the story of humankind's beginnings, found in the Bible's first book. While it is told in symbolic language, Catholics believe that this story nonetheless recounts primeval events that continue to explain human nature and shape human history.

We learn from the Bible that God created men and women to be his children, to live in love with him in the garden paradise of this world. This paradise was shattered by the first humans' sin, prompted by the devil, a rebellious angel whom Jesus called "the father of lies" and "a murderer from the beginning." In the guise of a serpent, the devil tempted the first couple, Adam and Eve, to do what God had forbidden them, promising that if they disobeyed God they would become "like God" themselves.

This moment and its consequences are captured in a pair of frescoes painted in the 1420s on the walls of the Brancacci Chapel, in Florence, Italy, which served as a "classroom" for later masters like Michelangelo, Raphael, and Leonardo da Vinci. The two masterpieces—*Temptation of Adam and Eve* by Masolino and Masaccio's *Expulsion of Adam and Eve*—tell the story of human beginnings.

There is a dreamy sensuality to Masolino's *Temptation.* Entwined around a thin, leafy tree, the comely serpent arches above the woman's head like a benign benefactor. The man and the woman are naked, and each holds a morsel of fruit while gazing at the other expectantly. Masaccio's *Expulsion* depicts the morning after that first night of sin. Adam and Eve are being marched out the gates of Eden by a red angel armed with a dark saber, their bodies convulsed with sobs, their faces masks of shame and pain.

These are the first portraits in the album of the human family. Descended from Eve, whom the Scriptures call the "mother of all living," we inherit the legacy of Adam and Eve's original sin. Conceived, in St. Paul's words, "under the power of sin," we are born with a propensity to sin—a tendency to want to deliberately reject God's will and commands.

The first thing to know about our world and ourselves, then, is that we hail from a long line of sinners. Because of original sin we will struggle with sin all the days of our lives. Every time we sin, we in effect reenact the sin of our first parents. We get suspicious that God might be holding something back. We do not look at him as our Father but instead set him up as a petty master, lording himself over us. We resent him for trying to hold us down, and we long to break free and go it alone.

Our sins are always personal. We make conscious decisions to abuse the freedom God gives us to pursue what we mistakenly identify as our own self-interest. Thus, St. Augustine could define sin as "love of oneself even to the point of *contempt of God.*"

But sin is never just a private affair. Our sins—what we do but should not, what we do not do but should—beget countless offenses and violences against loved ones and neighbors, even against people we will never see. That is why in the 1930s, when the *Times* (London) asked the Catholic essayist G. K. Chesterton and others to write on the topic of "What's Wrong with the World Today," Chesterton sent back a two-word response:

> Dear Sirs:
>
> I am.
>
> Sincerely, G. K. Chesterton

Sin is real. If you doubt it, check out the headlines on any given day or look inside yourself. Everywhere you will find sin and the fruits of sin—corruption, violence, injustice, lusts of the heart and lusts of the flesh. But if sin is our beginning, it is not meant to be our end.

Jesus broke sin's hold on our lives. He makes it possible for us to live as God intended. He was born of the Virgin Mary, and she was the only one among the billions born since the beginning of the world to be conceived without inheriting the curse of original sin. In God's plan, Mary was kept free from sin in order to bear the holy one who would take away the sin of the world.

Because of Jesus we can realize what the psalmist once sang, that the human person is made "a little lower than God, and crowned . . . with glory and honor." That is why Catholics call Adam and Eve's sin a "happy fault," or *felix culpa* in Latin. On Easter, we sing a hymn called the *Exsultet:* "O happy fault . . . which gained for us so great a Redeemer." Through Jesus humanity is led back from exile to the divine life intended by God.

Jesus shows us definitively that to be human is to be "a living being capable of being divine," as St. Gregory of Nazianzus used to say. We were made to be divinized—made divine—but not by any grasping or striving on our part. He who made us in his image and likeness by his grace will bring that image to perfection in each of us.

In the Womb, We Are Known

Because we are made in the divine image, all human life is sacred. For Catholics, every child is an image of the eternal Son of God, who came to us as an infant in the womb and grew from a child into a man. We believe that what God said of the prophet Jeremiah is true for all of us: "Before I formed you in the womb I knew you." We believe Jesus' promise—that whoever receives a child in his name receives him.

In his tender affection for children Jesus stood in radical contradiction to the attitudes and practices of the empire of his day. The Romans and Greeks held that children were inferior beings, something less than fully human. Plato, Aristotle, and other philosophers of the ancient world approved the killing of unwanted children through abortion and infanticide, and they saw nothing wrong with using children for sexual gratification.

Jesus said it would be better to have a millstone tied around your neck and be plunged into the depths of the sea than to suffer God's judgment for scandalizing one of his little ones. From the beginning, the church fiercely defended children, even the unborn. The *Didache* ("Teaching"), the oldest surviving manual of church life, written in the mid-first century, warns: "You shall not kill the embryo by abortion and shall not cause the newborn to perish." The Christian philosopher Athenagoras, in a plea to Emperor Marcus Aurelius in 175, explained: "We regard the very fetus in the womb as a created being and therefore an object of God's care."

Catholics honor everyone as an object of God's care, born with God-given dignity and the right to pursue his or her own unique relationship with God. Every person we meet brings us into contact with Jesus, who united himself with all humanity when he became man. We believe Jesus' promise that he comes to us especially in the poor and the hungry, the sick and the imprisoned.

This belief is one of the pillars of the Catholic approach to questions of social justice. St. John Chrysostom compared the "sacrament of the altar"—the Eucharist—to the "sacrament of our brothers and sisters." As he said:

> Do not pay him homage in the temple clad in silk only then to neglect him outside where he suffers cold and nakedness. He who said: "This is my body" is the same one who said: "You saw me hungry and you gave me no food," and "Whatever you did to the least of my brothers you did also

> to me." . . . What good is it if the Eucharistic table is overloaded with golden chalices, when he is dying of hunger? Start by satisfying his hunger and then with what is left you may adorn the altar as well.

Thus, Catholics since the days of the apostles have devoted themselves to works of mercy, charity, and justice. Because Jesus comes to us in the poor, we feed the hungry, nurse the sick, give hospitality to the homeless, fight social injustice, and work for the coming of God's kingdom on earth as it is in heaven.

We serve every man and woman as a brother or a sister, without regard to race or religion. As St. Gregory of Nyssa said in his treatise *On the Formation of Man,* written in the mid-fourth century:

> The gracious gift of likeness to God was not given to a mere section of humanity, to one individual man; no, it is a perfection that finds its way in equal measure to every member of the human race. . . . There is no difference between the first man that ever was and the last that will ever be: all bear the stamp of divinity.

We see life as a precious gift that God has bestowed upon each of us. That is why Catholics, from the first, opposed suicide, which like abortion and infanticide was a practice common in the ancient world. Defending this belief in the preciousness of life in the early 300s, an African Christian named Lactantius wrote:

> As we did not come into this life of our own accord, so . . . we can only withdraw from this habitation of the body . . . by

> the command of him who placed us in this body to inhabit it until he orders us to depart from it.

We Owe Him Our Lives

Because we experience our lives as a gift, we live in gratitude. We know there is no worship worthy of the One who has given us life except to offer ourselves to him. As François Fénelon, an archbishop in seventeenth-century France, put it, "I owe him not only all that I have but also all that I am."

We were made for this worship, this offering of ourselves to God. Jesus defined love as loving as he loved. He loved by laying down his life and offering it to God for us. That is how we are expected to live, loving God with all our hearts and minds and strength. As Jesus said, we must lose our lives to save them. Our lives are to become pure sacrifice. St. Augustine said, "Thus man himself, consecrated in the name of God and devoted to God, is a sacrifice inasmuch as he dies to the world so that he might live to God."

This is not a negative doctrine, a calling for us to negate or extinguish ourselves. It is a calling to love. Love is not selfish, but selfless. To love is to make oneself a gift to another. God is love, as the Scriptures tell us. And in our acts of self-offering, we move closer to the image of God in which we were created. We imitate the love of the Trinity, in which the Father gives life to the Son through the Spirit, and the Son in turn offers himself back to the Father in the love of the Spirit.

Since the earliest days, the church has venerated martyrs—those who make the ultimate self-sacrifice, giving up their own lives out of love for their neighbor or in witness to the truth. But self-sacrifice is not limited to martyrs; all of the church's teachings about both personal holiness and social responsibility are rooted in this idea of giving oneself to God. In early 260, when an epidemic was ravaging the Roman Empire, the persecuted Christian minority nursed the sick and dying and buried the dead. Non-Christians, by contrast, were so fearful of contracting the disease that they fled, many leaving their loved ones to suffer and die on the streets. Dionysius, a bishop in Alexandria, described the Christians' joyful service:

> Heedless of danger, they took charge of the sick, attending to their every need and ministering to them in Christ, and with them departed this life serenely happy. For they were infected by others with the disease, drawing on themselves the sickness of their neighbors and cheerfully accepting their pains. . . . The best of our brothers lost their lives in this manner . . . in every way the equal of martyrdom.

The self-offering to which we are called includes all our normal chores and labors. In the beginning, human beings were given work to do as a way to collaborate with God in bringing his creation to its perfect glory. However, like everything else about the human condition, work was distorted by original sin. We see this in the world around us: made in the image of the Creator, we are able to create computers and skyscrapers, fly to the moon, compose great symphonies and masterpieces of literature and art. But our sinfulness often renders our work drudgery, an obsession or a menace. The things we make—our technologies, our systems of thought—can threaten and even enslave us.

Jesus restored the true meaning and potential of human labor. He worked as a carpenter, called working men and women to be his followers, and drew richly from the world of work to illustrate his teachings. Jesus sanctified work, made it more than simply something we do to put food on the table or keep idle hands busy. Work now is a means by which we serve and draw close to God.

The summit of human labor is reached in the Eucharist, when the priest offers bread and wine—the fruits of creation and the work of human hands—to be changed into the body and blood of Jesus. All our labors are in some way to be "Eucharistic"—offerings to God, to be taken up and transformed by him and used for his glory.

A Thanksgiving People

Our life is meant to be liturgy, an ancient Christian word that means "service of the people." In the beginning, God oriented all creation, with man and woman at its pinnacle, toward the seventh day, the Sabbath. The Sabbath was the sign of God's covenant of love with the world. He established it as a weekly feast of communion between him and his creatures, a day when we put down our tools, rest, and give him praise.

"The sabbath," Jesus said, "was made for humankind." It is a sign of what we are here for, that we are made for worship. But as Paul explained, the Sabbath that sealed God's covenant in the beginning was "only a shadow of what is to come." Jesus brought a new Sabbath—the "eighth day," the Lord's Day, the day of his resurrection and the first day of God's new creation. Jesus gave us a new form of worship for this new Sabbath, a festival of love we call simply the Eucharist ("thanksgiving").

Catholics are thanksgiving people. In our worship we are people of praise, our hearts lifted up in humble thanks for the gift of eternal life offered in Jesus. Liturgy and worship are the only proper responses to the loving call the Father issues to us. St. Augustine's famously tender words belong here: "You have made us for yourself, and our heart is restless until it rests in You." Worship is the repose of our restless hearts in the One who made us for himself.

An ancient characteristic of Catholic worship is the antiphon, a word that means "answering back." It is the pattern of liturgical call-and-response, as when the priest prays, "The Lord be with you," and the worshipers answer back, "And also with your spirit." This prayerful dialogue reflects a fundamental Catholic understanding of what it means to be human. We are "antiphonal" beings in conversation with our Creator—listening for God's call and answering him with our lives.

Inside each of us, God has carved out a space for this antiphonal conversation. That space is called the conscience. "Conscience," St. Bonaventure said, "is like God's herald and messenger. It does not command things on its own authority, but commands them as coming from God's authority, like a herald when he proclaims the edict of the king."

Our conscience is an echo of God's voice within us. It proclaims what is right and warns us against what is wrong. Conscience is not about rules and regulations. It is a spiritual law that God writes on every heart, binding us to him as his children. What our conscience commands as "right" is that which keeps us alive in our Father's love. What our conscience calls "wrong" is that which pushes us away from his fatherly embrace.

God gave us conscience so that we would be able to find our way to him. John Henry Newman followed his conscience to become the most famous and influential convert to Catholicism in nineteenth-century England. He described the conscience this way:

> A man is at once thrown out of himself by the very voice which speaks within him. . . . That inward sense (the conscience) does not allow him to rest in itself, but sends him forth again from home to seek abroad for him who has put his word in him.

The Truth about Freedom

We can follow our conscience because God has created us to be free. Our freedom is perhaps the greatest sign of the image of God in which we are made. We are made free to decide whether to seek God or ignore him. In his *Oration on the Dignity of Man,* written in 1486, the great Italian humanist Giovanni Pico della Mirandola imagines God speaking this to Adam—that is, to each of us:

> O Adam . . . the rest of creatures are determined according to the laws of their nature . . . but you are not limited by any boundary. Rather you are to establish your own nature through your own free will, upon which I have made your destiny in life depend. . . . You are free to be perverted into subhuman forms, but you are equally free to be reborn in higher divine forms through your own decision.

It is deadly illusion to think that we are free just because we can make choices. Freedom is not the power to do what we please. Such was the false freedom the father of lies offered to Adam and

Eve. Freedom pursued that way leads to slavery to sin, to our own insatiable desires. In such circumstances, people become like "animals turning around a mill," as St. Gregory of Nyssa vividly described it: "With our eyes blinded we walk around the mill of life, always treading the same circular path and returning to the same things . . . appetite, satiety, sleeping, waking up, emptiness, fullness."

Jesus said, "The truth will make you free." We are truly free only if we are living according to the truth Jesus revealed about human nature. Indeed, the most exalted expression of human freedom is the act of faith—the choice *for God.* Catholics have always held up Jesus' mother as the clearest model for human freedom and faith. Mary, according to the Scriptures, is "she who believed." Mary was the first to believe in God's word about Jesus, and she was his first disciple, freely giving herself to God and uniting her will to his.

God will never force us to choose him. We have to decide for ourselves to be for him or against him, to believe him or not. This choice is between life and death, really. We can love and live or choose not to.

Body and Soul

We are born free and called to choose communion with God. And this is the stuff we are made of: a mortal body and an immortal soul. This too is symbolized in the Bible's first pages, as God fashions Adam out of dust from the ground and animates him with the Spirit of life.

We are not just bodies—muscle, bone, and blood—as Harry Wu's captors supposed. However, our bodies might have evolved from other forms of life. The Scriptures tell us that God used elements of matter he had already created—the dust of the ground—to fashion the first person. It could very well be that God guided the evolution of that matter through various animal forms until he saw that it was a body fit to be fused with a spiritual soul and bear his image and likeness.

But there are no accidents in God's creation. Things may evolve, but nature takes its course under the care and direction of the Creator. The human species is not the product of some random process of natural selection marked by a pointless struggle among lower life-forms. We are not animals, but the crowning glory of creation. God had a hand in creating each of us. The Scriptures speak of God "knitting" the person in the womb. He personally put the spiritual soul in each of us as we grew beneath our mothers' hearts.

The soul is the imperishable part of our makeup—it will live on forever after our body decays. But we are not just souls caged in bodies. Our soul is not who we are, and our body is not a shell we inhabit and then shed upon death. Better to think of ourselves as spirits-in-the-flesh, bodies shot through with soul. Our bodies are the "revelation" of who we are. Our bodies have a *language.* We are "expressed" in and through our bodies.

God's coming in the flesh reveals the meaning and destiny of the body. He promised that we will rise to eternal life in our bodies—as he did. "The flesh is the hinge of salvation," said Tertullian, the third-century African defender of the faith. Our bodies are not our private property. Paul said that our bodies are meant for the Lord and our Lord for our bodies. "Do you not know that . . . you are not your own?" he cried. "Therefore glorify God in your body."

In baptism each of us is grafted onto the body of Christ. Our bodies have been infused with divine energy, filled with the glorious possibility of God. We become a "temple of the Holy Spirit," as Paul described it. Indeed, Jesus' promise that he and the Father would make their abode within those who love him is no mere flourish of speech, but a basic truth of Catholic life.

The early Christians told the story of Leonides, who was beheaded by Emperor Septimius Severus. He left behind a wife and seven young children, including Origen, who went on to become a great evangelist and a martyr himself. In the evenings after putting his children to bed, Leonides used to watch them sleep. Thanking God, he would kiss each child's chest reverently because "it was the temple of a divine spirit."

Made to Be "One Flesh"

We are temples filled with divine spirit, made in God's image, made male and female. Perhaps the greatest artistic portrayal of this truth is *Ex Nihilo* ("Out of Nothing"). It is a vastly larger-than-life depiction of the creation of man and woman, sculpted by an American, Frederick Hart, probably the finest sculptor of the twentieth century. His work in stone, bronze, marble, and clear acrylic resin included exquisitely rendered ethereal nudes, grand public monuments, and transcendent religious images.

The story of *Ex Nihilo* is the stuff of romance and legend. Hart was an unknown thirty-one-year-old stone-carver's apprentice in 1974, when against all odds he won an international competition for the most important religious art commission of the century—to create the iconography for the west facade of the Gothic-style Washington National Cathedral.

During the eight years it took to complete the project, Hart himself became something of a new creation. Immersed in the Scriptures and Catholic writings about creation, Hart converted to Catholicism. He began to see his talent as reflecting the glorious image of the Creator. He devoted his art to expressing the beauty and nobility of the human spirit, and to reflecting what he called "the highest and most noble values of mankind and society." While meditating daily on the magnificent mystery of man and woman in the Creator's plan, Hart fell deeply in love with one of his models, Lindy Lain. The two were married, and her beauty would inspire his work until his death in 1999.

Standing fifteen feet high and twenty-one feet wide, *Ex Nihilo* was Hart's masterpiece. It evokes Michelangelo in its intense physicality and exalted sense of movement. But there is one big difference. In the legendary *Creation of Adam* in the Vatican's Sistine Chapel, Michelangelo depicts a one-on-one encounter between God and Adam, who is portrayed as self-aware and confident that he can reach out and touch the one who made him. Hart's creation scene is more primordial, all reverie and echo, like heartbeats heard in a dream. The taut, idealized human forms, emerge out of a whirlwind of rock, cloud, and seawater—nascence, awe, rapture, and ecstasy mingled on their lips and opening eyes.

What is striking in *Ex Nihilo* is how the figures fit together. The man and woman look as if they are a part of each other, only temporarily separated by the ravishing whir of creation and destined to be made whole again. It is a glorious depiction of the Catholic understanding of the "complementarity" of the sexes.

In God's plan, our sex is not something incidental to who we are. He made the human race "male and female," Scripture tells us. Our sex, then, is essential to our identity as creatures made in the divine image and likeness. But biology is not destiny. Man and woman are invested with the same spiritual dignity as children of the Father. Original sin disrupted this dignity by introducing a hierarchy of domination into relations between the sexes; however, by his affectionate friendships with women, by the respect he accorded women in his teaching, and in the responsibilities he gave them in his church, Jesus signaled the end of man's rule over woman. As Paul put it, "There is no longer male and female; for all of you are one in Christ Jesus."

Man and woman stand as equals before God. And they stand before each other as complementary beings. The man is made to "complete" the woman, and the woman is made to "complete" the man. St. Edith Stein, the philosopher and Catholic convert from Judaism who was martyred by the Nazis at Auschwitz, wrote that "man and woman are destined to live *one life* with one another, like a single being."

The beautiful symmetry we notice between the male and female bodies—the way they seem to be made to be joined together—hints at God's intentions. In the language of Genesis, he made the human person, male and female, to be reunited, rejoined literally as "one flesh." This communion of love is brought about in the sexual union of man and woman. It is a moment so sacred that God intended it from the beginning to take place only within the divinely established relationship of marriage. Men and women were made for this nuptial moment. In the words of Pope John Paul II, a "nuptial meaning" has been inscribed within our very bodies.

John Paul's "theology of the body" was a philosophical and theological breakthrough in our understanding of the mystery and destiny of the human person. It is a unique teaching, dense and provocative, that John Paul unfolded patiently nearly every Wednesday afternoon at the Vatican between 1979 and 1984.

In his teaching the pope recovered ancient scriptural and mystical insights about human love and sexuality in God's plan. While he drew from psychology, biology, philosophy, and the traditions of the church, he claimed to have learned the most from the young people he ministered to early in his career—from their search for beauty and true love. He told a journalist once: "As a young priest I learned to love human love. . . . If one loves human love, there naturally arises the need to commit oneself completely to the service of 'fair love,' because love is fair, it is beautiful."

The Thrill of Love

As John Paul expressed so well, the Catholic loves human love. Fair love, beautiful love, is a revelation of the love of God. When you are in love, your whole being is in thrall. Nothing is so important as to be near the beloved. These natural human sensations are given to us as a foretaste of the love that lies in the heart of Trinity, the love that God wants to share with all humanity in his church.

The most beautiful lyricist of the divine romance was the thirteenth-century Italian poet Dante Alighieri, best remembered for his late epic, *The Divine Comedy.* But he writes most memorably of love in his first book, *The New Life,* a series of sonnets and reminiscences published when he was twenty-eight.

In it he describes his love for the young maiden Beatrice, whom he first glimpsed in Florence when the two were nine years old. He recounts the tingle of excitement he would feel whenever he sensed her presence, how he longed to catch sight of her as she passed by in the streets. Dante soon discovered that the thrill of his love was just a glimmering token of a higher, more radiant love—the love of Love itself, the love of God. As he writes:

> At that moment I say truly that the Spirit of life, which dwells in the most secret chamber of the heart, began to tremble so strongly that it appeared terrifying in its smallest veins; and trembling it said these words: "Behold a God more powerful than I, who comes to rule over me." . . . I say that from that time forward, Love ruled over my soul, which was so early espoused to him, and he began to assume over me such assurance and such mastery. . . . In one of his hands he appeared to hold something all aflame, and he seemed to say to me these words: "Behold your heart."

In these delicate lines Dante captures the spirit of human love as God meant it to be. Human love is a divine gift that reflects on earth the beauties in the heart of God. Dante said his love for Beatrice set his heart on fire, leading to an "espousal"—a sort of spiritual marriage to God. All our human loves are meant to draw us into this espousal with Love. Some men and women are drawn to that espousal through a vow of virginity, making an exclusive, sacrificial offering of themselves to God. Most are called to offer themselves solely to another person.

Jesus said that in the beginning God made marriage a permanent sign of his love. In marriage, Jesus said, God joins together man and woman so that they form a new life as one:

"They are no longer two, but one flesh." Man and woman in holy matrimony become an icon of the Trinity, a single spiritual life made up of three "persons"—the man and the woman and God, who unites them in the bond of his love.

The marital act by which the marriage covenant is consummated is also a sign of the communion of love in the Trinity. As husband and wife give themselves to each other completely, each accepts the gift of the other in tender love.

God means sex to be an act of sacrifice and worship—husband and wife, shorn of all self-interest, offering body and soul to each other, loving wholly for the sake of the other, hearts penetrated with the love of God. We can hear an echo of this belief in a nuptial vow from the thirteenth century:

> With this ring I thee wed . . .
> and with my body I thee worship.

Creating Images of God

The love of spouses in their nuptial embrace can be truly "love making"—a love that makes new life. In this, our love is an image of the life-giving love of the Trinity that creates heaven and earth and all that is seen and unseen.

The image of God reaches its most radiant expression in the nuptial embrace. This communion reveals the fullness of our divine potential and destiny: we enter into the glorious possibility of participating in the Trinity's creative work. Becoming "one flesh," husband and wife are able to become "the begetter of humanity, the creator of images of God," in the phrase of the fourth-century bishop Amphilochius of Iconium.

The power to create new life, the yearnings that men and women feel for each other, the physical pleasure and emotional delight that sex brings—all these are natural signs of the divine blessings that God has given us in this wondrous gift. Naturally speaking, sex is intended to be a sweet and delightful moment of forever, the closest thing to heaven we can know on earth. But there is so much more to sex.

God also means sex to be supernatural, heavenly. Any two partners can experience the joy of the flesh that sex brings. But sex apart from the sacred context of man and woman joined in marriage will always be sex profaned, a sinful abuse of God's gift. If God's intentions are left out of sex, then the soul of each partner is left out too. Sex becomes only a function or performance, a coming together of parts of bodies.

A true union of bodies and souls that mirrors the divine love can only come in a covenant relationship between husband and wife vowed for life in the sight of God. That is why, following the teaching of Jesus, the church has always viewed certain practices as contrary to God's plan for creation and true human happiness and well-being: these practices include sex between unmarried partners and between persons of the same sex, masturbation, and the use of artificial contraception.

These are not arbitrary rules and regulations imposed from on high. They are better thought of as expressions of the sanctity of sex and its significance as a "sacramental gift." Hugh of Saint-Victor, a mystical theologian of the early twelfth century, said the sexual union of husband and wife was "the sacrament of the invisible community which must develop in spirit between God and the soul [and] . . . the sacrament of the visible participation which developed between Christ and the Church."

What We Are Made For

Sex is central to the Catholic vision of the human person because it is a supernatural sign, a mysterious sacrament that takes us back to "the beginning." The marriage of Adam and Eve in the Garden of Eden was a foreshadowing of the relationship that God wants with each of us. The apostle Paul said that the two becoming one flesh in the marital union is a symbol of Jesus' union with his church. He said all humanity, joined in the church, was to be made one flesh with Jesus. Paul added, not without a little understatement, "This is a great mystery."

We see this nuptial destiny of the human race in the Bible, which begins with the marriage of Adam and Eve and ends with Revelation's image of a kind of wedding en masse. The world, and each one of us, is made for this "marriage supper of the Lamb," the final communion of all humankind with the Father in the Spirit and through the Son. Israel's prophets looked for the Messiah to come as a divine bridegroom. The psalms and the biblical love poem, the Song of Songs, describe Israel as a princess being led from her bridal chamber into the palace of her Messiah-King. When the Messiah truly came, Jesus called himself the "bridegroom" and compared the kingdom of God to a wedding feast.

That is why Paul spoke of his missionary work as a sort of heavenly matchmaking—a "betrothing" of souls to Jesus. And in the early church, entrance into the faith was described in nuptial terms, as a wedding feast of the soul. Didymus the Blind, one of the most learned men in fourth-century Egypt, said, "In the baptismal pool, he who made our soul takes it for his bride." Saints and mystics down through the ages have used nuptial language to speak of spiritual relationships of indescribable intimacy. Of his life as a monk, St. Bernard of Clairvaux once wrote:

> Happy is the soul to whom it has been given to experience an embrace of such surpassing delight! This spiritual embrace is nothing else than a chaste and holy love, a love sweet and pleasant, a love perfectly serene and perfectly pure, a love that is intimate and strong, a love that joins two, not in one flesh, but in one spirit, that makes two to be no longer two but one undivided spirit, as witness St. Paul, where he says, "He who cleaves to the Lord is one spirit with him."

This sweet love, this spiritual embrace, is what we are made for. Harry Wu's captors were dead wrong. Human beings are made for so much more than what the dictators, terrorists, or social engineers of our day say we are. We are what the Word of God has revealed us to be—children made in God's image, each of us a unique and priceless expression of the love of God. Made by God and for God, we are destined in love for this spiritual embrace.

This is the proposal God has made to each of us in Jesus. And he awaits our response to his promise, given in the words of Paul: "What no eye has seen, nor ear heard, nor the human heart conceived, what God has prepared for those who love him."

→ IV ←

WHY THE CATHOLIC CHURCH?

Peter was old and his body bent. In the thirty years since the Master had been taken up to heaven in a cloud, Peter had crossed the empire, from Jerusalem to Antioch to Corinth and points between. In market squares, synagogues, jailhouses, ships, and homes, he told everyone he met the good news about Jesus.

When he preached, it was as if Jesus were speaking with *his* mouth. By a power he knew was not his, he could forgive sins, change bread and wine into Christ's body and blood, cure the incurable, even raise a woman from the dead. He had seen some hard traveling too. He had been beaten down and locked up, hounded and harassed in every city, all for the love of the Master. But he had succeeded in bringing the gospel to the heart of the empire—to Rome, which his fellow Christians called the great whore Babylon, the belly of the imperial beast, the heart of a civilization founded on power and might, false idols, and man-made gods.

Peter had first met Jesus one day while he and his brother, Andrew, were casting their nets into the Sea of Galilee. "Follow me," Jesus had called to them. For three years Peter had been

Jesus' right-hand man, the first among his twelve handpicked apostles. And Peter was following him years later as he slipped out of the city gates and up the Appian Way.

He was leaving Rome in secret. Parts of the city were smoldering, and a fever of bloodlust had been loosed in the streets. Peter's flock was under attack. The mad emperor Nero had blamed the Christians for a series of fires that had swept the city. The imperial historian Tacitus would later record that Nero had ordered a "vast multitude" of Christians to be tortured and killed "with most ingenious cruelty." Some were eaten alive by wild dogs; others were nailed to crosses and then set aflame.

Church elders had prevailed upon Peter to go into hiding until the persecution ended, and then return and lead whatever remnant of the church survived. Grudgingly, he had agreed. But to his amazement, on the road outside Rome he saw Jesus walking toward him. He fell to his knees.

"Lord, where are you going?" he asked.

"To Rome, Peter. I am being crucified again," his Lord replied. In an instant Jesus was gone, whisked into the clouds.

Peter knew immediately what his Lord's words meant—Jesus was suffering in the body of his persecuted church. Peter realized that where his Master was, he should be too. So with a joyous cry, he turned around and headed back to Rome, where he died a martyr's death.

This story circulated widely in the early church. Still today along the Appian Way you can visit Domine Quo Vadis, an ancient church named for Peter's question ("Lord, where are you going?"), built on the site where the two reportedly met.

It is a story that gives us insight into the mystery and meaning of the church. The church is a mystical communion between Jesus

Christ and all those who believe that he is the savior of humanity. In his church, Jesus continues to journey with us, pouring out the grace we need to become the holy people God created us to be. There is only one church, because there is only one Jesus. Over time the one visible church has splintered into a variety of expressions of Christian faith. There are Orthodox Christians and many kinds of Protestant Christians. But the church as Jesus intended it is most fully found in the Roman Catholic Church, established by Jesus on the foundations of Peter and the other apostles. By the apostles' words and deeds, handed down in the Catholic Church through the ages by men appointed as the apostles' successors, the saving work of Jesus continues in the world, guided by the Spirit of God.

The church remains like Peter on that highway back to Rome—an imperfect and at times weak people making its way through the world as a pilgrim, beset by hardship and persecution, always tempted to lose faith and betray Jesus; a people always seeking an answer to Peter's question: Where would you have us follow, Lord?

For the Sake of the World

The church is not something that came later, like an appendix to the life of Jesus. It is not a name to describe the voluntary association of people who believe in Jesus. Nor is it something intangible, like a state of mind or a set of shared beliefs.

The church, a visible human family uniting people of all nations and races, is the goal of Jesus' life, death, and resurrection. The world was made in anticipation of the coming of the church, the family of God. "It was for her sake that the world was created," according to *The Shepherd of Hermas,* an important second-century Christian writing.

Jesus did not come to save only those who personally heard his preaching and witnessed his miracles. He came to save every man and woman in every time and place. He does this through the community he called "my *church.*" The word comes from the Greek *ecclesia,* a word used to describe religious assemblies.

In the Greek rendering of the Hebrew Scriptures, *ecclesia* was used to translate *qahal,* the Hebrew term given to the gathering of Israel as God's elect, the people with whom he made his covenant. The church of Jesus is the new *qahal.* In the church, God's covenant promise to Israel is enlarged to include not only Israel but all nations. What he once said of Israel, from now on he will say of his church, the new Israel. "You are a chosen race, a royal priesthood, a holy nation, God's own people," Peter wrote from Rome.

The church is the everlasting kingdom of God that the prophets taught Israel to hope for. It is the kingdom the prophet Zechariah saw: "The LORD will become king over all the earth; on that day the LORD will be one and his name one." This kingdom is a family, a communion of love. Founded in the mind of God, the kingdom was brought down to earth and embedded in his church, the visible form of God's new covenant with humanity.

"The Church of today is the kingdom of Christ and the kingdom of heaven," St. Augustine said, describing a growing, supernatural society uniting the living, the dead, and the unborn. "Not only the believers who are alive today, but also those who have lived before us, and those who will come after us until the end of time."

The church is a society visible among other human organizations, but it nevertheless remains a mystery outside of time and space. It is part human, part divine; one foot in heaven, the other on earth; rooted in eternity, at work in history. The church is the kingdom come and not yet arrived. This is why Jesus taught his church to pray ceaselessly for the coming of the kingdom, though the kingdom is already in our midst in his church.

God's kingdom will grow for as long as he pleases, adding to its ranks, always awaiting the final coming of the Lord, who will bring down with him a new heaven and a new earth, a new Jerusalem, a kingdom that will have no end. Until that final day, the church will be what the fifth-century pope St. Leo the Great described it as: "the sacrament of man's salvation."

As a sacrament, the church is both a *sign* of Christ's promise for the world and the *instrument* by which he fulfills that promise. And the Father's promise is breathtaking. He intends to break down all barriers and make all humankind one family. We see this in a most dramatic way at Pentecost, which Catholics call the birthday of the church.

Pilgrims from all over the ancient world thronged Jerusalem that day, as the Acts of the Apostles tells it. Jesus' apostles, along with the women disciples and Mary, his mother, were at prayer in an upper room. Suddenly, with the sound of a rushing wind, the Holy Spirit was poured out on them as tongues of fire. They started praising God's salvation in "divided tongues," that is, in every language. The pilgrims were astonished: "How is it that we hear, each of us, in our own native language?" they marveled. "In our own languages we hear them speaking about God's deeds of power."

At Pentecost, the Holy Spirit was revealed to be the artisan of the church. St. Irenaeus said, "Wherever the Church is, the Spirit of God is also there, and wherever the Spirit of the Lord is, the Church is there, and every grace." The Holy Spirit sends the church forward into a world partitioned by nationality, race, and religion to translate the good news of God's mighty saving works into every tongue, to invite all to join together as children of the Father, brothers and sisters of Jesus, his only Son.

In the words of the seventh-century martyr St. Maximus the Confessor:

> Men, women, children, profoundly divided in nationality, race, language, walk of life, knowledge, rank or means . . . all these [the church] recreates in the Spirit. . . . She imprints a divine character. All receive of her a single nature which cannot be divided. . . . All are brought up and united in a truly catholic manner. . . . All are fused together, so to speak. . . . Christ is all in all.

What *Catholic* Means

The church is *catholic* because it unites all things in Jesus Christ. The church is *catholic* because Christ Jesus is there, as he promised he would be—in the Eucharist, in his Spirit given to the church at Pentecost. "Where there is Christ Jesus there is the Catholic Church," St. Ignatius of Antioch wrote around AD 100.

In the fourth century, St. Cyril of Jerusalem described the "catholicity" of the church in these terms:

> The Church is called *Catholic* because it has spread over the whole world, from one end to the other. Because it proclaims comprehensively and without defect all the doctrines of the faith which we must know, about the visible and the invisible, about heavenly and earthly things. Because it brings the whole human race—princes and subjects, the

> uneducated and the educated—to the right worship of God. And finally . . . because like a doctor it heals all sins which have been committed either with the soul or the body. It also possesses every kind of virtue—whatever it may be called in action and words—and every kind of spiritual gift.

In its "catholicity," its unity of all in one, the church reflects the glorious oneness of the three divine persons. As St. Cyprian of Carthage defined it in the third century, the Catholic Church is "a people made one with the unity of the Father and Son and the Holy Spirit." This was Jesus' final prayer—that all humanity would enter into the oneness of God: "That they may all be one. As you, Father, are in me and I am in you. . . . [T]hat they may be one, as we are one."

Jesus does not intend his church to be a drab uniformity in which the many differences of personality, culture, and race are absorbed into the "one." Jesus wants his church to be one as God is one—a unity in diversity, unique persons bound together in a communion of love.

The one Catholic Church contains a colorful array of particular churches living as part of one big family. The one Catholic Church includes the Western, or Latin, Church, which traces its origins to the missions of Peter and Paul to Jerusalem and Rome, and the Eastern Churches, which stem from the ancient cultural centers of Alexandria, Antioch, Byzantium, Chaldea, and Armenia. The names of these churches sound like poetry of the world's spiritual riches: Malabarese, Melkite and Ruthenian, Ethiopian and Belarusian.

Each of these particular churches has its own heritage, rites, customs, and ways of living the faith. But all are united by a common belief in the teachings, sacraments, and traditions handed on from Jesus to the apostles. There are many particular churches but only one church. That is why the apostles began the habit of addressing churches they established as "the church of God that is in Corinth" or "the church at Antioch."

What unites the church is the Eucharist. This is the new order of worship instituted by Jesus, in which we experience true communion with him by eating bread and wine miraculously changed into his flesh and blood. "Because there is one bread, we who are many are one body, for we all partake of the one bread," Paul said. The Eucharist makes the church one body with Jesus, a single new person, what Augustine called "the whole Christ."

Mother Church

The apostle Paul found out about this unity of Jesus and his church in a striking way. Paul had been a zealous Jew obsessed with destroying the new church of God. After overseeing the stoning death of the deacon Stephen and others, Paul was on his way to Damascus with orders to extradite Christians for trial before Jerusalem's high priest. Suddenly he was struck down and blinded by a light from heaven. He heard a voice: "I am Jesus, whom you are persecuting."

How close are Jesus and church? So close that when one member of the church is persecuted, Jesus is persecuted. Paul would later explain it this way: Jesus is one body with his church, as a groom and his bride become "one flesh" on their wedding night. Husband and wife remain individuals, but by their union they become a single new "person."

The church was born out of the pierced side of the crucified Jesus, just as the first woman was created from the side of the first man and made to be his bride. As Augustine said:

> Adam sleeps that Eve may be formed: Christ dies that the church may be formed. While Adam sleeps, Eve is formed in his side. When Christ is dead his side is smitten with a spear, that there may flow forth sacraments to form the church.

The church, then, is much more than a simple gathering of like-minded folks on a Sunday morning. In the church, each of us becomes a part of the mystery of creation and the history of salvation. Eve in the Scriptures was called the "mother of all living." And the church, like a new Eve, is the mother of all who are made alive in Christ. From the union of Christ and his bride, the church, a new human race is conceived by the gospel, born by baptism, nurtured and nourished by the sacraments, reared by teaching and example.

The motherhood of the church has long been understood as a continuation of the motherhood of Mary, who began the work of our salvation by giving flesh to Jesus in the womb. On the cross Jesus himself established a close connection between his mother and his church when he entrusted Mary to his beloved apostle John with the words, "Here is your mother."

The church, following the Son, finds the depths of its own character and mission in his mother. John called the church "the elect lady." Like Mary, the church is both mother and virgin. She is mother because she brings into being new children of God in baptism. She is virgin because she is a divine creation of the Spirit, existing by grace, protected from the corruption of error, desiring always to purify her members, to present them "holy and without blemish" to Christ.

The "People" of God

Living in our mother the church, each of us has a part to play in God's saving plan—to preach the gospel with our lives, to spread the kingdom of God. But our Catholic mother has always distinguished three basic ways of life, or roles, among her children. There is the clergy, those ordained for special leadership, who serve as priests and bishops, bringing the life-giving Word of God and his sacraments to the people. There are religious, or monastics—those set apart to bear witness to the radical possibilities of a life dedicated solely to the gospel. Finally, there is the laity.

Most of us fall into this third division. *Laity* means simply "the people." We are the ordinary faithful, the common children of our Catholic mother. Some of us are single; others are husbands and fathers, wives and mothers. We are found working in every profession and occupation. Our job is to bring the gospel into every corner of our workaday lives—in fields and factories, offices and legislatures, on stage and in laboratories, in studios, classrooms, and homes.

Jesus did not suffer and die to create a small band of "saved" people living in a ghetto amid a mass of the "unsaved." The mission of his church is to save the world, to change the way every man and woman thinks, acts, and lives. That is the paramount work of the laity. Through our friendships, associations, and work, we are to beget more children of mother church, to grow the family of God.

At the end of our lives, every layperson should be able to repeat the words of Papylus, a layman executed in the 160s during the persecution of Emperor Marcus Aurelius. The prosecutor-judge asked him about his children. He replied by pointing to the many he had led to baptism through his love and witness: "Know that I do not lie. In every province, in every town, I have children of God."

Church of the Apostles

In the order established by Jesus, the church's maternity flows from the paternity of her spiritual fathers—priests and bishops who trace their ministry and authority directly to Jesus' apostles.

Jesus intended his church to be "apostolic"—that is, built on the foundation of those known in the early church simply as the Twelve. An apostle is, literally, "one who is sent forth." Jesus himself was called "the apostle and high priest" of God. He chose the Twelve specially, instructed them privately, and sent them out with full authority to finish his work: "As the Father has sent me, so I send you." "Whoever receives one whom I send receives me; and whoever receives me receives him who sent me."

Jesus gave them immense responsibilities. They were to be prophets, bearing witness to him, teaching what he had taught them, and calling people to repentance and new life. They were to be priests—mediators through whom he would personally touch men and women, forgiving their sins and giving them new life. And they were to "sit on thrones judging" in his kingdom—that is, they were to be rulers of his church. For all this, he gave them the special gift of the Holy Spirit and reminded them that "apart from me you can do nothing."

The early records we have show the apostles carrying out their mission boldly, confident in their mandate and assured of the Lord's constant companionship. They preached, interpreted Scripture, baptized, absolved sinners, and celebrated the "breaking of the bread." As guardians of Christ's true teaching, they zealously combated heresies and false teachings. They founded local churches and established traditions of prayer and worship and rules of order and discipline. They wrote letters to clarify their teachings and met in councils to settle grave issues of doctrine and church practice.

Jesus did not intend them to be "founding fathers" who would get his church off the ground and then fade into the mists of pious memory. The mission he gave the Twelve—to preach the gospel to all creation, to make disciples of all nations—was so vast it could not possibly be completed in their lifetimes. When he promised, "I am with you always, to the end of the age," he was pledging to be not only with them, but also with those who would succeed them in this mission until his return at the end of time.

Thus, the Twelve arranged for their work to continue. They ordained priests and deacons to assist them and bishops to assume their apostolic functions in local churches. Writing in the mid-90s, St. Clement of Rome, the fourth pope and a disciple of Peter, explained the process of "apostolic succession" as a divinely instituted chain of command:

> Christ comes with a message from God and the apostles with a message from Christ. Both these orderly arrangements, therefore, originate from the will of God. . . . The apostles went forth, equipped with the fullness of the Holy Spirit, to preach the good news . . . and from their

> earliest converts appointed men whom they had tested by the Spirit to act as bishops . . . for the future believers. . . . Our apostles . . . went on to add an instruction that if these bishops should fall asleep, other accredited persons should succeed them in their office.

In the early days, bishops would gather at the funerals of brother bishops and choose their successors. The power of the Holy Spirit was conferred upon these new bishops by a solemn "laying on of hands." As a result, the new bishops possessed the same divine authority and responsibilities given to the apostles. St. Cyprian said: "The power to forgive sins has been given to the apostles, and to the churches which they established as commissioned by Christ, as well as to the bishops who succeed them in virtue of being appointed as their vicars."

The bishop "presides in the place of God," wrote St. Ignatius, a disciple of John, in the early 100s. He added, "Let everyone . . . revere the bishop as the image of the Father." Being bishop does not mean lording over the faithful. "To you I am the bishop, with you I am the Christian," St. Augustine wrote to his people. "The first is an office, the second a grace; the first a danger, the second salvation."

Calling the job dangerous is an understatement. Martyrdom was a common fate for these men—Ignatius torn apart by lions; Cyprian beheaded, as was Pope Fabian; St. Polycarp, bishop of Smyrna, burned alive in a stadium at the age of eighty-six. Such stories continue in our own day. Blessed Ignatius Maloyan, an Armenian Catholic bishop, was rounded up with other Catholics by a group of Muslims in a wave of terror in Turkey in 1915. He was pistol-whipped, dragged naked in chains, forced to watch soldiers kill five hundred of his friends and parishioners. When he still would not renounce his faith and convert to Islam, they shot him in the head as he cried out, "I take pride in the cross of my God and Lord!"

There will always be stories like this, because in every moment in history the bishop is the living sign of the church united with the cross of Jesus. The truth revealed by Jesus to the Twelve is transmitted to the church in every generation through the spiritual bloodline of bishops. St. Clement of Alexandria called the bishops "those masters who preserve the true tradition of the glorious teaching derived in a straight line from the holy apostles, Peter, James, John and Paul, transmitted from father to son . . . by God's grace."

A Kingdom Built on Solid Rock

This straight line of true tradition leads back to the apostle Peter. Peter was the unquestioned head of the Twelve; his name is found at the top of every list of the apostles in the Scriptures. In fact, after Jesus, Peter is by far the one mentioned most in the New Testament. The first among equals, Peter gets all the best lines, and he alone speaks in the name of the Twelve.

Peter is the only apostle who received his name directly from Jesus. In Scripture, when God changes a person's name—as when he changed Abram to Abraham, Sarai to Sarah, and Jacob to Israel—he is revealing that person's pivotal place in his plan of salvation. Jesus changed Simon's name to Peter (Petros in Greek, Cephas in the Aramaic dialect that Jesus spoke). The name means "rock." "You are Peter," Jesus said, "and on this rock I will build my church, and the gates of Hades will not prevail against it."

Jesus gave Peter what he called "the keys of the kingdom of heaven." In Israel's monarchy, keys were the symbol of the king's authority. When the prime minister or royal steward was entrusted with the keys, he had the power to rule in the name of the king. Isaiah prophesied that the Messiah would bestow "the key of the house of David" on a new royal steward: "He shall open, and no one shall shut; he shall shut, and no one shall open."

And when Jesus, the Messiah, came, he fulfilled this prophecy, giving Peter the power to open and shut the gates of the new kingdom. He also gave Peter the authority to make laws and judgments as ruler of his church: "Whatever you bind on earth will be bound in heaven, and whatever you loose on earth will be loosed in heaven." This "binding and loosing" was a technical phrase used to describe a rabbi's disciplinary and teaching authority. Like the rabbis, Peter was given the power to "bind" (to forbid or condemn) and to "loose" (to permit or absolve). What he deemed acceptable was believed to be acceptable to God. What he deemed unacceptable was not. Whom Peter excluded from communion with the church was believed to be excluded from communion with God. Whom Peter forgave was forgiven and welcomed back by God.

As with the other apostles, the special tasks given to Peter only make sense if the Lord intended them to endure after his death and to last to the end of the age. The Lord could not have wanted the keys to heaven to be lost upon Peter's dying. In the divine plan, Peter, the "rock," was to be the everlasting foundation of the church.

Indeed, Peter's special office continues in the "Holy See" of Rome. Peter went to Rome, as Paul did, because it was the capital of the empire. Like Paul he was martyred there. A small memorial marker was placed over Peter's grave, which lay on the slope of a hill in a large pagan graveyard. When the emperor Constantine converted to Christianity in the fourth century, he erected St. Peter's Basilica above the grave. The current St. Peter's Basilica was rebuilt in the sixteenth century, and the church's main altar now sits directly above a small marble box containing the bones of the "rock" on which Jesus built his church.

The basilica symbolizes the role played by the successor of Peter. From the start, Rome was the supreme capital of the church on earth, and its bishop was the supreme head of all the world's churches. *Ubi Petrus, ibi ecclesia* was the ancient motto—"Where Peter is, there is the church." And Peter was to be found in the "see," or seat, in Rome, where he presided. Peter's see is "the origin of the Church's unity," Cyprian wrote. And, as Pope St. Leo wrote, "the power and authority given to Peter is active and continues to live in his see."

Just as Peter was "first" of the apostles, so his successor had "primacy" over all bishops and churches. The bishop of Rome "presides in love, maintaining the law of Christ and bearing the Father's name," Ignatius said. Peter's authority was never contested by the other apostles, and there is no evidence of any dispute over the primacy of Rome in the early church.

In 95, when the church of Corinth was rocked by a scandal concerning priests who were arbitrarily defrocked, the bishop of Rome, Pope St. Clement I, stepped in and settled the matter decisively. He was expected to take action even though the apostle John was still living and the church of Corinth was an older and far more established church than the church of Rome.

Clement dealt with the Corinthian scandal in the matter-of-fact tone of one possessing authority from Jesus. Clement said his words were divinely inspired ("written through the Holy Spirit") and added, "If any disobey the words spoken by him [Christ] through us, let them know they will involve themselves in transgression and no small danger."

The bishop of Rome came to be called "pope," from the Latin word for father. And the pope has always been regarded as Peter was among the first Christians. In 451, after Pope Leo wrote an inspired letter explaining how Jesus Christ was both truly divine and truly human, the six hundred bishops assembled at the Council of Chalcedon declared: "This is the faith of the Fathers and the Apostles. . . . Peter has spoken through the mouth of Leo."

The Spirit of Truth

Following the example of the apostles, who convened at Jerusalem to decide critical questions related to gentile converts, in times of crisis the pope has always gathered the world's bishops in so-called ecumenical councils. In these councils, under the guidance of the Holy Spirit, the successors of the apostles have clarified essential beliefs that were under attack by heretics or widely misunderstood by the faithful.

As the church grew, a living teaching office developed, a "magisterium," expressed in council decisions, creeds, circular letters, and other authoritative writings from popes and bishops. This body of teachings, along with the authoritative power of the church's magisterium, and the Scriptures, sacraments, institutions, and rituals handed down from the apostles, form what is known as the sacred tradition of the church.

The church's magisterium is not a random accumulation of documents. Nor does it produce new truths or new revelations.

God has spoken once and for all in Jesus. But Jesus knew that the church had to do more than repeat his words and tell stories about his deeds and the adventures of the early community. That is why he gave his apostles and their successors "the Spirit of truth" to guide them as they sought to make his saving truths known in every time and place.

The successors of the apostles in every age teach with the Spirit's guidance and assistance. In fact, the church has always understood that the body of bishops cannot err when they teach on matters of belief and morality, so long as they agree among themselves and are unified with the pope.

This divine gift of inerrancy extends in a special way to the pope. As Peter's successor, he inherits the keys to heaven and the powers of binding and loosing that Jesus gave to the first pope. And just as Jesus prayed that Peter's faith not fail, so the successors of Peter are ensured that they will not fail to teach the true faith, that they will be "infallible" in their binding and loosing.

Infallibility is a deeply misunderstood concept. It does not mean that the pope is beyond reproach morally. It does not even guarantee that any given pope is a decent human being. The grace of inerrancy is given to the "office," not to the individual who holds the office. Infallibility means that even a scurrilous pope's teachings will be preserved from error. But does not infallibility mean that every word a pope utters on any subject is divinely inspired or true. Infallibility applies only to definitive pronouncements on "faith and morals"—that is, teachings regarding what we must believe and how we must live in order to gain salvation.

Popes do not proclaim new doctrines or teach whatever they want on issues of faith and morals. They are servants of the gospel, not masters of it. As a practical matter, popes always teach in consultation and in communion with their brother bishops. Their watchword is always that of St. Vincent of Lérins, who wrote in the fifth century that "our concern is to preserve what has been believed everywhere and always and by all, for this is what is, in the true and authentic sense, Catholic."

The church's teaching authority is a further expression of the divine care and love at the heart of God's plan for salvation. As a loving Father, God does not leave us groping for the truth, trying to sift through rival viewpoints and clashing interpretations of the Scriptures. He has left us the church, founded on the rock of Peter, to ensure that his saving truths come to us unadulterated.

The One True Path

Jesus is more than a great religious teacher, and his church is not merely one religious institution among many. Catholics believe that the church is the true religion, the one true way of salvation. All other religious figures and institutions are incomplete in comparison to the Catholic Church. How could they not be, if Jesus really is who he said he was, as Catholics believe?

The ancient religions of the world—especially Hinduism, Buddhism, and Islam—contain much that is beautiful, noble, and true. And these religions, especially, continue to impel people to heights of holiness, wisdom, and love. Catholics believe that all that is holy and true in these faiths is a gift of God, a reflection of the desire for God that he places in every human heart. But no matter how sublime the other religions of the world, only the

Catholic Church contains *all* the gifts that God wants to bestow on his children. Only the church can bring us to divine life.

That is why Peter and the early Christians compared the church to Noah's ark. We hear an echo of this idea in these lines from *The Divine Orpheus,* a sacred play written in the mid-seventeenth century by the Spanish master Pedro Calderón de la Barca:

> Let human nature board the ship of the Church.
> Good trip, happy crossing!
> Because the ship of the Church is the ship of life.
> Good trip, happy crossing!

Catholics believe that the church is the world's sole salvation. St. Cyprian stated the point strongly in the third century: "It is as possible for a man to be saved outside the Church as it was possible to be saved outside the ark of Noah."

This is, after all, what Jesus taught. He said that no one can go to the Father except through him. To be saved we have to be born again of water and Spirit in baptism. To have eternal life we have to eat his flesh and drink his blood in the Eucharist. Salvation, as our Lord revealed it, means meeting him in his church, which he established to continue his saving presence in history.

However, whom Jesus saves may not be limited to those we see being baptized and made a part of the Catholic Church. Those whom Jesus saves, those who are really "in" the church, remain a secret known only to God. "In the ineffable forethought of God, many who appear to be outside are within, while many who seem to be within are without—the Lord knows his own," Augustine once observed.

The church does not speculate about who is "in" and who is "out." The church has declared that Mary and scores of saints are certainly in heaven. But the church has never identified a single soul who has been damned by God, not even Judas Iscariot. The church's mission is to include, not exclude. And we still preach of Jesus what Peter preached at the dawn of the Catholic mission: "There is salvation in no one else, for there is no other name under heaven given among mortals by which we must be saved."

We know that God predestines no one for destruction and that, as Paul said, "God our Savior . . . desires everyone to be saved." We trust with the letter to the Hebrews that God "rewards those who seek him"; we trust with Peter that "in every nation anyone who fears him and does what is right is acceptable to him." Ours is a mission that hopes in the Lord's promise: "This is the will of him who sent me, that I should lose nothing of all that he has given me, but raise it up on the last day."

We have reason to hope that among those found in the Lord's possession on that last day will be many who sought God with a sincere heart and through no fault of their own never knew Christ or his church. We know that even if it was not God's will that they be joined in a visible way to his church, their salvation—as with every grace the Father bestows on the world—is poured out in the Spirit through his Son in his one Catholic Church.

The church leaves to God the ultimate judgment of souls. But the church cannot leave souls alone to follow their own private paths to God. We believe that all men and women can hope for salvation, yet we know of only one sure way to salvation, the way marked out by Jesus Christ. And that is the mission that Jesus has given us—to make disciples of all nations, baptizing them into the family of the church. This mission is not some vague institutional mandate or something pursued only by priests and bishops. It is a task given to every Catholic. "Nothing is more useless than a Christian who does not try to save others," John Chrysostom said. "It is part of the very essence of a Christian."

Some Christians do this by setting off on missions to distant lands. But most of us are called to be "missionaries without a boat," in the words of Madeleine Delbrêl. She did this during the time of the Second World War by bearing witness to the gospel among atheists in Ivry-sur-Seine, a Communist-run town outside of Paris. "Mission," Delbrêl said, "means doing the very work of Christ wherever we happen to be. We will not be the church and salvation will not reach the ends of the earth unless we help save people in the very situations in which we live."

So that is what we do. We do the work of Christ wherever we find ourselves—in our families and in our neighborhoods, in the places where we work and play. Our mission of love embraces the Jewish people in a special way. They are our elder brothers and sisters in the faith of Abraham, the people chosen by God to receive his revelation and to hear his word.

We know as Paul knew that the Jews will always be God's "beloved," that the "gifts and the calling of God are irrevocable," and that "all Israel will be saved." So we try to serve our common Father shoulder to shoulder with the sons and daughters of Israel as we await the coming day of the Lord, when all nations will worship the God of Abraham, Isaac, and Jacob in the new Jerusalem.

Our mission also includes praying and working to restore the unity of the one church. We echo Paul's plaintive cry against fissures in the early church—"Has Christ been divided?" Why

God has allowed the painful divisions of Christianity is a great unknown in his plan of salvation. We do know with Origen that "where there are sins, there are also divisions, schisms, heresies and disputes." And we are painfully aware that, along with the failings and sins of schismatics, too often the failings and sins of Catholics have contributed to the wounding of the Body of Christ.

We embrace all who are baptized as our brothers and sisters in Christ. We see the Spirit of the Lord at work in their churches and communities, making men and women holy, spreading the good news of salvation. In ways known only to God, their evangelical power flows from the grace given by Jesus to his one Catholic Church.

Yet we know that Jesus established one church, not many. And his final prayer was for one visible church to stand before the world as a testament of the Father's plan of love: "That they may become completely one, so that the world may know that you have sent me and have loved them even as you have loved me." The church is to be one so that all the world might believe in him and the One who sent him.

A Communion of Saints and Sinners

Jesus left the gift of the Eucharist as the sign and promise of our communion with him in his one church. Eastern Catholic Churches retain the ancient custom of crying out during their Eucharistic celebrations: *"Sancta sanctis!"* ("God's holy gifts for God's holy people!"). Our sharing in the holy gifts of bread and wine makes us a communion of holy people, a "communion of saints."

The Catholic mission is to bring all men and women into this communion of saints, the church. The motive of our love is that of Nicetas, an early fifth-century bishop in what is today Serbia:

> What is the Church if not the assembly of saints? Since the beginning of the world, the patriarchs . . . the prophets, the martyrs and all the just . . . form *one single Church*. . . . Believe, therefore that in this one Church you have attained the Communion of Saints. Know, too, that this Catholic Church is one, established all over the world. You must hold fast and resolutely to communion with her.

The church is a communion of saints, and also a society of sinners. She is the divine ark of salvation, but inescapably she also looks something like a convict ship, a vessel captained by sinners and sometimes by fools. This is perhaps the most difficult of the mysteries of the church—that it is both holy and divine and yet at the same time sinful and human.

The earliest confessions of faith reverenced the "holy Catholic Church." She is holy because she is the divine creation of Jesus, animated by the Holy Spirit. But the church is nonetheless made up of people like you and me—sinners big and small. St. Josemaría Escrivá, who founded Opus Dei, a twentieth-century movement of laypeople and priests seeking holiness, used to pray the Apostles' Creed every day this way: "I believe in the holy Catholic Church *in spite of everything*." A friend once asked him what he meant, and he replied, "I mean in spite of my sins and yours."

Even Jesus' chosen apostles showed themselves to be by turns dull witted, envious, petty, power hungry, deceitful, and cowardly. That in itself is a lesson. According to a first-century tract attributed to Barnabas, a coworker of Paul, "He chose men who were the worst kind of sinners in order to show that he came not to call the righteous but sinners."

Frail apostles have been followed by bad popes, avaricious bishops, missionaries who make converts by violence, laypeople who lie, abuse, and torture. These things do not shake our faith. The church does not cease to be holy because it embraces sinners any more than Christ was less holy for supping with tax collectors and sinners.

Jesus compared the church to a field sown with both fine wheat and weeds. The wheat and the weeds will grow together until the end of time. Then the divine harvest master will separate the good from the bad. Jesus told us that there would be scandals in his church, that our worst enemies would come from within our own household. But he promised, too, that the gates of hell would not prevail against her.

In the church's darkest hours, the Lord has always raised up saints and prophets to call her pastors and people to repentance. One of these holy reformers was St. Bridget of Sweden, who in the fourteenth century brought Pope Gregory XI this message from Jesus that she received in a vision:

> You, O prideful one, rob me of my sheep! . . . Begin at last to renew my church. . . . Is that Church a holy, venerable mother? No, it is now a house of ill-repute!

For all the failings of Catholics down through the centuries, Jesus has been true to his promise—his Spirit still guides the church into all truth. Nothing of his divine teaching has been lost. We can affirm today with even greater forcefulness what Cyprian said before he was martyred:

> It may be that there are betrayers in the Church . . . but with a great number, there remains a sincere and pure religion, a heart devoted to her Lord, a Christian faith which the infidelity of others has not caused to waver, but which, on the contrary, finds occasion in it to be strengthened.

The Beauty of the Church

The mission of the church is to save the world through the beauty of her saints. The names of her betrayers are long forgotten; the names of her saints are revered even by nonbelievers. Who has not heard of, let alone been touched by, the story of the poor man of Assisi, St. Francis? Or, closer to our own day, Blessed Mother Teresa of Calcutta? As St. Ambrose once said, "It is in the saints that the Church is beautiful."

In her saints, the church calls you and me, sinners though we are, to holiness. In the church, Jesus himself comes to men and women of every age just as he came to the Twelve. And he asks us to make a choice—to follow him or be left behind.

Those were the last words he spoke to Peter in the Scriptures: "Follow me." It was the third time he had appeared to his apostles after his resurrection. They had just finished breakfast on the shores of the Galilee—bread and fish cooked over a charcoal fire. Three times Jesus asked Peter, "Do you love me?" Three times Peter said yes. Then Jesus told Peter what this love would require of him. "When you grow old," Jesus said, "you will stretch out your hands, and someone else will fasten a belt around you and take you where you do not wish to go."

The early church remembered those words in the year 67, when Peter returned to Rome after meeting Jesus along the Appian Way. Peter was seized by Nero's soldiers—bound, imprisoned, whipped with stripes. They brought him to be crucified, and he asked to be nailed to the cross upside down, his head facing the dust from which all men and women are made. And that was how he died, hung upside down, with words of praise on his lips.

After he was gone, the streets of Rome ran with the blood of his fellow Christians, and their blood became the seed of a mighty church that now extends to the ends of the earth and beyond.

→ V ←

THE SIGNS AND WONDERS OF THE SACRAMENTAL LIFE

A Catholic can find God in the making of a liverwurst sandwich. Not a reminder of God, or a figment, or some trace evidence of divine beneficence, but contact with the living God, really and truly. Listen as the writer Andre Dubus describes making lunches for his daughters:

> A sacrament is physical and within it is God's love; as a sandwich is physical and nutritious and pleasurable, and within it is love, if someone makes it for you and gives it to you with love—even harried or tired or impatient love, but with love's direction and concern, love's again and again wavering and distorted focus on goodness; then God's love too is in the sandwich. . . .
>
> And each motion is a sacrament, this holding of plastic bags, of knives, of bread, of cutting board . . . this spreading of mustard on bread, this trimming of liverwurst, of ham. All sacraments, as putting the lunches into a zippered book bag is. . . .

> I drive on the highway, to the girls' town, to their school, and this is not simply a transition: it is my love moving by car from a place where my girls are not to a place where they are; even if I do not feel or acknowledge it, this is a sacrament. If I remember it, then I feel it too. Feeling it does not always mean that I am a happy man driving in traffic; it simply means that I know what I am doing in the presence of God.

That is a Catholic talking, one who was baptized into the sacramental life as a baby and nourished by the Eucharist nearly every day until his death in 1999. Dubus was a master of the short story. He wrote about ordinary people: the way they laugh and fall in love, their banality and venality, the desperate secrets that gnaw them, their unseen braveries and quiet decencies. His fictional world is much like the real world—peopled by men and women of weak flesh and willing spirits, often so anxious about the business of living that they do not see the signs of the divine surrounding them.

A Catholic sees those signs because he or she lives by the signs of the sacraments. The Catholic sees the world upheld by a Creator who wants us to live in his good graces. It is a way of seeing that comes only from believing every day that a miracle occurs on the altar—that bread and wine are truly changed into the body and blood of Christ.

Of course you do not find sandwich making in the official list of the sacraments of the Catholic Church. There are seven entries on that list—baptism, confirmation, Eucharist, penance, holy orders, matrimony, and anointing of the sick. The Catholic believes that Jesus established these as physical signs by which his church would bring us into contact with the living God and his saving power.

The sacraments are not ends in themselves. They are gateways to a new life—a life in which everything is bathed in the pure light of the divine. In the early church, those preparing to be baptized were called *photizomenoi,* a Greek term that means "those who are coming into the light." That is what happens to the Catholic who lives by the sacraments. The sacraments give us new eyes, new ears, a new sense of touch and smell. Even the humblest of chores, like making a sandwich and driving it across town in traffic, can become "sacramental"—a moment in which the veil of what we think is real is lifted, revealing a world alive with the glory of God.

The seven sacraments of the church are not just words and gestures. Nor are they just symbols or rites of passage. They are all that and more. The sacraments are signs that make wonders happen, signs that bring into being what they signify or point to—promises that make good on what they say they are going to do.

In the sacramental economy of the church, God continues the saving work that he began in creation. In the Scriptures, God's word is his command. When God speaks, things come into being, lives are changed, people are saved. He says, "Let there be," and the universe is created. When he was among us on earth, the word of Jesus, too, created new realities. By his word he forgave sins, caused the dead to rise. By his touch, he healed. When Jesus rose from the dead, he showed his apostles his wounded side and then breathed the Holy Spirit into them, giving his church the power to bring the saving waters of baptism and the saving cup of the Eucharist to a world thirsting for salvation. Jesus told his apostles that when they spoke, their words would be his words.

That the sins they forgave would be forgiven by him. That in their hands the bread and wine would become his flesh and blood.

The sacraments continue that work of Christ, through his instruments the priests. How this happens is a mystery. In fact, the sacraments were known to the first Christians as *mysterion,* "mystery," a term still used by Catholics in the East. The holy mysteries are the way we enter into what St. Paul called "the mystery hidden for ages in God."

By the second century, church teachers were translating *mysterion* with *sacramentum,* a Latin word used to designate a binding oath or promise of fidelity. This highlights another aspect of the sacraments. By Jesus' death on the cross, God made a new and everlasting covenant with the world—a new promise to be our Father, to make us his sons and daughters, to bring us to eternal life. We enter into that new covenant with God through the sacraments of baptism and confirmation, and we renew our covenant and rededicate ourselves to God in each Eucharist.

Into the River of Life

Our new life in Christ begins in baptism. Since the time of the apostles, Catholics have baptized their children within days of their birth. In many of our families, a child's baptismal day is celebrated as his or her true birthday, the day he or she was written into what the Bible calls "the book of life."

We baptize newborns because every child is born in chains, heir to the original sin of Adam and Eve. By baptism, we change ancestors. We are thrust into the waters as children of Adam; we emerge as children of God. "Here it is that Christ washes away in the river the sin of Adam," reads an inscription on an ancient baptismal pool in the German city of Mainz.

Early baptismal rites graphically displayed this truth. An adult seeking baptism stood before the bishop on a coarse hair rug. This was a symbol of the animal skins that Adam and Eve wore when God banished them from Eden. It was also a reminder of the "slavery in which the Devil holds him captive," said Theodore of Mopsuestia, a fourth-century Syrian bishop whose account of how the sacrament was celebrated is among the oldest that survives.

Facing west, the symbolic dominion of the devil, candidates renounced the evil one. Turning east, toward the paradise lost by Adam and Eve, they professed faith in Jesus. Then they stripped off their tunics, figuratively shedding the inheritance of the "old man" and reclaiming the original innocence of Adam and Eve, who before their sin felt no shame at being naked.

The naked candidate was then fully plunged into a pool of water three times—in the name of the Father, Son, and Holy Spirit. This was to symbolize not only the Trinity, the divine life the candidate was entering into, but also the three days Christ spent in the tomb and the candidate's death as a child of Adam. Rising from the waters, as Christ was raised from the dead, the candidate was dressed in a brilliant white robe. This was a "sign of that shining world, of that kind of life to which you have already come by means of symbols," as Theodore explained to those he had newly baptized.

In today's baptismal rite we find the same symbolic elements and many of the same prayers of Theodore's time. The baptismal rite is rich in symbolism but is not purely symbolic. Like all the sacraments, baptism brings us new life *by means of symbols,* as Theodore said.

In baptism we really and truly enter into the death and resurrection of Christ. We were baptized into his death, Paul said, "so that, just as Christ was raised from the dead by the glory of the Father, so we too might walk in newness of life." This is not a fancy figure of speech. It describes a real transfiguration that takes place when we are baptized—our human lives are united with the divine life of Christ. In a sermon to those he had just baptized, St. Cyril, a bishop in fourth-century Jerusalem, marveled at this mystery:

> What a wonder and a paradox! We have not actually died, we have not really been buried, and we have not in reality, after having been crucified, risen again. But the imitation is effected in an image, salvation in reality! Christ was really crucified, really placed in the tomb; he really rose again. . . . For us, on the one hand, there is imitation of his death and his sufferings and, on the other, not imitation, but the reality of salvation.

Born of Divine Strain

By our baptism, our lives are joined to Christ's life. We are made a part of his body, as Paul liked to say. We are made beloved sons and daughters of God—like Jesus and in Jesus. An ancient Easter homily describes our new identity: we are "creatures newly formed: children born from the life-giving font of holy Church, born anew with the simplicity of little ones."

In a very real sense, each of us becomes in baptism a "Christ"—literally, an "anointed one." "Let us rejoice and give thanks!"

St. Augustine exulted. "We have not only become Christians, but Christ himself! . . . Stand in awe and rejoice: We have become Christ!" In this astounding new life we are strengthened and empowered by the sacrament we call confirmation, which from the start has been closely associated with baptism. In the early church this sacrament was called chrismation, and it is still called that by Catholics in the East.

In this sacrament we are anointed with oil, as Jesus was. The oil is a sign of the divine stamp of approval that God puts on our lives. In the Old Testament, priests and kings were anointed as a sign that they had been set apart for special service to God. By our confirmation each of us becomes a part of what Peter called a "royal priesthood"—men and women given the grace and the spiritual strength needed to live for God alone, to offer ourselves as "spiritual sacrifices acceptable to God through Jesus Christ."

By baptism and confirmation our lives are forever changed. From this moment on our lives have a new trajectory and purpose. We are to be progressively deified, or divinized. We are to grow more divine, more like God, by becoming more like Jesus, whose life was given to us in baptism. The purpose of our lives can be summed up in a line by the twentieth-century spiritual master Blessed Columba Marmion: "Never let us forget that all Christian life, all holiness, is *being by grace what Jesus is by nature:* the Son of God."

In baptism, God becomes our Father, and the church, the bride of Christ and the body of Christ, becomes our mother. At the Lateran Basilica in Rome, considered the "mother" of all the world's churches, the baptismal font is inscribed with words written by Pope Sixtus III in 432: "Unto heaven is born a people of divine strain, begotten by the Holy Spirit who makes the waters fruitful. Amidst the waves, Mother Church brings forth her unspotted offspring conceived by virtue of the Holy Spirit."

By our baptism, the psalmist's prophecy is fulfilled in each of us: "I say, 'You are gods, children of the Most High, all of you.'" We are "gods" in the same way that a child "is" his or her parents. Born of the flesh and blood of the parents, the child is a unique and unrepeatable creature, yet bears their resemblance, carries their genes. In the same way, each of us is formed in the image of our heavenly Father in the womb of our mother the church. "The womb of the Church is for us what the womb of the most holy Virgin was for [Jesus]," St. Leo said.

Absorbing the Creator

Our mother the church wants us to grow into mature sons and daughters of our Father. The church helps us do this through the sacraments, especially the Eucharist. Just as a mother nourishes the infant at her breast, just as God fed his chosen people with manna in the wilderness, so the church feeds us with her own body in the Eucharist, the body of Christ. The Eucharist is a pledge of our salvation, a daily sign of the tender mercies of God. He who was beaten and killed for our sake now becomes food for all who hunger for God. The Lord of the universe comes to us in a tiny piece of bread and a sip of wine.

In the twilight of his life, the French novelist François Mauriac, the 1952 Nobel Prize winner in literature, still stood in awe of the mystery he was introduced to on the day of his first Holy Communion:

> Each one alone with his Creator . . . reduced to the proportions of the most insignificant man and the poorest woman, to the degree of giving himself to them as food if they want him. . . . I feel a deep satisfaction in this absorption of the Creator by the creature. How many times since the twelfth of May 1896, when I made a good first communion, have I repeated and marveled at the words of Gounod's hymn sung on that morning: "Even to me you can descend, humility of my Savior!"

In the Eucharist, we are changed by what we eat. Jesus promised that the Eucharist would bring us into his divine life and at the same time would bring his divine life into us: "Those who eat my flesh and drink my blood abide in me, and I in them." Later he told St. Augustine: "I am the food of the strong. Have faith and eat me. But you will not change me into you. It is you who will be transformed into me."

Every Eucharist, celebrated worthily, makes us more like Jesus. Our goal is that pinnacle reached by Paul: "It is no longer I who live, but it is Christ who lives in me." By the Eucharist, we are drawn into what the early creeds called the communion of saints—all those children of the church, living and dead, who have been nourished by his body and blood.

"The communion of saints is the *truth* of the sacraments," one of the great bishops of the church, St. Yves of Chartres, France, said in the eleventh century. The sacramental life is a call to saintliness, to live as Jesus lived. As sons and daughters of God, our lives are to be lived "Eucharistically." That is, we are to make our lives a "living sacrifice" of praise and thanksgiving to the Father. "Let your heart be an altar," St. Peter Chrysologus used to say.

"Present your body for sacrifice. God desires not death, but faith; God thirsts not for blood, but for self-surrender; God is appeased not by slaughter, but by the offering of your free will."

The Kiss of Christ

The sacraments cannot transform us overnight into saintly sons and daughters of God. The sacraments do not work that way. They are gifts of divine power and possibility. They make us "capable of God," in the words of St. Thomas Aquinas.

But we are still human. And God knows it is a struggle to be human. Temptations and sorrow, loss and rage, anguish and agony, thirst and exhaustion—he has known it all in the flesh of Christ. God also knew that even after baptism we would struggle with the weakness and proneness to sin that are part of our human makeup. The sad truth is that we can fall out of God's good graces. We can break faith with God and break fellowship with those to whom we have been united by the Eucharist. We can, in a word, sin.

There are small sins and large sins—venial sins and mortal sins, in the language of the church. Venial sins, everyday failings to love, sap our spiritual energies. Mortal sins, serious offenses against God's law as revealed in the Ten Commandments, choke off the Christ-life inside us.

Many of us will never commit sins so grave that they mortally wound us, resulting in our spiritual death, in the loss of the life of grace given to us in baptism. But even our seemingly trifling sins have a way of piling up. The little infidelities and bad habits we indulge weaken our affection for God. And as St. James wrote, "Sin, when it is fully grown, gives birth to death."

This is why Jesus taught his followers to pray for the forgiveness of sins and for deliverance from temptation and evil. To assist us in our struggles he entrusted to his church the sacrament of penance, what Paul called "the ministry of reconciliation." Penance repairs the damage we have done to our relationship with God; it reconciles us with him and restores our communion with his church.

Only the Father in heaven can forgive us our trespasses, and only the Son has the authority on earth to forgive sins. He now exercises that authority through his church, in the person of his priests. He entrusted them with this sacrament when he told the apostles before ascending to heaven: "Receive the Holy Spirit. If you forgive the sins of any, they are forgiven them; if you retain the sins of any, they are retained."

With this sacrament, the all-merciful Father ensures that sin never has to be the last word in our lives. If we confess our sins to his priest with a contrite heart and hear the word of his forgiveness, the last word will always be that of Jesus: "Your sins are forgiven."

In the confessional, we are penitents at the feet of the Lord. We are talking not to a priest but to God. The priest is only his instrument. We are like the woman at Jacob's well, face-to-face with Jesus, who knows "everything I have ever done!" We come to him in true sorrow, confessing all our failures to live as children of God, all our failures to love. We come not before a harsh accuser or a hanging judge but before a loving Father who has anxiously awaited our return, who wants us to grow up in his love.

Every confession is like the homecoming of the prodigal son in Jesus' parable. "See, the Father comes out to meet you," St. Ambrose said. "He will fall on your neck and give you a kiss, the pledge of love and tenderness. You are afraid of hearing words filled with anger, and he prepares a banquet for you!"

Russians call this sacrament "the kiss of Christ." The Russian-born writer Catherine de Hueck Doherty said that her mother taught her to talk to Jesus in confession as if she were talking to her own father:

> I would . . . tell him how sorry I was for having done something he didn't like. In my imagination, Christ hugged me and said something like, "That's all right, little girl. I know it's not easy to always do the right thing." Then he would kiss me and bless me and say, "Now go and play."

This sacrament is another sign of God's immense love for his children. No matter what we have done, he is always ready in the confessional to forgive us, to wipe the slate clean. The power of love communicated in this sacrament is one of the reasons G. K. Chesterton cited for becoming Catholic. The Catholic, he once wrote, "believes that in that dim corner, and in that brief ritual, God has really remade him in his own image. . . . The accumulations of time can no longer terrify. He may be great and gouty, but he is only five minutes old."

Marriage: A Great Mystery

By baptism, each of us has been given a particular mission in life, a vocation or calling—to glorify him as his holy sons and daughters in the ordinary circumstances of our lives and to spread the good news of Jesus and the kingdom.

But the church designates two states of life—marriage and priesthood (also known as holy orders)—as sacraments because they have a special connection to the saving work of Jesus and the mission of his church. This does not mean that Catholics who are not married or who are not priests are second-class believers. Every baptized person is called to be a "sacrament," an instrument through which God's salvation is offered to others. Baptized persons who are also called by God to marriage or the priesthood receive a special assignment, a further consecration.

Both marriage and holy orders are sacraments of spiritual paternity. They consecrate people to assume special responsibility for rearing new children of God. In marriage two baptized persons become one, and from their love springs new life. The priest too becomes a parent as he brings the people of God to life through the sacraments. Not every believer is called to be a priest, and not every believer is called to marriage. These are deeply personal callings, bound up with God's mysterious plan for each person and for the church.

God does not fall in and out of love with us. Christ does not love his bride for the time being or until something better comes along. His covenant of love is for all time, to be consummated at the end of the world in the "marriage supper of the Lamb," in Christ's final betrothal to his people. Marriage, the sacrament of God's covenant, is likewise an unbreakable bond, a promise for all time. What God has joined, Jesus said, no human authority, not even the highest authority of the church, can dissolve.

However, we can go through the ritual motions of any sacrament and not receive the grace God offers because of our ignorance or our hardness of heart. Marriage is no exception. The church recognizes that some apparent marriages will fail because they are in actuality not marriages at all, because one or both of the partners have made the sacrament null and void by lack of love or lack of faith.

In a true marriage, the man and the woman relinquish their cherished individualities and offer themselves as gifts to each other. They receive the gift of the other's life with all its strengths and limitations, joys and sorrows. The space that once stood between them is filled with Christ, who in the sacrament comes to dwell with them. The separate roads they once traveled merge into a single way, the way of his cross. In this sacrament, they are given the grace they need to follow together in his footsteps, to bear each other's burdens, to forgive each other's trespasses, to work for each other's salvation, to bring each other to heaven.

The sacrament creates from the two a single new being—a holy trinity composed of man and woman and the Spirit of love that unites them. In a poem on the beauty of marriage, St. Gregory of Nazianzus describes the couple as a church, a holy dwelling of the glory of God:

> Marriage is . . . the seal of unbreakable friendship.
> Those who are united in the flesh make but one soul,
> And they raise a like spire of their piety
> By their mutual love.

The sacrament is consummated in the marital embrace. The marriage bed is made an altar upon which husband and wife offer themselves body and soul as a loving oblation to God. Coventry Patmore, a nineteenth-century poet who wrote exquisitely of nuptial love, said that husband and wife become "priest and priestess to each other of relations inherent in the Divinity itself."

By their sweet love, their sacrifice of desire, their ecstasy of self-surrender and communion, the couple comes to know in their bodies what it is to love as God loves. They know, as Patmore put it, "that for the season at least, they justify the words *I have said, Ye are gods.*"

Like the love of God, which overflows in creation, the love of husband and wife should be fruitful. The first married followers of the Lord rejected the unusual and cruel birth-control methods of their time. In the same way, Catholics today refuse to defile their wedding beds with contrivances or artifices that would frustrate their love's God-given power to create new life. They want their love to be like that of God—extravagant, bountiful, unencumbered by selfishness or fear. Catholic couples see their lovemaking as a sort of attentive dialogue with God, in which he speaks through the natural rhythms of fertility and infertility in the woman's body, in a language that is both physical and spiritual.

And if God wills, by their communion of flesh and spirit the spouses become partners with him in the creation of new life. They are allowed to take part in a miracle, the glorious coming to be of a new person, made in the image and likeness of God. Of giving birth to her daughter, Dorothy Day once wrote:

> If I had written the greatest book, composed the greatest symphony, painted the most beautiful painting or carved the most exquisite figure, I could not have felt more the exalted creator than I did when they placed my child in my arms. To think that this thing of beauty, sighing gently in my arms, reaching her little mouth for my breast, clutching at me with her tiny beautiful hands, had come from my

> flesh, was my own child! Such a great feeling of happiness and joy filled me that I was hungry for Someone to thank, to love, even to worship, for so great a good that had been bestowed upon me.

Every child is a "sacrament"—a living sign that the creator of the universe entered the world by way of a human mother, that he called us to be "born from above" in baptism and to enter his kingdom as his little children.

In bringing a new child into the world, spouses enter more deeply into the mystery of God's saving plan and his plan for their own lives. The child born of their love was destined by God to be born since before the foundation of the world. The spouses realize that one of the reasons they were born and joined in marriage was to help God bring into being this particular child. They are to be for this child a herald and a teacher of the Father's love, raising the child up to fulfill the purpose for which he or she was created.

Yet even Catholic marriages that are not blessed with children are also sacred, life-giving places of generosity and overflowing love, with spouses often reaching out to adopt orphans or opening their lives to service to the poor. Every marriage is to be a covenant of love, what the church calls an *ecclesia domestica,* a "domestic church"—a sign, Paul said, of the living presence of "the Father, from whom every family in heaven and on earth takes its name."

The Fatherhood of Priests

Catholics call their priests "Father" because through them God brings us to divine life in the womb of our mother the church.

That is why St. Paul spoke of the Corinthians he converted and baptized as his "beloved children," reminding them: "In Christ Jesus I became your father through the gospel."

The priest's authority flows from the Father through the Son. Seated at the right hand of the Father in heaven, Jesus is the "high priest" who "always lives to make intercession" for "those who approach God through him," as the letter to the Hebrews puts it.

He continues his saving work of drawing men and women to God through his priests on earth. He entrusted this priestly work to his twelve apostles. He gave them the power and the commission to proclaim the gospel, baptize, forgive sins, celebrate the Eucharist, and govern his church. He established a divine link between himself and the Twelve and between them and God: "Whoever welcomes you welcomes me, and whoever welcomes me welcomes the one who sent me."

The authority of the Twelve was passed on to their successors, the bishops of the church, who have in turn ordained priests to be their coworkers. Every priest today is consecrated for service by a bishop who traces his own power and authority in a direct line to the Twelve and to Christ. Thus, four hundred years after Christ's death, St. Augustine said this to the baptized:

> The apostles begot you: they preached, they are the fathers. . . . The apostles were sent as fathers. To replace those apostles, sons were born to you who were constituted bishops. . . . Do not, therefore, consider yourself abandoned because you no longer see Peter in person, or Paul, or because you no longer see those to whom you owe your [spiritual] birth. A fatherhood has arisen for you. . . . Such is the Catholic Church.

> She has given birth to sons who, through all the earth, continue the work of her first fathers.

What Augustine said in the fifth century is just as true in the twenty-first. Through the ministry of our priests, we are made a part of the family of God begun by the apostles. We are the descendants of Peter, James, John, and the rest.

The Twelve called by Jesus were men, and the sacrament of priestly ordination has always been reserved for men alone. As they do today, women, including the mother of Jesus, held prominent roles in the early church as evangelists, teachers, and patrons. But Jesus did not call any women for the specific ministry that he entrusted to the Twelve. And the Twelve he chose, guided by his example and by the Spirit he said would lead them in all truth, in turn selected only men to be their collaborators and successors in the ministries given to them.

That has been the unbroken practice and teaching of the church ever since. The church would never think of celebrating the Eucharist with anything but bread and wine, because these were the elements used by Jesus. Likewise, the church feels bound to Jesus' choice of men alone, finding in that choice an expression of divine intent that can never be changed.

Since its earliest days, the church has also asked its bishops and priests to be celibate. The church believes this to be a most admirable imitation of Christ's celibacy and a sign of a man's total dedication to what Paul called "the affairs of the Lord." A council of North African bishops meeting in Carthage in 390 described this requirement as "what the apostles taught." The council explained that it is "fitting that . . . those who are in the service of the divine sacraments observe perfect continence so that they may obtain in all simplicity what they are asking from God."

The church in the West still regards celibacy as the most fitting lifestyle for holy men called to the priesthood. In Eastern Catholic Churches, bishops continue the ancient practice of celibacy, but ordinary priests are free to marry. However, in both the East and the West, celibacy remains what it was for Jesus—not an imposed discipline but a radical sign of self-offering, of a man's utter availability for the service of God "for the sake of the kingdom of heaven."

In giving up the great goods of marriage and fatherhood, the priest becomes a father of many in the Spirit. The fourth-century bishop Eusebius of Caesarea, one of the first church historians, wrote that priests "are engaged in a work of divine and spiritual generation. It is not one or two children, it is an innumerable multitude whom they have the mission to raise, to form according to the divine teachings and to direct in the other areas of life."

When a bishop ordains a man to the priesthood, Christ sends his Spirit upon the man, setting a divine seal on him and giving him sacred powers and a new identity. By this ordination he is consecrated to act *in persona Christi Capitis*—literally "in the person of Christ the Head." He becomes a living image of Christ, the high priest and head of the church, and a mediator of Christ's life-giving mysteries. The priest looks like an ordinary man, just as the body and blood of Christ at the Eucharistic table look like ordinary bread and wine. But, as St. Gregory of Nyssa said, "his invisible soul, by an invisible power and grace, has been transformed into a higher state."

And Catholics see their priests as the early Christians saw Paul and the other apostles: "as Christ Jesus." In celebrating the mysteries, especially the Eucharist, "the priest truly acts in the place of Christ," Cyprian of Carthage said. John Chrysostom said: "When the priest gives you [Eucharistic] bread do not think that the action is his. The hand stretched out to you is Christ's. And when the priest baptizes, it is not he who in reality baptizes, but God who holds your head by his invisible power."

Yet the priest has no messiah complex. He knows he has been given a sacred character. But he knows too that he is only a man, fallible and weak and in need of the nourishment of the Eucharist and the healing power of penance as much as any other Catholic. He is under no delusions that his priestly powers are his own. It is Christ who performs the sacraments. The priest knows that he is just an instrument through which God works. He is called to holiness just as every baptized Catholic is called, but he knows that even if he becomes the most scandalous of sinners, God can still use him to bring divine life to his people.

Augustine put this point starkly: "They whom a drunkard baptized, those whom a murderer baptized, those whom an adulterer baptized, if it was the baptism of Christ, were baptized by Christ. I do not fear the adulterer, the drunkard or the murderer, because I give heed to the Dove [the Holy Spirit], through whom it is said to me: This is He which baptizeth."

The priest, indeed, knows better than anybody the truth of what Christ said to the Twelve: "Apart from me you can do nothing." The priest is nothing without Christ. But with him, he is everything. Sharing in the priesthood of Christ, the priest is a redeemer of the world and a sanctifier of souls. Asked once what a priest is, St. Gregory of Nazianzus replied, "He refashions creation, restores it in God's image, recreates it for the world on high and, even greater, is divinized and divinizes."

All Is Grace

The sacraments are the means the Father uses to recreate and refashion us, to divinize us and make us children of a love divine. And the sacraments follow us through our days—from the cradle of our mother's arms at the baptismal font to the final breath we take before the grave.

The final sacrament is anointing of the sick. It is available to all the sick and infirm but is most often associated with mortal illness. Jesus anointed the sick with oil, and he instructed his apostles to do the same. St. James explained that in the sacrament the sick person is freed from sin and raised up by the Lord.

By this sacrament, our life in the Spirit comes full circle. In the beginning we are baptized into the death and resurrection of Christ; in our sickness and infirmity at the end of life we come to know the suffering of his passion and crucifixion in our own bodies. In a mysterious way our sufferings take on a salvific hue. We can fashion out of our anguished bodies and minds an offering of love to the Father for the sake of the church. The sacrament of anointing of the sick gives us the grace to join our sufferings to Jesus for the salvation of the world. We can say with St. Paul: "In my flesh I am completing what is lacking in Christ's afflictions for the sake of his body, that is, the church."

Anointing of the sick gives us the grace to face our helplessness with courage and hope. We can call on our Father as Jesus did in his agony. By this sacrament, our experience of the cross can give way to our hope for resurrection. In this sacrament the

Lord makes us the promise he made to the good thief who hung next to him: "Today you will be with me in Paradise."

Before her death of tuberculosis in 1897, St. Thérèse of Lisieux endured an agonizing three months in the convent infirmary. Without pain medication she underwent the primitive treatments for the disease, such as having her skin repeatedly punctured with red-hot needles. In her torment she suffered a long trial of faith and a sense of abandonment by God. Finally, she grew so weak that she was unable to swallow the Eucharist. But in one of her last conversations, she said this:

> If you find me dead one morning, do not be troubled: it is because Papa God will have come to get me. Without a doubt, it is a great grace to receive the sacraments; but when God does not allow it, it is good just the same—everything is grace.

To live by the sacraments is to see everything in our lives—even our death—with the eyes of a child. Through the sacraments, we can live as Thérèse said she did—as "a little child before God." Asked on her deathbed what she meant by that, she replied, "It means recognizing your nothingness, expecting everything of the good God, just as a little child expects everything of his Father."

This view is not a sentimental flight from reality. The Catholic is the keenest of realists. To live in the world of the sacraments is to live in the real world. Jesus said that to see with the eyes of babes is to see and understand things the Father keeps hidden from the wise. By the sacraments we see with the eyes of Christ. The poet Paul Claudel said: "The eye of the Christian does not remain on the surface of things, but sees through to the bottom. He knows that the man sitting across from us in this train compartment . . . is our brother, he is an irreplaceable image of God."

The child of God glimpses the secret infrastructure at the heart of the world, hears the rumors of glory in details of the everyday, finds meaning in the often incomprehensible diminishments and sufferings of our lives. With the eyes given us by the sacramental life we see finally that *our* will does not matter, that a divine will is unfolding quite apart from our schemes and plans, fears and anxieties. We understand that though we perceive it dimly and at times live in rebellion against it, we are all caught up in the mystery of God.

For Andre Dubus, the inscrutable unfolding of God's will meant being struck by a car as he tried to help an injured woman on the edge of a highway outside Boston in 1986. He pushed the woman out of the way and saved her life. But he was nearly killed. Hospitalized for three months, he underwent ten operations. One of his legs was amputated, and he lost the use of the other one. He was confined to a wheelchair for the final thirteen years of his life.

There is no happy ending to this story, no glib lessons about the life of faith. Dubus kept on living, kept on writing stories of unusual compassion and depth. He listened to Red Sox baseball games on the radio, struggled to forgive the driver who hit him, learned how to be a father without legs. He learned how to drive himself to church every morning to receive his Lord in the Eucharist. And he wrote about it all in essays of rare candor and humor.

"Living in the world as a cripple," he wrote after his accident,

> allows you to see more clearly the crippled hearts of some people whose bodies are whole and sound. . . . And while

> most of us, nearly all of us, have compassion and love in our hearts, we cannot or will not see these barely visible wounds of other human beings, and so cannot or will not pick up the telephone or travel to someone's home or write a note or make some other seemingly trifling gesture to give to someone what only we, and God, can give: an hour's respite, or a day's, or a night's; and sometimes more than respite: sometimes joy.

Those are the words of a Catholic—a man born again and nourished on the sacraments, a grown man living as a little child, the son of the Most High. He sees the barely visible wounds in others and the ties that bind us together. He sees that God wants to use each one of us as a "sacrament," to express his love through us. He sees that there is so much more to this world than meets the eye.

VI

THE WORD OF LIFE

"Tolle, lege! Tolle, lege!" The singsong wafted over the wall and into the garden where a man sat alone, weeping.

It might have been a little girl singing to her doll, enchanted by the Latin syllables rolling off her tongue: *"Tolle, lege! Tolle, lege!"* The words probably meant nothing to her. Perhaps she heard them in the market while shopping with her parents. Sometimes street-corner evangelists would harangue the crowds to heed the sacred Scriptures and be converted: *"Tolle, lege!"* ("Take, read!"). But the thirty-two-year-old man in the garden heard her chant as a personal message delivered straight from God.

The winding path that brought St. Augustine to the garden of that rented house in Milan in August 386 is one of the great tales in Western letters. Born and bred in the North African coastal colony of Numidia, Augustine was a well-educated if sporadically employed professor of rhetoric. He relished good company and a good philosophical debate, dabbled in trendy spiritualities and subversive political sects, and confessed to a consuming appetite for sensual pleasures.

After dallying with a string of lovers, he settled down at age eighteen with a woman who bore him a son. They lived together unmarried for fourteen years, until one day Augustine abruptly threw her out, keeping custody of their beloved son and announcing his intentions to wed a wealthy heiress who could finance his faltering career.

Then his world started falling apart. His wedding was delayed, so he took up with a new mistress. But this brought him little consolation. He felt as if he were being pulled apart from the inside. His inveterate religious seeking had unexpectedly brought him to a crisis point. He sensed that his whole life had been misshapen by sin, that he had made himself a captive of lust and weakness.

He felt the pull of the Christian faith, which was being urged on him by his long-suffering mother, Monica, and her friend St. Ambrose, the eloquent bishop of Milan. But the cost of conversion, the price of discipleship, was too high: he would have to abandon his wanton ways. He was afraid.

At the moment the child's song touched his ears—*"Tolle, lege! Tolle, lege!"*—he was feeling as if he would go mad or die. We pick up the story in Augustine's *Confessions,* one of the first autobiographies:

> Damming back the flood of my tears I arose, interpreting the incident as quite certainly a divine command to open my book of Scripture and read the passage at which I should open. . . . I snatched it up, opened it and in silence read the passage upon which my eyes first fell: *Not in rioting and drunkenness, not in chambering and impurities, not in contention and envy, but put ye on the Lord Jesus Christ and make not provision for the flesh in its concupiscence.*

> I had no wish to read further, and no need. For in that instance, with the very ending of the sentence, it was as though a light of utter confidence shone in all my heart, and all the darkness of uncertainty vanished away.

Augustine's encounter with the Bible—specifically with a verse from Paul's letter to the Romans—changed his life. It also changed history. Augustine was baptized by Ambrose the following Easter, was later ordained a priest and then a bishop, and went on to become probably the most influential figure in church history. The five million words he wrote—homilies, theological treatises, letters, polemics, and testimonials—shaped the intellectual development of Western civilization in areas from psychology and philosophy to political theory and theology.

It all started with a book. Not just any book, but *the* book. For Catholics, the Bible (from the Greek word for "books") is authored by God. As Augustine did, we believe it is the word of God, spoken personally to every man and woman and collectively to all humanity in every time and place. In the pages of the Bible, the Father is bending down like a loving parent, revealing his heart to us, asking us to give our hearts to him. In the words on the sacred page God calls to us as he did to Augustine: *"Tolle! Lege!"* We take and we read. And when we do, our lives become open books. The Bible is the autobiography of God. But it is also the journal of every soul.

The Story of the Word

Jesus never wrote a single word, yet he was intimately conversant with the sacred texts of his people. He could debate the proper interpretation of the law of Moses with the most learned lawyers and scribes of his day. When he spoke and when he prayed, his words dovetailed effortlessly with echoes and extracts from the prophets and psalms.

He spoke of himself in terms drawn from the Scriptures, and his actions evoked scriptural stories. When his disciples were criticized for picking grain and eating it on the Sabbath, he defended them by appealing to a story from the life of King David. He compared his body to the temple at Jerusalem and his impending death to Jonah's experience in the belly of the whale.

But he never put any of his own teachings in writing. Nor did he ask his followers to. Instead he established what he called "my church," giving his twelve apostles a mission to preach the gospel, literally the "good news" about him. He promised not to leave them alone in this task, that he would send his Holy Spirit to remind them of his words, to teach and guide them "into all the truth." On Pentecost he made good on his promise.

From that day forward the Twelve preached boldly and fearlessly what they called "the word of God." They told anyone who would listen about the amazing things they had seen and heard at Jesus' side and about God's mighty work in raising him from the dead. They made their case that Jesus was who he told them he was—the final fulfillment of all that God had promised in the Scriptures of their ancestors.

The apostles saw their "ministry of the word" as continuing the divine speech that God had been speaking since the beginning of time. Jesus, they preached, was the very Word of God through whom the universe had been created. He was the Word that God had spoken to Israel through the prophets. With the coming of

Jesus, God was no longer putting divine words in human mouths. In Jesus, he was speaking personally in the flesh.

Chosen to hear that word and taught to understand it, the apostles were to speak it in the power of the Spirit to the ends of the earth—person to person, friend to friend, heart to heart. Thus, the gospel is unlike any other words we hear and read. It is a word *about* Jesus. But it is also the word *of* Jesus. It is a mysterious but real encounter with the risen Lord.

Like the word of God that created the world in the beginning, the gospel has the power to give life, to fashion new lives out of the ashes of the old. We see this in the ministry of Jesus and the Twelve. When they spoke the word, lives were transformed, the sick healed, the dead raised. That is why, since the time of the apostles, Catholics have revered the gospel as the "word of life." We believe what the apostles taught—that this word gives life to those who receive it in faith; that, as Peter said, people are "born anew" through this "living and enduring word of God."

The word the apostles preached always cut to the core and always called for a response. "What should we do?" the people cried when they heard Peter's preaching on Pentecost. "Repent, and be baptized," he replied. In the apostles' preaching, the word always seeks conversion, always leads to the sacraments—especially the sacraments of baptism and the Eucharist, the breaking of the bread. "Those who welcomed his message were baptized," it is written of that first sermon by Peter. "They devoted themselves to the apostles' teaching and fellowship, to the breaking of bread and the prayers." Two thousand years later, to accept the word of God still means to be baptized and become part of the Eucharistic family founded by the apostles' preaching.

Writing the Good News

As the church grew over time, Jesus' apostles and close followers began to put down the gospel in writing. Letters written by St. Paul to the churches he established began circulating early, as did "Gospels"—accounts of the words and deeds of Christ.

The oldest records we have on the beginnings of the written Gospels come from the recollections of St. Papias, a bishop in what is now Turkey, written around 125. Papias had heard the preaching of the apostle John, was friends with the apostle Philip's family, and made a determined effort to interview as many of those who had heard the Twelve as he could.

From Papias comes the tradition that John's Gospel was published while he was still alive, that Matthew's Gospel was originally written in Hebrew, and that the Gospel of Mark was composed by a disciple of Peter and based on extensive interviews with the apostle. Other documents from this period corroborate Papias's testimony and identify the Gospel of Luke and the Acts of the Apostles as the work of a Syrian physician who was one of Paul's fellow travelers.

These Gospels and letters were never meant to replace the unwritten prayers, disciplines, practices, and institutions established by the apostles and early church elders. The Scriptures and those traditions were seen as forming a single, indivisible inheritance passed down literally from the lips of Christ to the apostles and from their lips and pens to the church for all ages.

Paul used his letters to clear up misunderstandings and to reinforce his preaching. He never intended to write a detailed manual of church practices or to codify what he had taught them in person. In fact, he told the Thessalonians: "Stand firm and hold fast to the traditions that you were taught by us, either by word of mouth or by our letter." When he was asked to mediate a dispute about the Lord's Supper in Corinth, he did not repeat what he had told them in person about how to celebrate the Eucharist. He only reminded them that the tradition he passed on was exactly what the apostles had received from Jesus: "I received from the Lord what I also handed on to you."

In the same way, the Gospels were not intended to be read as authorized biographies of Jesus of Nazareth. St. John admitted that his Gospel contained just a fraction of what Jesus had said and done. And it is obvious from even a casual reading that the evangelists did not sit down together and try to get their story straight so there would be no apparent discrepancies in their reports.

The Gospels are loving reminiscences, selective remembrances, partial glimpses seen from different angles. They are stories told from different perspectives to different audiences with different concerns. What Papias said about Mark's Gospel could easily be said about each of them:

> He . . . adapted his teaching to the needs of his hearers . . . but with no intention of giving a connected account of the Lord's discourses. . . . He was careful of one thing—not to omit any of the things which he had heard, and not to state any of them falsely.

Catholics accept the Gospels as they were accepted in the early community—as true and accurate accounts written under the inspiration of the Holy Spirit. Our watchword is that of St. Jerome, among the most renowned Bible scholars and translators in the early church: "Ignorance of the scriptures is ignorance of Christ."

The Gospels do contain a wealth of facts about the religious and political situation at the time of Jesus. But the task for the Gospel writers was not to write a "just the facts" account of a dead historical personage. The Gospels are a translation of God's Word, an explanation of what God was "saying" in the person of Jesus. The evangelists wrote to win souls, to invite people into a relationship with a living Person. Their words, John said, were "written so that you may come to believe that Jesus is the Messiah, the Son of God, and that through believing you may have life in his name."

A "God-Breathed" Canon

Early on, the church faced the challenge of determining which texts were to be regarded as authoritative. Rival factions drew up their own versions of the life and meaning of Jesus. Christians were confronted with a variety of competing "scriptures"—gospels, epistles, acts, and apocalypses—many purporting to be the handiwork of the apostles themselves. Some claimed to document "secret sayings" of Jesus; others detailed supposed events from his childhood. In the face of this anarchy of authorities, the church's bishops sought to establish a canon—a list of Scriptures deemed to be authentic products of the apostolic church and teaching.

It was not a question of carving out turf or consolidating power. Rather it was a matter of being faithful to their solemn duty of passing on what Paul called "the word . . . in accordance with the teaching" of Jesus. Only this word about the real Jesus has the power to save. To believe other words—no matter how beautiful or inspirational—was to risk believing a lie.

By the middle of the second century, early church leaders had settled on a canon that included almost all the books found in today's New Testament. The introduction to this collection, which is called the Muratorian Canon, writes off the texts that failed to make the cut with poetic flourish, saying that the rejected texts "cannot be received into the Catholic Church, for it is not suitable for gall to be mingled with honey."

By the time of St. Augustine in the fourth century, the Bible as we know it today was firmly set in place. It was composed of the twenty-seven books of the New Testament and the forty-six books of the Old Testament. The Old Testament canon consisted of the Greek translation of the Hebrew Scriptures that was in circulation at the time of Jesus.

Catholics believe that every word in the canonical Scriptures is "inspired by God," as Paul put it. The Greek word translated "inspired" literally means "God-breathed." We believe that the breath of God, the Holy Spirit, moves in the lines on the sacred page. This is the same Spirit that moved over the face of the deep in the beginning, the same Spirit that God breathed into the first human being. To breathe the air of Scripture is to take in the same Spirit that spoke through the prophets, overshadowed the Virgin Mary, raised Jesus from the dead, and lifted him into glory. It is the same Spirit that came upon the apostles at Pentecost and will abide with the church until the end of time.

That does not mean the writers of Scripture were merely taking divine dictation or writing in some God-induced trance. They wrote freely, using their God-given artistic and literary talents, expressing their own passions and preoccupations, their own unique outlooks and personalities. All the while they were writing words that conveyed exactly what God wanted them to convey.

Catholics believe that everything written in the pages of Scripture is true and free from error because God is its ultimate author, and God, by his nature, cannot tell a lie or make a mistake. Between the Bible's covers are all the truths necessary for our salvation, everything we need to know in order to inherit eternal life. In a beautiful homily preached in the early 400s, the Egyptian bishop St. Cyril of Alexandria explained this principle:

> Not all that the Lord did has been put down in writing, but only what was thought sufficient, either for practice or belief, for men to reach the heavenly city, shining with good works and virtues, so that they may be reunited to the city of the first-born [Jesus].

Children of the Witnesses

Establishing a canon did not mean the bishops started handing out Bibles. Most people in the fourth century did not know how to read, and it would be another thousand years before the technology for mass-producing books was developed. For centuries the Scriptures were circulated in hand-copied manuscripts and guarded lovingly by local churches.

But even if they could have put a Bible in each person's hands, the successors of the apostles would never have thought that to be sufficient. Scripture was never envisioned as standing apart from the church in which it was born, apart from the tradition—the new way of life handed on by the apostles.

The Catholic does not limit the word of God to only the words found in the Bible. As St. Bernard of Clairvaux said, the word is "not a written and mute word, but the Word which is incarnate and living." Catholics are not "people of the book." We are children of the witnesses, begotten of the words and deeds of those who first saw the risen Lord.

Parents do not raise children only by lecturing them about right and wrong and repeating stories and words of wisdom handed down from long-dead relatives. Instead, they build a home life in which the family's character and values are passed on as much by shared experience and example as by words. It is the same with the family of God, the church. Our life in Christ grows not only through reading the words of our ancestors in the faith, but also by doing the things they did, sharing in the rituals and practices they received from Christ.

For centuries the written word of God was heard more than it was read. Most believers heard the Scriptures on the Lord's Day, when the church gathered to celebrate the Eucharist. In the Mass, the whole of the apostolic tradition was brought together—the prayers, the sacraments, the common life, the priestly office, the Scriptures, the confession of faith, and more—to form a single memorial of the salvation announced and accomplished by Jesus. In the Mass, that salvation is communicated both in the Scriptures and in the bread and wine transformed into the body and blood of Christ.

The liturgy of the early Christians is not much different from the Catholic Mass today. It had two parts, "the ministry of the Word and the offering of the sacrifice," according to Tertullian. During the ministry of the word, St. Justin wrote from Rome in 155, "the memoirs of the apostles or the writings of the prophets are read. . . . Then, when the reader has finished, the presider instructs and exhorts them to imitate these good things."

Similarly, the Mass today includes readings from both the "prophets" and the "memoirs of the apostles"—the Old Testament and the New Testament. The readings are carefully selected and arranged, as they have been since apostolic times, so that they explain and interpret one another. In the liturgy, the word is heard as a personal and living encounter with the mystery of God. This is seen vividly in Byzantine Catholic liturgies where the book of Scriptures is enthroned in a place of honor at the beginning of each Mass. Before each reading, the words "Wisdom! Be attentive!" are intoned, reminding the people that the Word of God is truly speaking.

The hearing of this word has changed countless lives. At Mass one day in third-century Egypt, St. Anthony heard the Gospel passage in which Jesus tells a rich young man to sell all his possessions and follow him. According to Anthony's biographer, he "received the word of the gospel as a sign to himself, and he reflected that this reading had not taken place as a matter of chance."

After the Eucharist, he headed home, parceled out his large estate of three hundred farms among his neighbors, and sold all he had, giving the proceeds to the poor. The word led Anthony into the desert to a life of prayer, fasting, and solitude. He is remembered today as one of the first Christian monks.

The Devil Has Quoted Scripture

Early church leaders insisted that the Scriptures be read and understood within the context of the church's tradition. They had learned by experience. Many of the problems and heresies of the early church had stemmed from a rejection of this principle, as charismatic leaders and sects advanced wild theories and fanciful speculations they said were based on the Bible.

"The Devil himself has quoted Scripture texts," Jerome noted ruefully, referring to Satan's temptation of Jesus in Matthew's Gospel. "We could all, while preserving the letter of Scripture, read into it some novel doctrine."

But God did not send his word into the world only to leave it alone to be interpreted according to the whims, dictates, and tastes of whoever heard it. That is why the word was given to us in the church. This is the message of a dramatic scene in the Acts of the Apostles. The Holy Spirit tells the apostle Philip to strike up a conversation with an official of the queen of Ethiopia's court. Seated in his chariot, the official is reading the prophet Isaiah. "Do you understand what you are reading?" Philip asks. The official replies, "How can I, unless someone guides me?" So Philip interprets the Scriptures—"starting with this scripture, he proclaimed to him the good news about Jesus." Then the man asks to be baptized.

For the early church, and for Catholics today, the Bible was meant to be read with the apostles, in the church. As Peter said bluntly, "No prophecy of scripture is a matter of one's own interpretation." The apostles alone had learned the proper reading of Scripture from the mouth of the Master. They alone had been given what Paul called "the mind of Christ" and the Spirit to guide them deeper into its truths and mysteries. This understanding in the Spirit had been passed on to the bishops, who were entrusted with the apostles' "own position of teaching authority," as St. Irenaeus, the great apologist and bishop of Lyons, said in the second century.

The ancient principle known as the "ecclesiastical rule" states that the church has the final say over how Scripture is construed and interpreted. This does not at all discourage Catholics from reading or studying the Bible on our own. Indeed, the church's "rule" is aimed at ensuring that what we read is truly the word of God. What St. Clement of Alexandria in 215 called "the interpretation that the Lord has given of the Scriptures" is a matter of life and death for Catholics. To have the wrong interpretation of Scripture is to know a counterfeit Jesus. To not know the living God who comes to us in Scripture is to risk our eternal soul, not to mention our happiness in this life.

More than that even, Catholics cannot live without the word. "The Word of God," St. Ambrose said, "is the vital sustenance of the soul. It feeds it, pastures it and guides it. Nothing can keep the human soul alive except the word of God." Catholics from the start were urged to probe God's words, to read Scripture as "a letter from God Almighty to his creature," as St. Gregory the Great put it. "In it we come to know God's heart through God's words."

In giving spiritual guidance to a physician named Theodore, Gregory once chided him for being "so taken up with worldly business and too many state occasions that he neglects the reading of his Redeemer's words." Gregory's advice was widespread in the early church: "Be sure to ponder your Creator's words every day."

Scripture remains the soul of all Catholic prayer, worship, and teaching. The church's earliest creeds were composed from passages of Scripture and represent the church's definitive interpretations of those Scriptures. The monks early on established a cycle of daily chanting the entire book of Psalms. Ordinary believers were encouraged to use the sacred words as the touchstones for prayer and private meditation. A fresco in the tomb of St. Petronilla, dating from the early fourth century, shows the saint leading a woman named Veneranda, who carries a box that contains "the Holy Books which will open heaven to her."

Ancient devotions such as the rosary and the stations of the cross are essentially prayerful meditations on passages of Scripture. The words of the church's sacramental liturgy, especially the Mass, are inspired by and in many cases drawn directly from Scripture. Indeed, the use of the word of God from Scripture is what gives the church's sacraments their power to bring us into communion with the true and living presence of Jesus. Our worship can be life-transforming only because we hear the biblical word "not as a human word but as what it really is, God's word," as Paul said. Ordinary human language, no matter how beautiful or persuasive, cannot communicate God's grace. Only the inspired word of God can perform the divine action of forgiving sins or transforming bread and wine into the body and blood of our Lord.

This is why the proper interpretation of Scripture was so critical. This is why early martyrs often died clutching copies of the Scriptures in their hands. Without a rule of faith, the Catholic knows, the unity of the word would splinter, reducing the saving truth to a scattering of partial truths and individual theses.

A One-Word Book

How do Catholics read and interpret the Bible? We begin by believing that the Bible is one book that tells a single story, and that it is a book that is only one word long.

The canon assembled by the early church fathers is a remarkably diverse library of some of the finest literature ever written: histories, epics, and legends; exquisite poetry of heartache and loss; lyrics of exultation and desire; soulful letters and sage advice; mystical visions, parables, and sermons. Between the covers of the Bible are dozens of authors who wrote in different languages and literary styles over a period of more than sixteen hundred years.

The biblical canon has hundreds of supporting characters and intricate scenes, but essentially it tells a single story, a history of the world in seventy-three chapters. It is the story of God's love for the children he created, how they ran away from him and squandered their divine inheritance, how he tried down through the ages to lead them back home, finally sending his only Son to show them the way.

For all its pathos and drama, the Bible is a story that is only one word long. And that word is Jesus. He is the point of the story, the One whom every incident and every character points to. Hugh of Saint-Victor put it this way: "All of divine Scripture is one book and that one book is Christ, because all of divine Scripture speaks of Christ and all of divine Scripture is fulfilled in Christ." The church learned to read Scripture this way from the New Testament writers, who had learned to read and write this way from Jesus.

Jesus' first actions upon being raised from the dead included teaching the disciples how to interpret the Scriptures and celebrating the Eucharist. On the first Easter afternoon, he met up with two despondent disciples making their way to Emmaus. And "beginning with Moses and all the prophets," he interpreted the Scriptures of what we call the Old Testament. Then, Luke's Gospel tells us, at table he "took bread, blessed and broke it, and gave it to them." And he was "made known to them in the breaking of the bread."

Later that first Easter night, Jesus appeared to his apostles. And again, he taught them how to understand the Scriptures, saying that "everything written about me in the law of Moses, the prophets, and the psalms must be fulfilled." What he was saying was that the entire body of Hebrew Scriptures pointed to his coming and to the establishment of his church.

That does not mean that the church sees no other value in the Hebrew Scriptures than their prophecies of Christ. Indeed, one of the earliest heresies put down by church leaders was that of the Marcionites, Christians who wanted to throw out the Old Testament as misguided reflections of those who worshiped a lesser god.

For the leaders of the early church, Israel's story was their family story. Jesus was a son of the Jewish people, and so were his twelve apostles and his greatest missionary, St. Paul. Following Jesus' example, the early leaders recognized the authority of the Hebrew Scriptures as God's word. They appealed to the law of Moses and the prophets in their teachings on morality and drew on Old Testament history for practical lessons and wisdom. They prayed with the words of the Old Testament and from the start incorporated these Scriptures into their own worship.

They saw in the Old Testament texts the beginning of salvation history, the patient unfolding of God's gracious and merciful plan to fashion the human race into a family of God that worships and dwells with him. As they saw it, salvation history reached its apex in Jesus. That did not make the earlier days of that history less important, but more.

The church saw an even deeper meaning in the words and deeds, historical figures, and events in the Old Testament. The Flood and Noah's ark were "types," or signs, to prepare us to understand the saving work of baptism. The manna God gave the Israelites in the desert was also a "type"—of the true bread from heaven that God would give us in the Eucharist.

How could real historical events and persons at the same time be symbols or signs of other or future realities? Because God is the ultimate author of Scripture, St. Thomas Aquinas liked to answer. God inspired the words written on the sacred page. But he was also the creator or "author" of the actual people and events recorded in those pages. As the words on the page are "signs" that refer to the actual people and events, so too are the events and people "signs" of invisible or supernatural realities.

"How to Go to Heaven— Not How the Heavens Go"

From Jesus, the apostles learned that the divine word has both a *letter* and a *spirit,* that Scripture has two basic "senses," or meanings—one literal and the other spiritual. The spiritual sense is to the literal as the soul is to the body. We think of the sacred page as the scroll that John the apostle saw being opened in the book of Revelation. It was "written on the inside and on the back." The spiritual is the divine meaning that lies beneath and shines through the surface of the words on the page.

We always begin our reading of Scripture with the literal sense, trying to understand the direct meaning of any passage—what the sacred author was trying to say to the audience he was writing to at the time and what those words mean for us. We do not take every line of Scripture literally. Sometimes what is written on the page is a figure of speech, as when Jesus says that believers will be able to take up deadly snakes and drink poisons.

Also, reading for the literal sense does not mean we look to the literal words to teach us things that God does not intend to teach in Scripture. For instance, we do not read the first three chapters of Genesis as a lesson in astronomy, biology, or geology. There is an important Catholic truth in the quip cited during the Galileo controversy in the seventeenth century and attributed to the Italian church historian Cardinal Cesare Baronius: "The Scriptures tell us how to go to heaven—not how the heavens go."

Though the Bible is not intended as a science or history text, its accounts of God's mighty works are not to be dismissed as myths or pious fictions. "The point to chase down in this religion is history," Augustine said. One of the signposts on the road to Augustine's conversion was his realization that much of what he took as "fact" and "truth" he took on faith, not on evidence or experience.

> I began to consider the countless things I believed which I had not seen, or which had happened with me not there—so many things in the history of nations, so many facts about places and cities which I had never seen, so many things told me by friends, by doctors, by this man, by that man. And unless we accepted these things, we should do nothing at all in this life. Most strongly of all it struck me how firmly and unshakably I believed that I was born of a particular father and mother, which I could not possibly know unless I believed it upon the word of others.

It is that way with Scripture. The God of the Bible is a God who acts in history, a God of miracles, a God who has done certain deeds at particular moments in time and in particular places. If we do not believe the Bible is based on fact and truth, if we do not believe that God actually did the things the Bible says he did—create men and women, liberate the oppressed, send his Spirit into the womb of a virgin, raise his only Son from the dead—then there is really not much sense in reading the book.

When we seek the spiritual sense of the text, we are looking for what St. Gregory of Nyssa described as an "understanding of the spirit of history without losing its historical reality." The spiritual sense is not a meaning we "read into" the words or the way the words make us "feel" when we read it, nor is it hunting for a secret message encoded in the text.

The spiritual sense is the sense given by the Spirit, the meaning that God intends the passage to have for the church today in light of the divine plan revealed by the coming of Jesus. To read for the spiritual sense of Scripture is to read the way Jesus read the Scriptures and the way he taught his disciples to read. Jesus revealed that the Father was unfolding his saving plan in a succession of divine words and deeds that became symbols, or "types," of the saving realities that would be fully understood only with the coming of Jesus and his church.

God had revealed this "typological" understanding of history to Israel's prophets centuries earlier. As it is used in the Bible, typology is far more than a literary device. It reflects a worldview, a fundamental belief in how God acts in human affairs. Throughout the Old Testament, God's works are interpreted in light of his past actions in Scripture. The Flood in the time of Noah is depicted as a reprise of the creation of the world; the temple that Solomon builds is described as a new Garden of Eden. The prophets saw in God's great deeds of the past—especially the creation of the world, the exodus from Egypt, and the kingdom of David—the shape of things to come in the future. Isaiah, Ezekiel, and others foretold the coming of a new Moses who would lead a new exodus that would inaugurate a new kingdom and a new creation.

The New Testament is filled with similar typological interpretations of the Old Testament. The Gospels describe Jesus as the new Moses expected by the prophets; they speak of his death on the cross as a new passover and exodus. In his letters Paul likewise describes the Christian sacramental life as participation in a new exodus. He says that baptism corresponds to the Israelites' passing through the waters of the Red Sea, and compares the Eucharist to the manna and water that God miraculously gave to the Israelites in the desert. This same "typology" runs through the New Testament, with the Bible's last book describing the end of the world as all that the prophets had foreseen—a new exodus, a new creation, and a new kingdom.

Reading with the Four Senses

Based on the apostolic tradition, the church fathers—the second generation of Bible interpreters—distinguished three "spiritual senses" of Scripture in addition to the literal sense. In the Middle Ages these four senses were explained in this ditty:

> The letter teaches God's deeds;
> the allegorical sense what to believe;
> the moral sense how to act;
> the anagogical sense for what higher goal to strive.

When Paul and Peter compare baptism to the Flood and the Exodus, they are reading the allegorical sense—using the events as symbols or foreshadowings of the sacrament. When Jesus compares the three days Jonah spent in the belly of the whale to the three days he will spend in the tomb, he is using a type of allegory, as he is when he compares the Eucharist to the manna in the desert.

When he uses the Genesis account of Adam and Eve to teach about marriage and divorce, Jesus is reading the "moral" sense—finding in Scripture a lesson for the church. Paul does the same thing when he uses the story of the Israelites' wandering in the desert to teach the Corinthians about avoiding immorality and temptation. We do not "read into" the texts a moral sense. Rather, with the help of the Spirit, we try to draw out from the texts the moral message that God intends.

Reading the "anagogic" sense is like watching the ascension of Christ. Our gaze is lifted toward heaven, and we are given a glimpse of the things of heaven or of what is to come at the end of time. When Paul quotes the prophet Isaiah ("He will swallow up death forever") in his letter to the Corinthians, he is making an anagogic reading—using the text to disclose how it will be in the resurrection of the dead, when the Lord comes again. The book of Revelation is like one long anagogic Scripture, revealing in symbolic language that the Mass we celebrate on earth is a gateway to a never-ending celestial liturgy, a "marriage supper of the Lamb" to be unveiled definitively at Jesus' second coming.

Our spiritual reading of the Bible is not limited to our readings of the Old Testament in light of the New Testament. The word that God speaks to us is not only about what he has done in the past. His saving work did not end with the writing of the last syllable of Revelation. In fact, the Bible's entire last book points us to a day that is yet to come. So our dialogue with God in the pages of Scripture is bound to continue until that last day.

Jesus told his apostles that there was much more he had yet to tell them. He promised to give them his Spirit to lead them into the deeper truths of his words and actions. The Spirit, he vowed, "will take what is mine and declare it to you." That is why Origen said, "The spiritual sense is what the Spirit gives to the Church."

Jesus' word to the church continues especially in the liturgy. In celebrating the Eucharist and the other sacraments, we are made heirs to the promises of Scripture—the saving works and promises of God are made real in our lives. The divine word comes to us, too, in our private reading of the Bible. For many Catholics the daily reading of Scripture becomes a form of meditation and prayer in which the words pour off the page as a love letter written personally from the Lord to each one of us. Through *lectio divina,* or "sacred reading," we ask the Spirit's guidance as we contemplate the Scriptures, seeking greater knowledge of God and his plan for our lives. Augustine never studied or prayed over the Scriptures without imploring God's help:

> O Lord, perfect me and reveal those pages to me! . . . May the inner secrets of your words be laid open to me when I know. This I beg you by our Lord Jesus Christ . . . in whom are hidden all the treasures of wisdom and knowledge. These are the treasures I seek in your books.

Take! Read!

Sixteen centuries after Augustine, we take and read, confident that the word we hold in our hands is the word the Father wants to speak to us. This is the Word that he sent in the flesh, the word spoken to the Twelve and written down for us. This is the word they preserved and sheltered from heretics, the word that many martyrs died for.

We read with the help of the Spirit and with the help of the community of faith that has given us the Scriptures. When we take and read we do so in light of the way these Scriptures have been used in the church's liturgy and in the writings of saints and mystics—people whose lives have been changed and made holy by this word. These people include the holy widow Melania the Younger, who moved from Rome in the 400s to live on the Mount of Olives, where Jesus spent his last quiet moments in prayer. "The Bible never left her holy hands," it is said of her. Her mentor, St. Jerome, gave us our marching orders: "Love to occupy your mind with the reading of Scripture."

We take and read as did Julian Green, one of the finest Catholic novelists of the twentieth century. He painstakingly taught himself Hebrew in order to read and pray the Old Testament in its original tongue. "Every time I open the Bible, I find an allusion to my life, to my problems," he once wrote.

The Bible is a book for everyone. You do not have to be a scholar or a saint to read it. Its treasures are open to all who seek them. "The Word increases or diminishes according to the capacity" of the reader, St. Ambrose said. What is important is that we are trying to live the life that the Scriptures depict, a life of prayer and ever-increasing devotion to the will of God. Mary's words to the angel of the Lord become ours: "Let it be with me according to your word."

Jesus held his mother up as our model for acceptance of the word: "Blessed . . . are those who hear the word of God and obey it!" As she did, we strive to keep his word ever close to us. We know the Father wants to mark every human heart as his own.

That was the meaning of the prophecy of the "new covenant": "I will put my law within them, and I will write it on their hearts. . . . They shall all know me, from the least of them to the greatest."

This was the new covenant written in Jesus' blood, the gospel preached by the apostles and proclaimed through the ages by the church. This is why the Bible was written, preserved, studied, and preached. God desires to "rewrite" us in the image of the Word. God wants to say of us—and all people—what Paul said of those who first heard the word and believed:

> You are a letter of Christ, prepared by us, written not with ink but with the Spirit of the living God, not on tablets of stone but on tablets of human hearts.

God wrote his word on Augustine's heart, and he became one of the church's greatest interpreters of the sacred page. But Augustine always pointed us to the day when the word we read on the sacred page will give way to the Word of God we contemplate face-to-face in heaven:

> Then, when that day comes there will be no more need for lamps. We shall no longer listen to the prophet nor open the book of the Apostle. We shall not require the testimony of John, and we shall have no further need even of the Gospel. Then all the Scriptures will vanish away, which have blazed like lamps for us in the darkness of this world, for we shall no longer be in darkness.

⇾ VII ⇽

THE POSSIBILITY OF PRAYER

On one of her missionary journeys, St. Teresa of Ávila was pitched from her mule into a stream. Sitting in the mud, she turned her eyes to the sky and said, "Lord, if this is how you treat your friends, no wonder you have so few of them."

Though she lived in the 1500s, Teresa was the most modern of saints: a mix of lofty ambition and high anxiety, of ironic detachment and longing for community and connection. She was a shrewd and creative entrepreneur, reforming the flagging Carmelite religious order and founding numerous new convents around the Spanish countryside. She was also a sardonic comedienne, mischievous and playful, with a self-deprecating wit. As a young nun, she scandalized her superiors one night after dinner by getting up and doing a passionate dance to the clickety-clack of castanets. "One must do things sometimes to make life bearable," she deadpanned.

She once prayed, tongue only slightly in cheek, "From silly devotions and sour-faced saints, good Lord deliver us." Teresa was perhaps the greatest Catholic master of prayer—one of a mere handful of solemnly declared "doctors" of the church, which means that her life and teaching are held up for special study and emulation.

Teresa was given in prayer an exalted experience of union with God. Gian Lorenzo Bernini's famous sculpture *The Ecstasy of St. Teresa* (1645–52) captures the rapturous heights to which she could climb in prayer. The artist shows her body thrown back and ravished, as if swept up in the arms of a lover, her delicate fingers barely able to hold on, her mouth open in an expression of sweet delight.

Most of us have to settle for a more down-to-earth kind of prayer life. But in Christ each of us receives the extraordinary gift of ordinary prayer—the ability to live in conversation with the One Jesus taught us to call "our Father." Prayer does not require a cloister. It does not mean out-of-body transport. Teresa described prayer quite simply, as "nothing else than an intimate friendship, a frequent heart-to-heart conversation with him by whom we know ourselves to be loved."

For Teresa, God was somebody who knows you inside and out, somebody to whom you can pour out your heart, somebody you can joke with when you have been knocked flat on your rear. The Catholic spiritual masters all agree on the essence of prayer. It is a relationship, a living and growing dialogue with God. "Prayer is conversation with God," said St. Clement of Alexandria, an Egyptian philosopher-convert, in the early third century.

This conversation begins early. Newborn Catholics hear the warm rhythms of prayer while cradled in their mothers' arms at Sunday Mass. In every language, the Catholic grows up speaking the loving tongue of prayer: "Padre nuestro, que estás en el cielo . . ." in San Salvador; "Ár nAthair, atá ar neamh . . ." in Gaelic homes in Ireland; "Notre Père qui es aux cieux . . ." in Paris;

"Our Father, who art in heaven . . ." in Erie, Pennsylvania; "Ama Namin, sumasalangit ka . . ." in the Philippines; "Baba Yetu uliye mbinguni . . ." in the Democratic Republic of the Congo.

Prayer marks the passing of our days: "Bless us, O Lord, and these Thy gifts" at mealtimes; "Angel of God, my guardian dear" before falling to sleep; the sign of the cross and the prayers of the rosary—the Our Father, the Hail Mary, the Glory Be to the Father—throughout the day.

The prayers of our youth make furrows in our souls, imperceptibly planting the deep grammar we need for a grown-up relationship with God. As our vocabulary of prayer grows, we move to a more personal experience of prayer. We find that there are as many varieties of prayer as there are shades of human need and emotion. And if we are open and listening, we find God leading each of us into our own individual style of talking with him.

Prayer is conversation, but it is not idle chitchat. We need prayer as we need air. To pray is to breathe. Not to pray is to slowly suffocate, to choke off connection with the source of life itself. The Catholic masters of prayer are emphatic, even graphic, on this point: "The soul without prayer is dead and emits an offensive odor," said St. John Chrysostom, the great patriarch of Eastern Catholicism.

Our Father . . .

How do we pray? When Jesus' disciples asked him that question, he responded by teaching them the Lord's Prayer, or the Our Father.

The Our Father is both a model for prayer and a lesson in Christian character development. Each phrase illuminates what prayer is all about. At the same time, it teaches us the attitudes and virtues we need in order to live as children of the Father. In the 1960s, Blessed Pope John XXIII wrote in his spiritual journal, "To know how to say the Our Father and to know how to put it into practice—this is the perfection of the Christian life."

From that first word—*Our*—Jesus begins to unfold the mystery of the life of prayer. We never pray alone. You pray with me and I pray with you, though a continent may lie between us, though we may speak in different tongues.

Like their Master, the apostles gathered morning, noon, and night to pray the Psalms, the prayer book of the Old Testament. The believer "should pray to God no less often than three times a day since he is in debt to the three Persons, the Father, the Son and the Holy Spirit," Tertullian wrote in the early third century. Over time, this public prayer of the Psalms developed into what we today call the Divine Office, or the Liturgy of the Hours, a daily cycle of prayers that aims to consecrate every minute of the day to the Trinity.

In our praying of the Psalms together, we draw deeper into the mysteries of God's love and his continued saving presence among us. Even when we pray alone, we pray together. We are members of a family, a "communion of saints." The *Our* of our prayer is like a family-loyalty oath—a pledge to stick together, to stick up for, worry about, and never forget one another.

We pray for one another, as Jesus taught us. Prayer of petition and intercessory prayer—seeking some favor from God for ourselves or another person—are probably the most widely understood experiences of prayer. One of our earliest depictions of prayer is a painting found in the Catacombs of St. Priscilla, an ancient burial ground on the outskirts of Rome. It shows a woman standing with her arms stretched wide, hands turned up, eyes lifted to the heavens, imploring the Lord. This anonymous woman was confident that God heard her prayers, as we are confident that he hears ours.

We pray with the knowledge that God does not always give us the answer we hope for, knowing that we will receive what is best for us. "We must never pray for a favor for any one, except conditionally, saying, 'If it please God,'" said St. Philip Neri, a master of prayer in sixteenth-century Rome.

We pray for the living and we pray for the dead. We forget no one in the family of prayer. In our private prayers and at Mass we tell the Lord of our love for our departed and of our fervent wish that one day we will join them in heaven. This Catholic intuition that we are bound together in an invisible web of prayer both in life and in death is tenderly evoked in the final words of St. Monica, the beloved mother of St. Augustine. "Lay this body anywhere, let not care for it trouble you at all," she told her son. "This only do I ask, that you will remember me at the altar of the Lord wherever you may be."

For the Catholic, the life of prayer continues after we die. The Lord hears the prayers of the living for the dead, and the prayers of the dead for the living, especially the prayers of saints and martyrs. The book of Revelation describes the Lord taking up golden bowls filled with "the prayers of the saints." In graffiti they scratched on the walls of the tombs of their dead, the first Christians begged the intercession of the saints. The catacombs are filled with such writings: "Marcellinus and Peter, intercede for Gallicanus the Christian!"

The early Christians sought especially the intercession of the Blessed Virgin Mary. So do we. "O holy Mother of God," we cry, using the same words believers used in third-century Egypt, imploring her "patronage," her assistance. Though we ask them for help, we never pray to Mary and the saints as if they are in any way a substitute for God. They have no powers to grant our prayer. We ask something humbler, more fitting—that they hear us, that they include a small prayer for us in those golden bowls they present to the Lord.

Who Art in Heaven . . .

Prayer never starts with us. Our prayer is always a response to the call made personally to each of us by the Father. Our prayers are possible because we have been made brothers and sisters in Christ. God is "my Father and your Father," Jesus said. "Because you are children," Paul wrote, "God has sent the Spirit of his Son into our hearts, crying, 'Abba! Father!'"

In our prayer we are like little children crying out to the Father, who is also calling for us. We pray with the wondrous knowledge that we are his children, desired and loved, as St. Basil marveled: "For You know each one by name and all the years of their lives even from their mother's womb!"

There is no place on earth where our Father is not near to us, no time when he cannot hear us. As Paul told the philosophers at Athens, "He is not far from each one of us. For 'In him we live and move and have our being.'" We do not have to reach up to heaven to seek the Father. By the gift of baptism, our Father has made each one of us a temple in which he dwells. St. Isaac of Nineveh, a monk in seventh-century Syria, said that "the ladder leading into the kingdom of heaven is hidden within you, in your heart." To pray is to climb down that ladder, deep inside ourselves, to find the Trinity dwelling there. When we pray, St. Gregory of

Nazianzus said, we experience "the union of the entire holy, royal Trinity . . . with the whole human spirit."

This was the insight of Catherine de Hueck Doherty. A Russian baroness driven into exile by the Bolshevik Revolution in 1917, Doherty came penniless to Canada. She underwent a profound conversion experience and went on to establish houses of prayer and ministries to the poor throughout North America. At the core of her spiritual life was an experience she called *poustinia,* the Russian word for "desert." Doherty said that this is the place inside each of us where God dwells in magnificent silence:

> "When you pray, go into your room, close the door, and pray to your Father in secret." These words of our Lord mean that you must enter into yourself and make a sanctuary there; the secret place is the human heart. . . .
>
> Prayer is inside. I am a church. I am a temple of the Father, the Son and the Holy Spirit. They came to me. The Lord said that he and his Father would come and make their dwelling with me. I do not have to go anywhere. . . . There is a *poustinia* of the heart.

Speaking to us in the desert of our hearts, our heavenly Father guides our gaze toward him. A beautiful illustration of prayer is found in the so-called Luttrell Psalter, a tiny, illuminated prayer book commissioned by a wealthy English landowner, Geoffrey Luttrell, in the 1320s. One page of the Psalter depicts a naked man on his knees, palms pressed together in front of him. He is looking intently upon the large, bearded face of the Father, who peers down from out of mist and firmament. They regard each other in solemn familiarity, unable to take their eyes off each other. The praying man looks up with the expectant eyes of a child, eyes that seem to say, "I want to be like you one day."

Hallowed Be Thy Name . . .

The Our Father continues with a statement of fact: "Hallowed be thy name." This reminds us that though we are privileged to call God "Father," he remains the all-powerful and all-holy maker of the universe. We are called to intimacy with God, not to irreverent familiarity.

Our conversations with God must always begin in *hallowing*—acknowledging that we are creatures and he is the Creator. We start our prayer in thanksgiving and adoration. We adore him as the Almighty, giving praise and glory to his name for all the wonders of his creation, thanking him for the mercy and compassion he showed in sending us his only Son.

When we pray, "Hallowed be thy name," we fulfill the promise God spoke through the prophet Ezekiel: "I will sanctify my great name . . . and the nations shall know that I am the LORD." Jesus reveals the holy name of God. His name, Jesus, which means "God saves," is at the heart of all our prayers. Everything we ask for we ask in his name; everything we do, we do in his name.

This name, Catholics believe, contains the real presence and power of God. It is so powerful that some teach that repeating the holy name "Jesus" or the divine title "Lord" is the only prayer necessary. In the deserts of fourth-century Africa, the abbot Macarius told his disciples, "There is no need of much speaking in prayer, but often stretch out thy hands and say, 'Lord, as

Thou wilt and as Thou knowest, have mercy upon me.'" Around the same time, Bishop Diadochus of Photice said his followers should only pray what he called the "Lord Jesus" prayer.

Many Catholics today, especially those in the East, practice this "prayer of the heart," silently repeating the words "Lord Jesus Christ, Son of God" as they inhale and the words "Have mercy on me, a sinner" as they exhale. The practice seems to have begun as a means of fulfilling Jesus' command to "pray always," a teaching echoed by St. Paul, who said we must "pray without ceasing."

Those who pray this way say it helps them live in the presence of God at all times. They say that the repetition of the holy name forms an inaudible interior "sound track" that runs underneath their daily thoughts and activities. It is a prayer that can keep us tied fast to the Lord even in the depths of suffering and despair. Lashed to the stake, flames rising about her, St. Joan of Arc died with this one-word prayer on her lips: "Jesus."

No matter how we pray, we must hallow his name. By this name the universe was created and is sustained. By this name each of us was made. And by this name we are to be remade. So in our prayer we perform an act of self-consecration, pledging each day to lead lives worthy of that name. As explained by St. Peter Chrysologus, a fifth-century Italian bishop known for his golden-tongued preaching:

> It is this name that gives salvation to a lost world. But we ask that this name of God should be hallowed in us through our actions. For God's name is blessed when we live well, but is blasphemed when we live wickedly.

Thy Kingdom Come, Thy Will Be Done . . .

We pray as missionaries who want to spread this holy name to the ends of this lost world. We pray as ambassadors from a heavenly kingdom that was brought to earth in the person of the Son.

As children of the kingdom, we pray in a strange state, in a time that can only be described as "already not yet." It is *already* because the kingdom is actually here. By his coming, Jesus has already brought the heavenly kingdom into our earthly midst. He has planted it as a seed and entrusted its nurture and increase to his church. It is *not yet* because he has yet to return for the final harvest.

Our prayer is a watchful desire for the coming of the Lord. This experience of "already not yet" is captured in a short Aramaic phrase that the first Christians prayed at each Eucharist: *Maranatha.* It can be translated both as "Our Lord, come!" and as "Our Lord has come."

As we pray for his coming, we pray that the Father's will be done. There is no question that his will *will* be done. What is always tenuous is our part in the accomplishment of his intentions. What we pray for is our entrance into his will and our acceptance of his will for our lives. God will never make us do what he wants. We can always say to God, "I will not."

So we pray for the grace to know his divine will, to want what he wants, to walk in the paths he sets before us. We pray for the grace to be able to say, as Mary said, "Here am I, the servant of the Lord; let it be with me according to your word." We pray for a child's trust in our Father's goodness, for confidence that our happiness will be found in doing his will. We pray that even in our sufferings we may be able to say, "Yet not what I want but what you want"—as our Lord prayed in the garden on the night before he was put to death.

But what does the Father want from us? Paul described "the mystery of his will" as God's fatherly plan to make all men and women his sons and daughters. What is our place in this grand plan? Paul told us that too: "This is the will of God, your sanctification." God wants to make us his holy sons and daughters. That is his will, and that is what we pray for. What is holiness? Loving God and one another as he has loved us.

We ask the Lord in prayer, What is your will? And he always replies, "Just as I have loved you, you also should love one another." The Catholic life of prayer aims to turn life itself into a prayer, an offering of love. We pray to live every moment in love, to do even the littlest things out of love for God. In the words of Brother Lawrence, who worked for more than forty years in the kitchen of a Carmelite monastery in seventeenth-century Paris:

> In the ways of God, thoughts amount to little whereas love counts for everything. And it is not necessary to have important things to do. I flip my little omelet in the frying pan for the love of God, and when it is done, if I have nothing to do, I prostrate myself on the floor and adore my God who gave me the grace to do it, after which I get up happier than a king. When I can do nothing else, it is enough for me to pick up a straw from the ground for the love of God.

Give Us This Day Our Daily Bread

How strange: we go from prostrating ourselves before his holy name to making demands of him. We ask him to *give* us things. No "please." No "thank you." Just bald stipulation: Give us our daily bread—right here and now.

We can talk to God this way in prayer. "Speak to God as a child does to his mother: 'Give me a piece of bread. Give me your hand. Kiss me,'" said St. John Vianney, an extraordinary priest who labored in the French village of Ars in the generation after the bloody anticlerical Revolution of the 1780s.

Indeed, Jesus told us that God wants us to pray as if we are desperate, as people whose demands cannot wait. He told us to bang on the Father's door at all hours, even when it is bolted shut and he is fast asleep. The Father will rise and give us what we need. St. Alphonsus de' Liguori, an eighteenth-century Italian revered, as is John Vianney, as one of the church's great priests, said that the Father "finds his delight in having you treat him personally and in all confidence. Speak to him often of your business, your plans, your troubles, your fears—of everything that concerns you."

When we pray this way, we are not telling the Father things he does not already know about us. We pray this way to keep ourselves honest, to come to the Father without pretense or self-delusion. This kind of honesty in prayer teaches us humility, which is the virtue of seeing ourselves as God sees us, as we truly are. We bring nothing to the table when we come to the Father. We come with empty pockets, as beggars and seekers.

All that we need—food, shelter, and clothing; justice, love, and community—comes from the Father. All these staples of existence are symbolized in the simple word *bread,* the most basic of human needs. We pray as people who know we depend on God for this bread. We pray for those who have only crumbs and scraps of this bread, and we promise by this prayer to share our bread with them through works of self-sacrifice and charity.

Yet we also pray knowing that it is not by bread alone that men and women live, but by every word that proceeds from the mouth of God. As St. Bernard of Clairvaux said: "The famine in the land is the lack of the Word of God in the human spirit. It is . . . hunger for hearing the Word of God. . . . The Word of God is bread since it gives and preserves life in us."

Our prayer is always nourished by the word of God, the sacred Scriptures. The spiritual masters compare the prayerful contemplation of Scripture—*lectio divina* ("sacred reading")—to eating the Eucharist. It is a transformative experience of the real presence of Christ. Guigo II, a French Carthusian monk and popular medieval spiritual writer, prayed this before reading the Scriptures:

> Lord Jesus, Son of the living God, O living Word, teach me to eat and to assimilate your Gospel so that it may transform me and make my spirit become entirely conformed to what you are and what you will.

When we pray for our daily bread, we pray to be transformed by that bread. "The Father in heaven urges us, as children of heaven, to ask for the bread of heaven," St. Peter Chrysologus said. "Christ himself is the bread who—sown in the Virgin, raised up in the flesh, kneaded in the passion, baked in the oven of the tomb, reserved in the churches, brought to altars—furnishes the faithful each day with food from heaven."

The Father feeds us with our daily bread as we make our way in the "already not yet" of the kingdom. The Greek word *epiousios,* which we translate as "daily" in the Lord's Prayer, does not appear anywhere else in the New Testament and is not found in any writings of the period. Literally the word means "super-essential"—most vital, something we need more than anything else in the world. This is how the early Christians described the Eucharist. This is why we pray the Lord's Prayer before consuming the bread and wine in communion.

During the emperor Diocletian's persecution of Christians in North Africa in the fourth century, about fifty Christians were rounded up after Mass one day in the town of Abitena, near Carthage. Given one last chance to renounce their faith, they replied with a prayer that sealed their fate as martyrs: "We cannot survive without the Lord's body."

Nor can we. So we pray for the super-essential bread of his flesh and blood, the bread that the Lord said we must eat to gain eternal life. We pray that he give us the bread of life eternal, the bread all men and women hunger for.

Forgive Us . . . as We Forgive . . .

At this point in the Lord's Prayer, we confront ourselves as sinners. Even the best among us should really begin our every prayer with the apostle Peter's lament: "Go away from me, Lord, for I am a sinful man!" On the other hand, we could offer up the witty but no less accurate toast of St. Teresa of Ávila: "May he be blessed forever who has put up with so much from me!"

To pray honestly we have to come into the Father's presence as grateful debtors who know that we have been forgiven a sum we could never have paid back. Jesus' promise was this: as often as we stumble we can turn to the Father in contrition, confident that we will hear the word of his forgiveness, the word he spoke to the woman caught in adultery—"Go . . . and from now on do not sin again."

But there is a catch—"*as we forgive those . . .*" To receive forgiveness, we have to give forgiveness. How many times do we have to forgive those who trespass against us? When Peter asked Jesus, he replied, "Not seven times, but, I tell you, seventy-seven times." In other words, *every time.*

This petition reminds us that there is more to the life of prayer than our private audiences with the Father. Remember, it is not only "you" or "I" who prays. *We* pray to *our* Father. If our prayer is to be one, if we are to be united as one family in love, we must be able to forgive and accept the forgiveness of others. The communion of love that God intends for his creation is maintained and replenished by forgiveness—his forgiveness of me and my forgiveness of you.

If you say you love God but hate your brother or sister, you are a liar, the apostle John said. Such hardness of heart could cost us our eternal salvation. This is the stern warning of Jesus' parable about the wicked servant who, though his entire debt was canceled by his master, ruthlessly punished those who were indebted to him.

So we pray for the Master's forgiveness. We pray for the grace that animated one of the last century's most venerated saints, Maria Goretti, a conscientious, prayerful twelve-year-old Italian peasant girl murdered by a neighbor in an attempted rape in 1902.

As she lay dying from multiple stab wounds, Maria prayed for her killer. "May God forgive him, because I already have forgiven him." More remarkable though less well known is the story of Maria's mother, Assunta. When her daughter's remorseful killer was released after serving twenty-seven years in jail, Assunta assured him of her forgiveness. And in 1937, the mother and her daughter's killer attended midnight Mass on Christmas Eve, in a local shrine erected to honor the slain Maria.

Most of us are asked to make much humbler acts of forgiveness. But even these acts we cannot do under our own power. Forgiveness is possible through God's grace alone. So we pray for the grace to forgive, knowing that our own forgiveness depends upon it.

And Lead Us Not into Temptation . . .

To be human is to feel temptation. That is because to be human is to be born free. We are always able to choose between living with God and living apart from him. Temptation is the attraction we feel for what is not of God. God never tempts us. The Greek phrase we translate as "Lead us not into temptation" means something closer to "Do not let me fall into, do not let me yield to" temptation. We fall because we are frail. Our human nature has been weakened by original sin.

We fall too because we are tempted by the devil, our adversary in the spiritual life. This seems especially true of those who dedicate themselves to living a lofty spiritual life. The writings of saints and spiritual masters are filled with gritty accounts of spiritual warfare. "What a strange thing!" St. Teresa of Ávila once remarked. "It is as though the devil tempts only those who take the path of prayer."

The devil cannot *make* us do anything. So he works more subtly in our lives, just as he did in the garden with Adam and Eve, sowing doubts about God's promises, tempting us to think we can live without God.

Perhaps the most insidious temptation is to stop praying. Often, this temptation comes in a deceptively "practical" guise—the all-too-common feeling of not having enough time to pray. The usually mild-mannered Blessed Columba Marmion became irate when he heard this excuse: "It is a snare of the devil!" he snapped. "For without prayer, without contact of heart and soul with God, one never rises beyond mediocrity. It is during these moments of union of soul that God communicates his light and his life, although at times in an imperceptible manner."

When we say that we do not have time to pray, we are really saying that we do not think that prayer is worth our time. We are making a calculation that the "benefits" that accrue from praying are not commensurate with the "costs," that is, the time we invest in it. But that is the wrong way to think about prayer. We cannot come to prayer asking, what is in it for me? We cannot pray as if we are reading a wish list. Prayer is not about "getting things" from God. When we approach prayer this way, it is easy to abandon it when we do not get "results."

We pray not to fall into that temptation, the most fundamental of all temptations—the trap of cutting off talks with God because we do not "feel" anything or "get" anything out of our prayer.

But Deliver Us from Evil . . .

Our prayer to be delivered from all evil takes us back to earth, tells us about the world we live in. It is a beautiful world, created and redeemed by the love of God. But it is also a world groaning in travail, a world where the Evil One, whom Christ called "the ruler of this world," still tries to frustrate the coming of the kingdom. It is a world where many are held in bondage to sin, in spiritual prisons made out of their own disordered desires. It is a world too where many are oppressed by evil social structures, economic or political systems created by the sins and corruption of others.

The book of Psalms describes it as a world caught in a struggle between two ways—the way of life and the way of death, the way of the just and the way of the wicked. The Psalter is the book of the believer trying to live a holy life in an unholy world. We pray the Psalms as a cycle of 150 prayers about the struggle for deliverance from evil—from the first psalm, which speaks of a blessed one who strives against "the advice of the wicked," to the last, in which the evildoers have been bound up, and "everything that breathes" gives praise to the Lord.

Prayer helps us face the evils of the world with hope. We pray to walk with the Lord in what the psalmist calls the path of righteousness, committing ourselves to the Lord's struggle to deliver this world from evil and death. We pray, confident in our salvation because Christ has defeated the devil and "conquered the world."

Amen

Evil never gets the last word. Not in the world and not in prayer. The last word is always *Amen*—a word that means "It is true." God's promise is real. When we pray, "Amen," we make an act of faith. We say, "I believe in your promise, delivered by your Son." With our "Amen" we pledge to live as children who call on our Father, who see him in everything and know he is near us at all times.

Speaking of herself, St. Teresa of Ávila once marveled that "the Lord makes a little old woman wiser in this science of prayer than the theologians!" But that is what prayer does. It makes it possible for us, though mere men and women, to be made friends of God.

⇝ VIII ⇜

THE MIRACLE AND MEANING OF THE MASS

In Olivier Messiaen's music, time does not so much stand still as touch eternity.

A visionary musician and perhaps the most original composer of the twentieth century, Messiaen drew inspiration from exotic birdsongs, Hindu worship music, the plainchant melodies of medieval monks, and the meters of Greek drama. But what made his art so hauntingly strange, and seemingly able to transport the listener to a place outside time and space, was the Mass—the ancient and mysterious locus of Catholic worship, in which the coming of the eternal God into human history is celebrated and renewed as bread and wine become the body and blood of Jesus Christ.

For nearly sixty years, Messiaen was the organist at the Church of La Trinité, in Paris. The job meant that he spent hours each week playing and improvising at Mass and daily prayer services. He rarely gave concerts, often saying he did his best playing in church. He compared himself to another French composer and organist: "When [Charles] Tournemire improvised in a concert, it was good," Messiaen said. "But the improvisations were much more beautiful during Masses at St. Clotilde, when he had the Blessed Sacrament in front of him. I think I resemble him somewhat in this respect."

From his first composition, *The Celestial Banquet* (1928), to his sprawling late opera, *St. Francis of Assisi* (1983), Messiaen's work breathed with awe at the nearness of God in the Mass. The themes his compositions returned to again and again—the glories of creation, the ecstasies of nuptial desire, the Trinity, the resurrection of the body—are truths that resound at the heart of the Mass.

Messiaen's most radical and enduring accomplishment was his development of tonal modes and rhythmic patterns that created a sense of time interrupted, of the body being lifted beyond the confines of place and time. He captured in sound the mysterious essence of the Mass. "I'm not a theorist," he once remarked, "only a believer, a believer dazzled by the infinity of God."

The Celestial Banquet

Messiaen's music takes us to the eternal present of heaven, as every Mass does. Heaven is not static and changeless. In his revelation to the apostle John in the Bible's last book, Jesus shows him that heaven is a never-ending liturgy in which angels and saints praise and glorify God before the altar of the Lamb.

Jesus shows him something else too: that every time we celebrate the Mass on earth we participate in that liturgy going on in heaven. In the Mass, heaven and earth embrace, human and divine touch in communion. To make that embrace and communion possible was the reason Jesus gave us the Mass as his final gift. It was the reason he became flesh and dwelled among us in the first place.

The Mass is a remembrance of things past—how in rising from the dead Jesus destroyed the dominion of time and obliterated the borders between heaven and earth. The first Christians called Sunday the "Lord's Day" and made every Mass an Easter party, a celebration of life's victory over death, eternity's triumph over time.

"We live according to the Lord's Day, on which our life has also risen! How could we ever live without it?" exclaimed St. Ignatius of Antioch. The Mass is also "a pledge of the life to come," as an ancient prayer from the liturgy puts it. No longer must we live our days in the shadow of an inevitable death, the Mass proclaims.

These are the deep mysteries that Catholics celebrate in every Mass. And these mysteries are made real right before our eyes in every Mass. This is why our Lord gave it to us, commanding his apostles to "do this in remembrance of me."

Everywhere from East to West

From its first celebration by Jesus on the night he was betrayed, the Mass has spread throughout all creation. Jesus intended it to be the heart of his continuing mission to the world. Indeed, the word *Mass* is derived from the final words of the celebration in Latin—*"Ite missa est"*—which send us out into the world to invite everyone we meet to this heavenly banquet.

Within a century of Jesus' last supper, an itinerant Christian preacher named St. Justin surveyed the Roman Empire and concluded that "there is not one single race . . . among whom prayers and Eucharist are not offered through the name of the crucified Jesus." Two thousand years later, we can say the same thing. The Mass, or Eucharist (from the Greek word for "thanksgiving"), is celebrated every day everywhere from east to west, by people of every tribe and tongue, of every race and nationality.

Most Catholics experience the Mass as Olivier Messiaen did—once every seven days, on the Lord's Day, in a church near our home. We follow the advice given in the *Didascalia,* a third-century manual of church worship:

> Leave everything on the Lord's Day and run diligently to your assembly because it is your praise of God. . . . Hear the Word of Life and feed on the divine nourishment which lasts forever.

The Mass we celebrate on Sunday is not much different from the Mass the early Christians ran to. It still consists of two basic parts—the reading of the sacred Scriptures and the sacrificial offering of bread and wine. Our Mass has the same pattern as those joyful meals Jesus shared with his apostles in the days after he rose from the dead. As Luke tells us, first he "interpreted to them the things about himself in all the scriptures." After that, "at the table with them, he took bread, blessed and broke it, and gave it to them. . . . He had been made known to them in the breaking of the bread."

The oldest, most complete description of the Mass comes from a report filed by St. Justin with the Roman emperor Antoninus Pius in the year 155. The Mass we celebrate in the early twenty-first century is remarkably similar to the Mass Justin observed.

As those early Christians did, we gather on "the day of the sun" and listen to the reading of "memoirs of the apostles or the writings of the prophets." The priest preaches, challenging us to "imitate these beautiful things" we hear in the readings. After this, we stand and offer prayers for ourselves and the world, that all may know "eternal salvation." Then bread "and a cup of water and wine mixed together" are brought forward. The priest "takes them and offers praise and glory to the Father of the universe, through the name of the Son and of the Holy Spirit." Then we pray and eat what Justin called the "eucharisted" bread.

The Table Is Prepared

The Mass we come to today can be seen as a magnificent, centuries-old mosaic of materials from the Scriptures and from the writings, hymns, and devotional instructions of the apostles and early church leaders. Every word and gesture of the Mass is there for a reason—to bring us into a deep communion with the living God, a sharing in his life and love.

We begin each Mass by making the sign of the cross as we repeat the words "In the name of the Father and of the Son and of the Holy Spirit." By this act we take our place in the worship of God in heaven. We stand in the company of angels and saints who have "his name and his Father's name written on their foreheads." These words from the Bible's last book, Revelation, are an ancient designation for the sign of the cross.

What we see in the Mass is a lot like what John saw in his revelation of heaven: an altar of gold, chalices, incense, candles, and robed priests; the sign of the cross; penitential rituals and the reading of the sacred scrolls; the invocation of the Blessed Virgin and the saints; choirs singing, "Holy, holy, holy" and crying, "Amen" and "Alleluia"; the eating of "hidden manna." This is what goes on in the liturgy in heaven. And this is what goes on in the liturgy on earth.

No matter where or when you gather to celebrate the Eucharist, you share in that liturgy going on in heaven. The Mass does not *remind* us of heaven. The Mass *brings* us to heaven. When one comes to Mass, St. Ambrose wrote in the fourth century, "he makes haste toward the heavenly banquet, and seeing the most holy altar made ready, he cries: 'Thou preparest a table before me!'"

From start to finish, the Mass is a hymn of praise to the heavenly Trinity. Every prayer is made *to* the Father, *through* the Son, *in, with,* or *by* the power of the Holy Spirit. There is even a trinitarian cadence to many of the petitions and offerings the priest makes throughout the Mass.

In our worship we confess that the world and everything in it is a gift and an icon of the Trinity's boundless love—that all things come from the Father almighty through the Son in the Spirit of love. Our worship in the Mass is the offering of spiritual sacrifice. Through the Spirit and in the name of the Son, we offer ourselves to the Father in thanksgiving for everything he has given us.

The Lord Be with Us

After we make the sign of the cross, the priest speaks the fundamental truth of the Mass. He may speak a Trinitarian summons drawn from the letters of St. Paul: "The grace of the Lord Jesus Christ, the love of God, and the communion of the Holy Spirit be with you." Or he may say the same thing more succinctly: "The LORD be with you."

In the Mass, the Lord God is with us. He promised he would be whenever two or three were gathered in his name. Whether we stand in a towering cathedral in a capital city or in a tiny chapel in a remote village, the Lord comes to us—as he came to the apostles on that first Easter night, passing through the doors they had bolted in fear. Our Lord wants to be with us, to be friends with us, to see and touch us, to become flesh in us. "It is the law of friendship that friends should live together," St. Thomas Aquinas said. "Christ has not left us without his bodily presence in this our pilgrimage, but he joins us to himself in this sacrament, in the reality of his body and blood."

Since the Lord truly comes to meet us, we must bring our offerings to his altar in all honesty. That is why we confess our sins and beg his mercy at the start of each Mass. Again, this is something Catholics have been doing since the first Mass. "On the Lord's Day . . . give thanks after having confessed your transgressions, that your sacrifice may be pure," advises the first-century *Didache.*

So we stand in his presence, joining the priest and fellow worshipers in a public confession: "I have sinned." We do not detail our personal faults or indulge in some sort of ritual self-abasement. Our penitential prayer expresses our desire to come clean before God: We are weak, we confess. But with his grace we know we can be made strong.

We confess *together,* believing that we are united in Christ—to one another and to those who have gone before us to heaven. We ask the prayers of our brothers and sisters gathered with us. We ask the Virgin Mary, the angels, and the saints to pray for us at the altar of the Lamb. And we pray to God directly, personally, asking mercy from each divine person of the Trinity:

> Lord, have mercy.
> Christ, have mercy.
> Lord, have mercy.

After seeking his mercy, we sing his praises. We sing the song the angels sang to announce Christ's birth at Bethlehem: "Glory to God in the highest," or, in Latin, *"Gloria in excelsis Deo."* The Gloria is a triumphant hymn to our God who comes in the flesh:

> Glory to God in the highest,
> and peace to his people on earth. . . .
> For you alone are the Holy One,
> you alone are the Lord,
> you alone are the Most High,
> Jesus Christ,
> with the Holy Spirit
> in the glory of God the Father.

The Gloria, like other key parts of the Mass, is meant to be sung. "To sing belongs to lovers," St. Augustine said. And these are our love songs to the Lord. Song is another way the Lord lifts us up to contemplate the heavenly mysteries.

Through their efforts to glorify God in the Mass, popes and bishops became the West's most influential patrons of classical music, commissioning sublime choral and polyphonic works from the world's most gifted composers. The Mass has inspired some of the highest achievements of human art—from the towering majesty of Ludwig van Beethoven's *Missa Solemnis* to the delicate luminosity of Giovanni Pierluigi da Palestrina's *Missa Papae Marcelli.*

This is as it should be. In the Mass, the glory of heaven meets the glory of earth. It is fitting that we who are made in the image of his heavenly glory pay tribute to him with the most beautiful and noble creations of our hearts, minds, and hands. We are bound for glory and made for the Gloria—"destined . . . so that we . . . might live for the praise of his glory," as St. Paul said. In the Mass we live this.

Hearing the Word

The Mass continues with the reading of the Bible. Every Sunday, the church presents us with three readings—one from the Old Testament, one from the Letters or Acts of the Apostles, and one from the Gospels; in between we sing one of the psalms. These readings are not random exhortations. Sunday by Sunday, we are reliving the life of Jesus and the great events in the history of salvation.

The priest reminds us that this is more than a Sunday Bible study: "The Lord be with you." The Word of God has come into our midst to tell us his story personally. We again mark ourselves with the sign of the cross and welcome his word with shouts of adoration—"Thanks be to God!" We cry out, "Alleluia!"—the word sung by angels and saints in the heavenly liturgy.

The word is read and preached by the priest to shed light on our daily struggles, to inspire us to offer our lives as a sacrifice of love, united to the sacrifice of Christ. Soon the Lord will feed us at his table with his body and blood. But at this point in the Mass, we are to savor the goodness of his word and all that he has done in history to prepare us to worship at this Mass. We do what

St. Ambrose said: "Drink Christ by drinking his words. . . . The Sacred Scriptures are drunk and the Sacred Scriptures are eaten when the sap of the Eternal Word descends into the veins of the spirit and into the powers of the soul."

The word of God always calls for a response. The Hebrew people responded to the reading of his covenant in one voice: "All the words . . . we will do." The Virgin Mary said to the angel, "Let it be with me according to your word." So we rise after the Bible readings to profess our faith, praying the Nicene Creed, drafted by the church's bishops in 325.

Just as John saw those "slaughtered for the word of God" worshiping at the altar in heaven, we pray the creed mindful of the millions who have given their lives for the faith—even today. We remember martyrs such as Blessed Miguel Pro, who stood without a blindfold before a Mexican firing squad in 1927, arms spread wide in the form of a cross, shouting with joy, "*¡Viva Cristo Rey!*" ("Long live Christ the King!").

Pro, a Jesuit priest, had defied the revolutionary government's edicts outlawing the church. He had taken his priestly ministry underground, bringing the Eucharist clandestinely to hundreds each day, carrying alms to the poor, and encouraging workers in their struggle for justice. In the weeks before he was executed, Blessed Miguel wrote a moving poem in which he prayed for the Eucharist's return to his suffering land:

> O Lord, Thy empty tabernacles mourn . . .
> As orphans we ask Thee, Jesus, to return
> And dwell again within Thy sanctuary. . . .
>
> O Lord, why has Thy presence from us fled? . . .
> Oh! come again. . . .

By the bitter tears of those who mourn their dead,
By our martyrs' blood for Thee shed joyfully,
By crimson stream with which Thy Heart has bled,
Return in haste to Thy dear sanctuary.

After we profess our faith, we offer prayers that this faith will be the salvation of a suffering world. We pray for the needs of the church, the country, and the world we live in, and for the afflicted and weak in our community.

Mystery in Bread and Wine

At this point in the Mass, we place our gifts on the altar of sacrifice. We ask the Father to accept the grain of the earth and the fruit of the vine, the work of our hands. We glorify him as the Lord of creation, the giver of every good gift. We use the triumphant words of the psalmist: "Blessed be God [forever]."

We pray that the bread and wine—and we ourselves—will be changed into the body of Christ. The priest makes this prayer for us as he pours a few drops of water into the chalice with the wine:

By the mystery of this water and wine,
may we come to share in the divinity of Christ,
who humbled himself to share in our humanity.

We hear in this petition an echo of the formula the church fathers used to sum up the Incarnation—"God passed into man so that man might pass over into God." In the Mass, we believe, that promise of divine-human communion is fulfilled and renewed in our lives.

This petition also brings us back to the first public miracle performed by Jesus—the changing of water into wine at the wedding feast at Cana. "Christ has changed water into wine, which is akin to blood, at Cana of Galilee," St. Cyril of Jerusalem preached in the 300s. "Invited to the visible wedding, he accomplished this first miracle. . . . [Now] he has given to the children of the bridal chamber the joy of his body and blood." In the Eucharist we are made members of the wedding, each of us seated at the head table of the marriage feast that Jesus called his "banquet" in his parables.

We enter into the depths of the communion of love that God intends for each person. In baptism each of us was promised "in marriage" to Christ, Paul said. We are made a part of "a great mystery"—the union of Christ the bridegroom with his beloved spouse, the church. Every Eucharist is our nuptial feast. "Every celebration," Augustine said, "is a celebration of marriage—the Church's nuptials are celebrated. The King's Son is about to marry a wife and . . . the guests frequenting the marriage are themselves the Bride. . . . For all the Church is Christ's Bride."

As Jesus offered himself for us on the cross, we are to offer ourselves on the altar. "Present your bodies as a living sacrifice, holy and acceptable to God, which is your spiritual worship," St. Paul urged. So we do. The priest bids us to rise with another exhortation drawn from Scripture: "Lift up your hearts." We lift up our hearts—all our desires and ambitions—and offer them to the Father. "The Lord be with you," the priest continues, reminding us again that the veil between heaven and earth has been rent.

"A person must be of stone, who at that hour believes he is still upon this earth," St. John Chrysostom said in explaining this part of the Mass. “The angels surround the priest. The whole sanctuary and the space before the altar is filled with the heavenly powers come to honor him.” We have reached the Eucharistic prayer—the summit of the Mass. In this ancient prayer we remember the salvation won for us by Jesus, and we share in it. The oldest form of the prayer dates to within the first three centuries after Christ, and it was originally modeled on Jesus’ prayer at the Last Supper.

The prayer begins with a reciting of a hymn to the Trinity that both the prophet Isaiah and the apostle John heard being sung in the heavenly liturgy:

> Holy, holy, holy Lord,
> God of power and might,
> Heaven and earth are full of your glory.

At this point in the Mass we are not only repeating angelic words. We are actually singing *with* the angels, glorifying God with them. To their heavenly hymn, we add a fragment from a thanksgiving psalm sung by Jews to conclude their Passover meals:

> Blessed is he who comes in the name of the Lord!
> Hosanna in the highest!

The disciples sang this song as Jesus entered Jerusalem to celebrate his final Passover. “Hosanna” is a Hebrew plea for God’s salvation. All this is about to happen in the Mass—the glory of heaven is about to fill the earth, and the blessings of salvation are about to come to us in the name of the Lord.

All we can do is fall on our knees. We are about to witness a miracle. It is a moment of high drama. The priest slowly extends his hands over the bread and wine on the altar before him. He begs the Father to send down his Spirit upon these gifts to make them holy.

We have laid our lives on the altar too, so our prayer is also a prayer for our own glorification. An ancient liturgy in Syria included this invocation: "Fill us also with thy glory which is with thee and deign to send thy Spirit upon these creatures." The Spirit we invoke is the same Spirit who hovered over the face of the deep at the dawn of creation, who came upon Mary, who descended upon Jesus in the River Jordan, who offered him to the Father on Calvary. The Spirit we invoke is the Spirit who raised Jesus from the tomb and took him up in glory, who descended on his church in tongues of fire at Pentecost, who still guides the church as a pillar of fire in the dark wilderness of the world.

At this moment in the Mass, we ask that our lives be folded into the mysterious life of this Spirit. We ask that the Lord be begotten among us and that our mortal flesh be vivified, filled with the divine glory. In the liturgy of Byzantine Catholics, which dates to the late third century, the priest prays in words that echo the angel's words to Mary: "The Holy Spirit will come upon you, and the power of the Most High will overshadow you." What is about to happen in the Mass continues the mystery of humankind's redemption begun in the Virgin of Nazareth. We will witness the coming of the Word in the flesh.

A Miracle of Remembrance

First, however, the priest recounts the story of our Lord's last night and how he gave us the Mass. The last week of Jesus' life coincided with the Jewish Feast of Passover, and he gathered his apostles in an upper room in Jerusalem to celebrate the feast.

Everyone at the table, pious Jews all, was intimately familiar with the meaning of the ritual meal they were about to eat. They had heard their fathers explain how the Lord God had instituted the Passover and commanded the people to celebrate it as a "day of remembrance" of their liberation from Egypt. Every year they recalled that first Passover, how their ancestors carried out God's order to kill an unblemished lamb, sprinkle its blood on the doorposts, and then eat it. They celebrated a miracle—how their ancestors' firstborn children were saved as God "passed over" and did not strike those homes signed with the blood of the lamb.

The Jews believed that through this celebration, they truly joined their lives to the covenant God had made with their forefathers. "In every generation, a man must so regard himself *as if he came forth himself out of Egypt,*" says the Mishna, an ancient corpus of Jewish traditions. In their prayers they said: "He performed these miracles for our fathers *and for us.* He has brought *us* forth from slavery to freedom." They believed that in this meal they were overshadowed by the Shekinah, the glorious cloud of the divine presence.

Jesus intended his last Passover meal to evoke all this heritage of Jewish belief and desire. By his words and actions and his command—"Do this in remembrance of me"—he was instituting a new passover. The Eucharist was to be the memorial of his passing over from death to life.

It was not meant as some symbolic reminiscence of glory days gone by. Like the Passover, the Eucharist is to be a memorial that brings us into the present of what is being remembered.

In the Eucharistic memorial, every person in every generation can regard himself or herself as having been personally saved by Jesus' sacrifice on the cross. We experience the miracle of his resurrection, which was performed for each of us personally.

That was Jesus' intention when he blessed the bread and said, "This is my body" and took wine and said, "Drink from it . . . for this is my blood of the covenant." His words still stop us in our tracks. They still cause us to look for some other possible meaning. But there is none. He did not say, "Let this bread and wine be a reminder to you, a symbol of my body and blood."

His words were plain. The Last Supper was not the time or place for metaphors or parables, for words that could be misconstrued or taken out of context. He was alone for the last time with his twelve closest friends and chosen followers. The "hour" that he had spoken of so often was drawing near. What he had to say he had to say quickly, clearly, and directly. By these words he made his last will and testament, confiding to his beloved apostles how he wanted to be remembered for all ages. He was leaving in their hands all that he had—his body and blood poured out in sacrifice for all.

The Twelve clearly understood what was being instituted and entrusted to them. They had been with him in the synagogue at Capernaum when protest broke out over his vivid description of his body and blood as heavenly food:

> I am the bread of life.
> I am the bread that came down from heaven.
> The bread that I will give for the life of the world is my flesh.

> Those who eat my flesh and drink my blood have eternal
> life.
> My flesh is true food and my blood is true drink.
> Whoever eats me will live because of me.

The crowd in Capernaum was horrified. "How can this man give us his flesh to eat?" they cried. But the Lord did not back down. Three times he repeated emphatically that they would have to eat his flesh and drink his blood if they wanted to live. Many of his disciples left him after that, shocked and indignant. But the Twelve remained. They had witnessed the miracle of his feeding five thousand people with five loaves and two fish. They were convinced that he would not deceive them, that his words were what he said they were—"spirit and life." Jesus gave them the chance to leave too. But Peter spoke for them all when he said: "Lord, to whom can we go? You have the words of eternal life."

We hear these words of eternal life in the Mass. They form the prayer of consecration by which the bread and wine are changed into his flesh and blood: "This is my body. . . . This is the cup of my blood." On our knees still, we respond in a shudder of astonishment, as did Thomas, who touched the marks where the nails had been. Our disbelief vanishes as a trembling confession rises from deep within: "My Lord and my God!"

He is here! In all his humanity and all his divinity. The Word of God is here in the bread and wine, as truly present as our neighbors beside us in the pew. He is here—the dead God who flung off his burial shroud, rolled away the stone, and came again, quiet and triumphant, to eat and drink with his friends. He is here—the Son who sits at the right hand of the Father, bearing the scars of his passion, returned in glory.

It is a moment captured in an astonishing way in Olivier Messiaen's last organ work, *The Book of the Blessed Sacrament.* The fruit of decades spent improvising before the Eucharist, this music is pure worship, the awe of a man who had entered into the holy sanctuary of heaven. Messiaen once scribbled on the top of one of his scores: "I sing the gift of the divine essence—the body of Jesus Christ, his body and his blood."

They Beheld God and Ate and Drank

As we kneel before the altar today, we are part of an unbroken chain of witnesses that runs back to the Last Supper. In the Scriptures, one of the first things Jesus is shown doing upon rising from the dead is celebrating the Eucharist with two disciples he meets on the road to Emmaus. He was "made known to them in the breaking of the bread," Luke reports. Peter would later describe the apostles as those "who ate and drank with him after he rose from the dead." He seemed to be trying to deliberately recall the experience of the elders who went to the mountain with Moses and "beheld God" and "ate and drank."

The Eucharist was the life-center of the new churches the apostles founded. They broke the bread secretly in private homes, in services celebrated by bishops ordained by Paul and the apostles. Believers observed a *disciplina arcani* ("discipline of the secret"), refusing to talk or write in detail about the sacred mysteries to those who had not been baptized.

But the apostles' writings and other first-century church documents brim with fragments of prayers and hymns used in these early celebrations. And they left us other little clues. The

Gospels recall how Jesus foretold the Eucharist in his miraculous multiplications of loaves. It is hard not to notice that in these stories, Jesus *takes* the bread, *blesses* it, *breaks* it, and *gives* it to the Twelve. We notice that these are the precise words, in the same order, used in the Last Supper and in his celebration of the Eucharist at Emmaus on the first Easter night. The blessing that Jesus uses is even described with the Greek word *Eucharistia.*

The apostles' account of the Last Supper was set down very early for use in worship. Paul inserted an account into his first letter to the Corinthians, written around AD 56 or 57. In giving detailed instructions for the celebration of the Eucharist, he used the technical terms rabbis used to describe the transmission of Jewish sacred traditions: "I *received* from the Lord what I also *handed on* to you, that the Lord Jesus on the night when he was betrayed took a loaf of bread, . . ."

For Paul and the Twelve, transmitting the Lord's teaching on the Eucharist was a divine commandment that was vital to their mission. And they did their job well. Two millennia later, their faith is our faith. We believe as they did that the bread and wine are truly changed into the body and blood of Christ. We say that "transubstantiation" has taken place: the "substance" of the bread and wine—what they really are—has changed, although what we see on the altar still looks like bread and wine. St. Justin, a disciple of the apostles, explained it this way:

> We do not receive these gifts as ordinary food or ordinary drink—but as Jesus Christ our Savior, who was made flesh through the Word of God and took flesh and blood for our salvation. In the same way, the food over

> which thanksgiving has been offered *(literally, "eucharisted bread")* . . . is, we are taught, the flesh and blood of Jesus who was made flesh.

This does not happen by magic. The word of God makes things what they are, and only that word can change what something is. By that word, the sun was set into the sky and oceans were formed. When the Word came among us in the flesh, he spoke, and blind eyes were opened, lepers were healed, the dead rose to life. His words "This is my body" have the same power and purpose as the Lord's "Let there be" in creation and the words spoken to Mary in the new creation: "You will conceive in your womb."

Spoken in the Mass, Christ's words transform bread and wine to bring each of us into what Paul called real "sharing" or "communion" in the body and the blood of Christ. The priest at the altar is essential, but only because he acts *in persona Christi,* in the person of Christ. All of us gathered at Mass are part of what Peter called "a kingdom, priests serving his God and Father." But the priest at the altar has been set apart. Only he has been ordained to "do" what Christ commanded to be done.

That is why the great twelfth-century reformer St. Hildegard of Bingen never tired of reminding priests of the mysterious grandeur of their office:

> You are the angels of the Lord of hosts. Because, as at the words of the angel Gabriel, God became incarnate of the Virgin Mary in order by his nativity, passion and ascension to save man who was lost, so at your words the same body and the same blood of the same Son of God, with

> the representation of his nativity, passion and resurrection, is brought for our salvation and for the salvation of all the faithful, both living and dead.

Hildegard was one of the boldest and most accomplished women of her time. A Benedictine abbess, she was also a painter, poet, playwright, and composer; she advised popes and kings and wrote one of the first medical textbooks in the West. What animated her every work was this belief in the tremendous mystery of God made flesh in Jesus, the mystery that culminates in the Eucharist.

Grinding the Wheat of God

At this point in the Eucharistic prayer, still on our knees, we marvel as Hildegard did at the love of God shown to the world in Jesus. We profess a short summary of what Paul called "the mystery of the faith": "Christ has died, Christ is risen, Christ will come again." In the Eucharist, Thomas Aquinas said, is the "entire mystery of our salvation." This is what Christ died for—to come again in this Eucharist, to give us his life.

We join St. Ignatius of Antioch in confessing "the Eucharist to be the flesh of our Savior Jesus Christ." Ignatius was willing to die for this belief, his flesh ripped from his bones by the emperor's lions. In a farewell letter to his congregation, he said he was thankful to be counted worthy to offer his body in sacrifice, as the Lord gave his body to him in the Eucharist:

> I shall die for God, unless you hinder me. I beg you not to. . . . I am the wheat of God, so let me be ground by the

> teeth of the wild beasts, that I may be found the pure bread of Christ.

As Ignatius did, we see in the Eucharist a model of what our lives are to be—a pure offering to God. In offering our lives to God in the Mass we receive the life of God. Our faith is the faith of the young deacon St. Tarsicius, who used to bring communion to Christians locked in Roman prisons. He was brutally beaten by a mob one day and died clutching the Eucharist to his breast. "The boy preferred to give up his life than yield the body of Christ to those rabid dogs," Pope Damasus I said in his eulogy.

With the glorified body of Christ in our midst, our Eucharistic prayer continues with a series of prayers of "remembrance." In memory of the Son, we ask the Spirit to unite in love all of us who share in this Eucharist. "Because there is one bread," St. Paul told the Corinthians for whom he celebrated Mass, "we who are many are one body, for we all partake of the one bread." That is a great mystical truth about the Eucharist. As we are transfigured, we are bound together as a single divine person.

Again, this is no metaphor. We really are one body. By this, we mean what Paul meant—that we are flesh and blood vivified by the divine Spirit. St. Irenaeus put it perfectly:

> [Paul] is not speaking of some spiritual and incorporeal kind of man, for spirits do not have flesh and bones. He is speaking of a real human body composed of flesh, sinews and bones, nourished by the chalice of Christ's blood and receiving growth from the bread which is his body.

Our prayers of remembrance continue with appeals for the church beyond the walls in which we worship. We pray for the pope, the bishops, and the clergy—the flesh-and-blood links to the origins of the church in that upper room in Jerusalem two thousand years ago. We pray especially for the dead, that they will be purified and brought into the light of God's presence. In his vision of the divine liturgy, John heard this prayer resounding in heaven: "Blessed are the dead who from now on die in the Lord. . . . They will rest from their labors, for their deeds follow them." We pray that we too keep the faith and be made worthy of life for all eternity, shared with Mary and the whole company of saints in heaven.

We conclude our Eucharistic prayer with a final appeal to the glory of the Trinity, adapted from one of Paul's prayers:

> Through him, with him, in him,
> in the unity of the Holy Spirit,
> all glory and honor is yours,
> Almighty Father,
> forever and ever.

As the priest lifts high the bread and wine, we shout a triumphant "Amen!" Our "Amen" is a cry of gratitude to the holy name of Jesus. In his humanity he became the great yes that reversed the no of Adam and Eve's sin. In his divinity, he was the great yes spoken by God to our race, the yes that forgives and welcomes us into the life of the Trinity. "In him it is always 'Yes,'" Paul wrote. "For in him every one of God's promises is a 'Yes.' For this reason it is through him that we say the 'Amen,' to the glory of God."

A Sign of Peace

We rise now to pray the prayer that Jesus taught his apostles. At this point in the Mass, the Lord's Prayer is a summation of all that has taken place thus far: we have glorified his name, prayed that his will be done in our lives, begged forgiveness of sins, and prayed for our daily bread and for deliverance from the final evil, death.

To the end of Jesus' prayer, we add a coda that may have been composed by the apostles for use in early celebrations of the Mass. It is found in its most primitive and beautiful form in the *Didache:*

> Remember, O Lord, your Church. Deliver it from every evil and perfect it in your love. Gather it from the four winds, sanctified for your kingdom, which you have prepared for it. For yours is the power and the glory forever.

After our "family prayer," we exchange a sign of peace with our brothers and sisters. This seemingly simple gesture is filled with significance. Jesus once said that our worship is halfhearted if we are not at peace with one another.

Jesus himself is "our peace," as St. Paul said. By his death and resurrection he tore down the walls dividing person from person, humanity from God. The Eucharist is the peace he gives us, the pledge of our reconciliation and communion with God. There is nothing casual about the sign of peace we offer, be it a kiss, a hug, or a handshake. This sign, St. Cyril of Jerusalem said, "unites souls to one another and destroys all resentment."

Our souls united, we fall to our knees again. The priest elevates the Host and says:

This is the Lamb of God
who takes away the sins of the world.
Happy are those who are called to his supper.

The prayer yokes two Scriptures—John the Baptist's first recognition of Christ as the Lamb of God, and a cry the apostle John heard in the heavenly liturgy. Together they form a magnificent, climactic disclosure of the meaning of Christ's sacrifice and the celebration of that sacrifice in the Mass.

As Paul said, "Our paschal lamb, Christ, has been sacrificed." The Mass explains why, in John's Gospel, Jesus is condemned to death near the hour when the Passover lambs were traditionally slaughtered by the priests in the temple. At the first Passover, Moses told the Israelites to sprinkle the blood of the lamb on the doorposts of their homes using a hyssop branch. And on the cross, John reports in an odd detail, Jesus is offered a wine-soaked sponge on a hyssop branch. Jesus' executioners do not break his legs because, as John states directly, the Paschal Lamb was to remain unblemished.

Jesus is portrayed in the Gospel as the sacrificial lamb of the new passover. The blood of the first Passover lamb spared the Israelites from death, and the blood of the new Lamb, shed on the cross, has saved all the world from death. The Eucharist is a memorial of his sacrifice, just as the Passover recalls the sacrifice that brought about the Exodus.

Moses sprinkled the Israelites with "the blood of the covenant." In the Eucharist we are sprinkled with what our Lord called "the new covenant in my blood." In the Mass, as the letter to the Hebrews tells us,

> you have come to Mount Zion and to the city of the living God, the heavenly Jerusalem, and to innumerable angels in festal gathering, and to the assembly of the firstborn who are enrolled in heaven, . . . and to the spirits of the righteous made perfect, and to Jesus, the mediator of a new covenant, and to the sprinkled blood that speaks a better word than the blood of Abel.

On our knees before the innocent "Lamb that was slaughtered," as John described him, we can say only one thing: we do not deserve to be here. So we turn to Scripture to find the right words to say. We adapt the Roman officer's plea for Jesus to heal his servant. We acknowledge our unworthiness and profess our faith in his healing and merciful love:

> Lord, I am not worthy to receive you,
> but only say the word and I shall be healed.

Only then do we approach the table to receive his body and blood. Ancient liturgies compared the Eucharistic host to the fiery coal that the angel took from the altar in heaven and placed on the tongue of the prophet Isaiah. The early church spoke too of the *sobria ebrietas,* the "sober inebriation" of drinking from the cup of the long-prophesied banquet of Wisdom.

As St. John of Damascus did in the middle of the eighth century, we "draw near to him with ardent desire and receive the divine coal, so that . . . our sins may be burnt from our hearts illuminated, and we may become so much inflamed in the exchange of fire as to become gods." We put the cup to our lips with the joy of St. Ambrose, drinking in "divine revelation, the sober inebriation which raises man from earthly to visible things."

Until Time Is No More

Mass ends as it began—with the blessing of the Trinity, in the name of the Father, the Son, and the Holy Spirit. We are sent out from Mass to bring the life of Christ to a world hungry and thirsty for God.

The Mass is missionary. Jesus gave his church the work of baptizing all men and women in the name of the Trinity. The Father wants us to extend the gift of salvation to everyone. We do this in the same way that Christians have always done, by bringing the Bread of Life to the world, serving the poor, performing works of mercy and love. And as Christians have always done, we keep rushing back to church on the Lord's Day. "For as often as you eat this bread and drink the cup, you proclaim the Lord's death until he comes," St. Paul said.

We pray for his coming into our midst on the altar. And we await his coming again in glory. This is what the first Christians prayed in their worship—*"Maranatha!"* ("Our Lord, come!"), an Aramaic word that probably came to them from the lips of the Lord himself. With every Eucharist we look forward to what the prophets called the "day of the Lord" and what the apostle Peter called "the coming of the day of God, because of which the heavens will be set ablaze and dissolved, and the elements will melt with fire."

On that day, as the angel declared in Revelation, time will be no more. That passage became the basis for Olivier Messiaen's most famous composition, *Quartet for the End of Time,* which some say was the last century's greatest piece of chamber music.

It was performed in 1941 in a Nazi concentration camp in Silesia, Germany, where Messiaen was being held with five thousand other prisoners of war. He wrote the piece for himself and three other musicians jailed with him. It was performed in camp on the only instruments available—a broken-down, out-of-tune upright piano, a cello with three strings, and a beat-up clarinet and violin.

It was the last music that many of those present would ever hear. And the quartet still stuns and surprises listeners today. In it, time does seem to end; the listener is transported high above the razor-wire fences, the stench of tyranny and death, the desperation of the doomed, the sin of the world. But this is no escapist fantasy. This is music as apocalypse, sound that lets us glimpse eternity. Messiaen's masterpiece is the music of the Mass—a confession of faith in the Lord of history, who has freed us from time and death.

We leave every Mass as if it were our last. We depart looking forward to drinking the fruit of the vine with Jesus in the eternal liturgy of the new Jerusalem. We make our way there communion by communion, following his voice, longing to rejoice in his song:

> I was dead, and see, I am alive forever and ever.

IX

THE LIFE OF THE WORLD TO COME

Mary walked the line with her Son every step of the way, from the greeting of the angel to the foot of the cross. She nursed him when he was an infant, helped him take his first steps, taught him to pray and to read the sacred scrolls. She followed in the crowds as they pressed in tight to hear his teachings. She watched him die and saw him raised from the dead. She was in the upper room with his chosen Twelve when he rained down his Spirit like tongues of fire and gave birth to his church.

"Blessed is she who believed that there would be a fulfillment of what was spoken to her by the Lord," the Scriptures say of her. Mary was named along with her Son in the earliest confessions of the faith. She was honored with the highest title a mortal could ever aspire to: "mother of God."

She lived a holy life, proclaiming the mighty things the Father had done in his mercy, the blessings of his Son, and the power of the Holy Spirit that had come upon her. Her last recorded words in Scripture actually come at the beginning of Jesus' ministry, at a wedding they attended in Galilee. Her words, as everything about her life, point us away from her and toward her Son: "Do whatever he tells you."

When her earthly life came to an end, Mary was taken up to heaven, body and soul. And the fifteenth of August, thought to be the anniversary of her assumption, became for early Christians a day of great celebration.

In an ode he wrote for the feast in the seventh century, St. Germanus I of Constantinople put these words on Jesus' lips: "You must be where I am, Mother, inseparable from her Son." In Armenia, Christians prayed on the Feast of the Assumption: "Today the flamelike choirs of the angelic spirits see our human nature, which was drawn out of the dust of the earth, and they tremble."

Mary's destiny, these early believers knew, was our destiny. She was the first to hear the gospel, and she was the first to experience the promised fruits of belief in that gospel, rising body and soul to everlasting life with God. Mary's assumption is a promise of the resurrection of our bodies. "This is *our* frame that we celebrate today, *our* formation," said St. Andrew of Crete in a seventh-century homily.

The End of Death

What happened to Mary will happen to us. We believe, as the first creeds professed, in "the resurrection of the body and life everlasting," and that Jesus will come again to announce the end of history and to "judge the living and the dead."

This is another of the Christian claims that find no parallel in the history of the world's religions. This claim—that not only our souls but also our bodies will rise to live forever—has shocked and repulsed and provoked protest ever since Christians began to make it. When the apostle Paul preached it to the philosophers of Athens, they laughed him out of town.

But this remains the substance of what we hope for. We are not created for ruin but for immortality. Our bodies will not disintegrate and be survived by our "essence" or "spirit." Our souls will not transmigrate in an eternal reincarnation into different bodily forms. Our whole beings—body and soul, spirit and matter, our human personalities—will live forever.

On the cross, Jesus destroyed our death. He freed us forever from the fear of death that still holds most of humankind in thrall. Rising from the dead, he restored our life. He returned the human condition to its original state, as God always meant it to be. God did not make men and women to die but to live forever in love with him. Death entered the world through the original sin of Adam and Eve. Jesus mastered sin in his life and thereby made death the gateway to everlasting life.

Jesus declared himself the gateway: "I am the resurrection and the life." He promised that if we believe in him and join our bodies to his by eating his body and drinking his blood in the Eucharist, he will raise us up when he comes again. Ignatius of Antioch went to his death proclaiming the Eucharist to be "the medicine of immortality, the antidote for death, and the food that makes us live for ever in Jesus Christ."

Those who enter by the narrow gate of Jesus can say confidently with Paul, "My desire is to depart and be with Christ." Yet death remains a mystery and a void. It dissolves our personality and ends our earthly bands of love. Catholic prayers for the dying confront the most painful and unyielding realities of death. We pray for final perseverance, for strength to ward off the devil's last temptations, for protection against the fierce natural feelings that rise up within us to protest our leaving this life.

But we know by faith that life is changed in death, not finished. Death for us is new birth. This is why the church commemorates the lives of saints on the day they died, not the day they were born. "Him it is I desire—who rose for us," Ignatius said on the eve of his martyrdom. "I am on the point of giving birth. . . . Let me receive pure light; when I shall have arrived there, then shall I be a man."

First Judgments

What happens in that new birth? What will it be like when we die? What we know for certain is that our soul departs from our body and we receive our personal judgment from the Lord.

It may well be that angels bear our soul away, as Jesus described angels carrying Lazarus to the bosom of Abraham. Early Christian prayers and liturgies for the dead speak of angels helping the dying in their final moments and guiding their souls into "holy light." The traditional Mass for the Dead prays: *"In Paradisum deducant te angeli"*—"May the angels lead you into paradise."

This will all happen in an instant, in the blink of an eye. "After that the judgment," the letter to the Hebrews says. At the moment of our death, we fly into holy light, appear in the presence of Jesus, and give account for the life we have lived. There will be no lengthy trial, no weighing of evidence, no appeals process. We go before God with all our deeds, all our attitudes and dispositions, all the secrets of our heart, all the good we have done or failed to do.

In his parable of the last judgment, Jesus said we would be judged according to our love and hospitality toward our neighbors, especially the poor, the hungry, the sick, the homeless, and the imprisoned: "Truly I tell you, just as you did it to one of the least of these . . . you did it to me." Our attitude toward the least of these will disclose whether we have accepted or refused the grace of God's love. As the apostle John wrote, "Those who do not love a brother or sister whom they have seen, cannot love God whom they have not seen."

Jesus is our judge, but Jesus does not really pass judgment on our lives. "I do not judge anyone who hears my words and does not keep them, for I came not to judge the world, but to save the world," he said. "The word that I have spoken will serve as judge." We will be judged by how well we measure up to Jesus' word of truth and love. We will live forever in the love of God in heaven if we have lived here on earth in the love of God. If we let his word fall on deaf ears, if we say no to the salvation and new life he offers us, that life will be closed off to us for eternity.

The Possibility of Hell

Hell—a state of eternal estrangement from the love of God—is a real possibility for everyone. Jesus warned of a state beyond the grave that awaits "evildoers"—the worthless servant, the rich man who ignores the beggar at his gate, those who refuse to love Jesus in the hungry and the thirsty, the stranger and the prisoner. "I never knew you; go away from me," he will say to these, and they will be sent away to what he called the "outer darkness," a "place of torment" and "unquenchable fire," that "eternal fire prepared for the devil and his angels."

To affirm the existence of hell is to affirm the grandeur and dignity of the human person. To God, our life is not a stage play.

He creates every person out of love and respects our freedom so deeply that he will never compel us to love him in return. Hell is the consequence of a lifetime of freely deciding to refuse God's love, to finally and forever say to God, "Leave me alone."

Probably the best definition of hell is in Georges Bernanos's great novel of spiritual warfare, *The Diary of a Country Priest,* where he describes a village pastor's ministrations to a rich woman who appears to have lost her faith. At one point the priest cries out to her: "Hell is not to love any more, madame. *Not to love any more!*" We make our own hell by refusing to love in this world.

We know that hell exists from Jesus, the apostles, and the constant teaching of the church. Yet we know nothing about the population of hell, who is there and how many. The church has never declared that anyone—not even Judas Iscariot—is actually "in hell." The church's task is not to sit in judgment or to threaten but to preach Jesus' "good news" to the ends of the earth and to make disciples of all nations. We preach the promise of a new life, not fire and brimstone. The gospel is joy and possibility, not fear and trembling.

Thus, there is no place in our preaching for speculating about who is "going" to hell. We have no room for anxiety and despair about our own salvation. God does not create in order to destroy. He has predestined no one for ruin. The possibility of hell reminds us that our lives are not a game. Our task is to conform ourselves to the image and the loving heart of Jesus. We trust in his mercy with St. Bonaventure: "I still know one thing—that the love and the merits that I intend to have, lead with certainty to eternal life."

If souls are lost, their hell is truly of their own making. But this also suggests that we are failing in the mission Jesus gave us—to make the gospel attractive and compelling, something worth living and dying for. Our mission is both universal and extremely personal: we are to save the entire world, and every person in the world counts. So long as one person is at risk of being lost, we cannot rest content. We feel as St. Catherine of Siena did:

> How could I ever reconcile myself, Lord, to the prospect that a single one of those whom, like me, You have created in Your image and likeness, should become lost and slip from Your hands? No, in absolutely no case do I want to see a single one of my brethren meet with ruin. . . . I want them all to be wrested from the grasp of the ancient enemy, so that they all become Yours.

Catherine's anxieties express well the longings of God. As the apostle Peter wrote, God does not desire "any to perish, but all to come to repentance." Jesus taught us to pray and work constantly for God's will to be done on earth. And we know, as Paul said, that "God our Savior . . . desires everyone to be saved and to come to the knowledge of the truth."

Even Voltaire Could Repent

God's mercy is limitless. We hope that no soul may perish. We are confident that no one, no matter how belligerent and defiant, no matter how resistant to the love of God, is beyond the pale of his redemption. Our confidence is bolstered by the testimony of the saints, who embody God's love for even his worst enemies, his pursuit of sinners down all their crooked paths, and his joy when they return to him.

We take heart from saints like John Bosco, the nineteenth-century Italian priest. Once he went to the bedside of a dying man who belonged to a militantly anti-Catholic secret society. "Do not speak to me of religion," the man cursed, threatening to shoot the priest. So instead, John talked to him about the career of Voltaire, the great French writer and philosopher who was a sworn, bitter foe of the church and the faith, which he ridiculed in his works as superstitious, intolerant, and corrupt.

"Some say that Voltaire never repented and had a bad death," the saint concluded. "This I do not say, because I do no not know." Hearing this, the dying man was incredulous, for the condemnations of Voltaire by high church leaders were widely known. "You mean," the man asked, "that even Voltaire could repent?" He then confessed his own repentance to the priest and died a peaceful death.

For the Catholic, no one is lost to the mercy of God. No one is born to die—not even a Voltaire, not even that dying man who threatened to shoot St. John Bosco. No matter what road we have been traveling in life, if we have true sorrow for our sins and a true desire for the love of God, we can trust in his mercy, even in our dying moments.

That was the prophetic message of St. Faustina Kowalska—the first saint canonized by the church in the twenty-first century. A Polish nun in the years just prior to the outbreak of the Second World War, Faustina was granted mystical visions of Jesus' boundless mercy for sinners. In vision after vision, he told her that even the worst sinners can turn to him in love:

> My daughter, know that my heart is mercy itself. No soul that has approached me has ever gone away unconsoled.

> Sooner would heaven and earth turn into nothingness than would my mercy not embrace a trusting soul.

The mercy of God is infinite. But this does not mean that we should take God's mercy for granted. Before his conversion, St. Augustine did precisely that. He would even beg God to let him cling to the pleasures of his sinful life for just a while longer. In his memoirs, he wrote: "Here I was still postponing the giving up of this world's happiness . . . saying 'Grant me chastity and continence, but not yet.' For I was afraid that You would hear my prayer too soon, and too soon would heal me."

But as Augustine came to know, eternal life is not a final examination that we can study for at the last minute. The fact is that change becomes more difficult as we grow older. We get stuck in our ways. In the language of the Scriptures, our hearts harden; we become less receptive to the tender mercies of the Father. If we have spent a lifetime resisting God's advances, we cannot be certain that in our final years or final moments we will have the capacity to accept his grace and turn to him.

This is why Catholic preaching is so urgent. The truth is that this moment could be your last. The time for repentance is now. Death will come as a thief in the night, the Lord said, and the work of conversion should not be put off. This was the message of Pope St. Clement I:

> While we are on earth, let us repent. We are clay in the hand of the craftsman. If a potter is making a pot and it goes wrong or comes apart in his hands, he refashions it; but when he reaches the point of putting it in the hot oven, there is no more he can do for it . . . similarly we

> can no longer confess or repent, once we have gone out of the world.

Where We All Belong

Heaven is where we belong. Heaven is what we were made for, and only heaven will satisfy our longings. Heaven is our goal, but what it is remains a mystery. St. John Chrysostom titled a series of sermons on the afterlife *On the Incomprehensible Nature of God.* He knew that many of our deepest questions will not be answered until we are beyond the grave.

What is certain is that heaven exists. Jesus called heaven "my Father's house." He ascended into heaven "to prepare a place for you. . . . So that where I am, there you may be also." We can go to heaven because Jesus has gone there first in his risen body, in the fullness of his glorified humanity. His ascension to what Paul called "the right hand of God" gave humanity a place within the very life of God.

In heaven "we will be like him, for we will see him as he is," John the apostle said. God comes to us in many ways throughout our lives—in other people, in the beauties of his creation, in the sacraments of his church. But in heaven we shall see him "face to face," as Paul said, with nothing standing between us. We look forward to this heavenly promise—that we will experience God as he truly is, that we will spend eternity in the bliss of God's own life. This is the prayer of every Catholic heart, beautifully expressed by Cardinal John Henry Newman:

> God alone is in heaven; God is all in all. . . . He fills Heaven, and all blessed creatures though they ever remain in their

> individuality, are . . . absorbed and, as it were, drowned in the fullness of Him. . . .
>
> If ever, through Thy grace, I attain to see Thee in heaven, I shall see nothing else but Thee, because I shall see all whom I see in Thee, and seeing them I shall see Thee. . . .
>
> O my God, what am I that Thou shouldst make my blessedness to consist in that which is Thy own! That Thou shouldst grant me to have not only the sight of Thee, but to share in Thy very own joy! O prepare me for it, teach me to thirst for it!

We are not turned into angels in heaven or made over into some generic "creature of heaven." We go to heaven in all our uniqueness and individuality. Who we are in this life is who we will be in the next—although in heaven we will be purified of sin. We were created to be a unique and irreplaceable image of God on earth; in heaven we will be the perfect likeness of God that we were intended to become.

Our Work in Heaven

Heaven is other people—Mary and the saints, not to mention the angels and the Trinity. During our earthly lives we are joined through the Eucharist in a mysterious unity with Catholics everywhere in the world. In heaven, we experience the "other side" of the communion of saints. "This is the joy of salvation, this is eternal life: to live with the just, with all the friends of God in the kingdom of immortality," St. Cyprian said.

But our relationships with those on earth are not severed once we reach heaven. On earth, we benefit from the holiness and love of the saints in heaven. They look out for us, listen to our prayers, intercede for us. In heaven we too will assume responsibility for caring and praying for the ones we leave behind. Jesus said in his parable of the talents that those entering into the joy of the Master will be given charge over many things. As on earth, we will have work to do in heaven, a part to play in his saving plan.

From heaven, we will watch over our brothers and sisters on earth, especially our loved ones. We will experience their joys and their sorrows, with ears open always to their pleas and petitions. We will intercede for them, bringing our prayers for them before the altar of the Most High, as John foresaw in his revelation. "All our friends who have arrived wait for us," St. Cyprian said of the saints in heaven. "They desire vividly that we participate in their own beatitude, and are full of solicitude for our regard."

Toward the end of her short life, St. Thérèse of Lisieux had a vision of heaven. In a dream she saw a group of saints in heaven, one of whom came forward to speak with her. She told Thérèse that her time was short and that God was well pleased with her. When Thérèse woke, she said: "I *believed,* I *felt* there was a heaven and that this heaven is peopled with souls who actually love me, who consider me their child." About a year later, three months before she died, Thérèse coughed up blood in the middle of the night and then gasped this promise to her nurse:

> I feel that I'm about to enter into my rest. But I feel especially that my mission is about to begin. . . . My heaven will be spent on earth until the end of the world. Yes, I want to spend my heaven in doing good on earth.

Doing good on earth will be our mission in heaven. And the stories of the saints give us countless examples.

Consider the story of Teresia Benedicta McCarthy. A two-year-old toddler in 1987, Teresia got hold of a bottle of Tylenol and ingested twenty times the lethal dosage. Her liver swelled to five times its normal size. Doctors told her parents that nothing could be done. But her parents and friends prayed to Edith Stein, the Jewish convert who became a Carmelite nun and was executed by the Nazis. Teresia's parents had a special devotion to Stein. Teresia had been born on the anniversary of Stein's death, and her parents had given her the name Stein took upon entering the Carmelite order.

Within two days Teresia recovered fully. Amazed doctors could offer no medical explanation. Following ten years of study—including an intensive review of the medical evidence—church officials ruled that her cure was a miracle worked by Christ through the heavenly intercession of Edith Stein. In 1998, when Edith Stein was officially canonized as a saint, Teresia, then twelve, attended the ceremonies in Rome.

We believe what St. Edith Stein herself once wrote about the power of the saints in heaven:

> You reign at the Father's right hand
> In the kingdom of his eternal glory. . . .
> You reign on the Almighty's throne
> Also in transfigured human form. . . .
> From where you are, there also are your own,
> Heaven is my glorious homeland,
> I share with you the Father's throne.

Purgatory, the Consuming Fire

Heaven will be our glorious homeland. But most of us will not reach it directly. Upon death, many will have fallen far short of that "holiness without which no one will see the Lord," as the letter to the Hebrews puts it. Even if we die in God's grace and friendship and are judged worthy of heaven, we will need to undergo purification to rid us of the stain of sin, to make us holy and capable of communion with God.

Jesus said that some of our sins would need to be forgiven or atoned for "in the age to come." Peter and Paul both taught that our life's works would be put to the test of a divine fire that would cleanse and purify us of all that is unworthy of God. And Catholics have always believed that after death there will remain imperfections in need of correcting before the soul can finish its journey to heaven.

We call that interim stage on the way to heaven *purgatory*. Purgatory is not a river of fire or a gulag of dread beyond the grave. Rather, it is a condition of penance, an aspect of our encounter with the judgment of God, who the prophets said is a "consuming fire." Purgatory is the gaze of the Lord Jesus, "the Son of God, who has eyes like a flame of fire," as the apostle John revealed.

Our lives are to be purified and tested in the fiery gaze of his love. "The fire will test what sort of work each has done," Paul said. What is not of God, all the edifices of our selfishness and vanity, will be painstakingly burned away until what survives is pure and precious. Purgatory finishes the work begun in baptism—that of transfiguring us into the image of Christ, who is the perfect image of God. As Origen wrote in the early third century:

> Our God is called "a consuming fire." This fire does not consume what has been created in God's image and likeness, the work of his own creation, but rather whatever wrongs we have piled upon it.

How this purification takes place, how long it lasts, what type of pain is involved—these questions remain among the incomprehensible mysteries. Paul said only that we would "suffer loss." Following a mystical vision of purgatory, St. Catherine of Genoa was convinced that the souls there submit to their sufferings with a joyful anticipation of heaven that grows "as God flows into these souls more and more, as the hindrance to his entrance is consumed. (Sin's rust is the hindrance, and the fire burns the rust away so that more and more the soul opens itself up to the divine inflowing.)"

The Refreshment of the Dead

What goes on in purgatory is a mystery. But Catholics have always been taught they have a duty to pray daily and offer sacrifices for the "refreshment" of those souls who have not yet reached "perpetual light."

Every Mass includes prayers for the dead. St. John Chrysostom said this practice was "ordained by the apostles." The dead are remembered at a point in the Mass after the bread and wine have been changed into the body and blood of Jesus. It is "a great benefit to the souls on whose behalf the supplication is offered, while the holy and tremendous Victim is present," explained St. Cyril of Jerusalem.

As she lay dying, St. Monica asked her son St. Augustine to pray for her when she was gone. Tertullian wrote in the second century: "The faithful wife will pray for the soul of her deceased husband. . . . If she fail to do so, she has repudiated her husband." The first Christians inscribed touching promises of their continued love and prayers on the tombs of their loved ones. One from the catacombs of Rome reads, "Calemira, may God refresh thy spirit, together with that of thy sister, Hilaria."

We pray for the refreshment of those in purgatory. We pray as did Judas the Maccabee in the Scriptures, "that they might be delivered from their sin" and granted the "splendid reward that is laid up for those who fall asleep in godliness." We pray out of love. We have no illusions that we can pull strings for them; the refreshment of their spirits comes as an unmerited gift from the mercy of the Father. Rather we pray for them because Jesus has joined living and dead in his one body. "We do not live to ourselves, and we do not die to ourselves," Paul said. We are not on our own. We will never know until the next life how much we have benefited from the prayers and sacrifices of others, living and dead. And we do not know how much others, living and dead, benefit from our works of love.

Through Jesus we live for one another. Paul said we are to "bear one another's burdens" and to "care for one another." He wrote, "If one member suffers, all suffer together with it; if one member is honored, all rejoice together with it." When we make sacrifices for other members of the body, we join ourselves in love to the redemptive work of Jesus. As Paul said, "I am now rejoicing in my sufferings for your sake, and in my flesh I am completing what is lacking in Christ's afflictions for the sake of his body, that is, the church."

The saints have been granted visions of what can be accomplished by our prayers. When St. Perpetua was waiting to be fed to the lions in late February 203, she dreamed she saw her dead younger brother in misery, hot and thirsty, dirty and clothed in rags, struggling to drink from a fountain that was too high for him to reach. For days, Perpetua prayed and made supplications for him. Just before her execution, she had another dream:

> I saw the place which I had before seen, and Dinocrates, clean of body, finely clothed, in comfort; and the font I had seen before, the edge of it being drawn down to the boy's navel; and he drew water thence which flowed without ceasing. . . . And being satisfied he departed away from the water and began to play as children will, joyfully. And I awoke. Then I understood that he was translated from his pains.

The End-Time

The life of the people of God will continue through time, but time will have an end. We do not know the minute or the hour when this will happen. Catholics do not waste time worrying or speculating about some supposed "rapture" or trying to "decode" biblical prophecies to predict when the end might come. We take Jesus at his word: "About that day or hour no one knows, neither the angels in heaven, nor the Son, but only the Father."

Following the judging of the dead, Christ will come again in glory to judge all the living. Some might be sentenced to "eternal punishment," Jesus warned; others to "eternal life." At the end of time love will be the measure. Our eternal destiny will depend on how much love we have shown for the Lord through our acts of love for our neighbors, especially the poor.

In this final hour, we look forward to what Paul called "the redemption of our bodies." The resurrection of the body will not be a reincarnation, our souls passing into new bodies. We will rise for the life to come as whole persons, body and soul. Our resurrected bodies will be the ones we lived and suffered and died in—only transformed, perfected, glorified, made heavenly.

As Paul described it, our resurrection will not consist of a reassembly of body parts, the resuscitation of our corpse, or the soul donning a new suit of flesh. The body of our resurrection will grow from out of the body that was laid in our grave, in the same way a plant grows from a seed, as Paul said.

God will raise us in power to new life in spiritual, heavenly bodies no longer subject to infirmity or decay. Babies who died in utero; those who suffered deformity and disability; St. Joan of Arc, who was burned at the stake and had her ashes littered in the River Seine—all will be raised body and soul to perfection, to the final divinization of our humanity. Our resurrected bodies will be different from our earthly bodies yet related to them, just as a plant is different from and yet continuous with the seed from which it shoots.

This transformation of our resurrected bodies mirrors the mysterious, miraculous transformation that takes place in every Eucharist. This is why St. Irenaeus said that every time we take the sacred bread and the sacred cup, we have a foretaste of the resurrection of our bodies:

> Just as bread that comes from the earth, after God's blessing has been invoked upon it, is no longer ordinary bread,

> but Eucharist, formed of two things, the one earthly and the other heavenly; so too our bodies, which partake of the Eucharist, are no longer corruptible, but possess the hope of resurrection.

New Heaven, New Earth

In the end, it will be revealed that what has happened at our altars every day since that first Easter night at Emmaus is the destiny of the whole world. This world will pass away, and there will come what Peter called "new heavens and a new earth"—a world transfigured, heaven and earth in full communion, all creation filled with the unsurpassable light of the Creator. God will be "all in all."

The purpose and meaning of God's plan will be unveiled in all its radiant splendor. As it was revealed to John in the Bible's last book, the end of the world will consummate in the marriage of the church to the lamb of God, Jesus.

We will understand then that all human history was intended to be a divine love affair, God's passionate courtship of his people. The covenant he desires with humanity, and with each of us, was symbolized in the marriage of Adam and Eve in Paradise. Since the dawn of creation he has been preparing all humanity for the great wedding feast of the end of time, the marriage of human and divine, spirit and flesh, heaven and earth.

In the church, God's covenant of love, revealed to his chosen people, Israel, finds fulfillment. Daughter Zion, as the prophets called Israel, offered herself to God in the person of Mary. And we, too, have sworn to offer ourselves to God, first in baptism and again in every Eucharist. In the end, we will see our wedding day, our divine espousal—when all who love him will gather at the wedding feast of the Lamb as a holy city, a new Jerusalem, a bride adorned in linen bright and pure.

That day will mark the start of a new creation. The earth will become the city of God, the temple of the living God. All creation will be made his dwelling—"the paradise of God," as Revelation sees it. And in this glorious city, we will eat from the tree of life planted in paradise at the world's beginning. What we were made to be in the beginning, we will be made in the end. Our eternal lives will be a never-ending liturgy of praise and thanksgiving to the Creator. John beheld countless people from every nation and race worshiping before the throne and altar of God and the Lamb, reigning forever as sons and daughters, priests and kings, over all creation. We will be among that number.

This is the world the Catholic looks forward to in every Mass, the world we are being made fit for by our prayer and devotion, our life of faith. This is the world that was announced at Nazareth twenty centuries ago, the new world begun in the womb of Mary, in her child waiting to be born, Jesus.

AFTERWORD

Love never ends. But as for prophecies, they will come to an end; as for tongues, they will cease; as for knowledge, it will come to an end.

—1 Corinthians 13:8

In the preceding pages, I have tried to offer an explanation and appreciation of the Catholic faith.

What it comes down to in the end is *love.*

Love is a word so overused and trivialized today that it no longer bears any resemblance to *love* in the biblical and Catholic sense. It has become a synonym for appetites and warm sentiments. But in the Bible and in the Catholic tradition, love is sacrifice, love is worship.

Love is the new commandment that Jesus gave us—to love as he loved, by offering our whole heart, strength, mind, and will for others and for God. In the love he showed for us on the cross, Jesus revealed that love is the name of God. Love is the reason he made the world. Love is the reason he called each one of us into being. We were made by love and for love. And in the simple, elegant formulation of St. John of the Cross: "At the evening of life, we shall be judged on our love."

If what the Catholic believes is true, there is nothing that God has not or will not do to win our love. In Origen's beautiful words from the third century, God bears for each one of us a *passio caritatis*—the passion of love:

> The Savior came down to earth out of compassion for the human race. He suffered our sufferings. . . . He underwent for our sake . . . the passion of love.

If there is one theme that runs through these pages, through all the Scriptures and the many Catholic lives and works discussed, it is this: God's passion of love continues in the Catholic Church. The Catholic passion is God's passion. In the work of the church and in our lives as Catholics, God meets us in our sufferings and in our joys, offers his life to us, and tries to teach us this passion of love.

Throughout this book I have deliberately not quoted from church teaching documents or catechisms in order to focus on how those teachings are expressed in the lives and works of Catholics. But we would do well to remember that everything in the church is ordered to this passion of love. In the Roman Catechism, issued after the Council of Trent (1545–63), we find this exhortation:

> The whole concern of doctrine and its teaching must be directed to the love that never ends. Whether something is proposed for belief, for hope or for action, the love of our Lord must always be made accessible, so that anyone can see that all the works of perfect Christian virtue spring from love and have no other objective than to arrive at love.

Everything Catholics believe and do springs from this love that never ends. And everything Catholics believe and do has the objective of inviting the world to share in this love—which begins in this life and continues without end in the life to come. The Catholic passion is an invitation to believe. And like all invitations, it awaits our reply.

✧

NOTES

The sources below are listed by chapter and page number. All Scripture quotations in the text are taken from the New Revised Standard Version (NRSV) of the Bible. References to direct quotes from the Bible are listed in boldface type.

I have tried to avoid citing materials that might only be found in scholarly libraries; the books and other resources included here should all be readily available. Most of the church documents and many of the saints' writings that I refer to are also available online, at sites such as www.vatican.va, www.ewtn.com, www.newadvent.org, and www.salvationhistory.com.

Preface

x *Overcome with wonder* Paul Claudel, *I Believe in God: A Meditation on the Apostles' Creed,* ed. Agnès du Sarment, trans. Helen Weaver (New York: Holt, Rinehart and Winston, 1963).

Chapter 1: Son of Mary, Man of Heaven

2 *to reproduce his life* Charles de Foucauld, *The Spiritual Autobiography of Charles de Foucauld,* ed. Jean-François Six, trans. J. Holland Smith (New York: P. J. Kenedy and Sons, 1964), 52–53, 129.

3 *names of Jesus* Theological-Historical Commission for the Great Jubilee of the Year 2000, *Jesus Christ, Word of the Father: The Savior of the World,* trans. Adrian Walker (New York: Crossroad, 1997), 49.

3 *Who am I?* St. Francis of Assisi, quoted in Yves Congar, *The Revelation of God,* trans. A. Manson and L. C. Sheppard (London: Darton, Longman and Todd, 1968), 85.

3 *Jesus' question* **Mark 8:29.**

3 *salvation* **John 4:22.**

5 *my wife forever* **Hosea 2:16, 19.**

5 *Mary's vow* **Luke 1:38.**

6 *mystery hidden* **Ephesians 3:9;** Colossians 1:26.

6 *blessed destiny* St. Maximus, quoted in Christoph von Schönborn, *God's Human Face: The Christ-Icon,* trans. Lothar Krauth (San Francisco: Ignatius Press, 1994), 122–23.

7 *Isaiah's cry* **Isaiah 64:1.**

8 *Sick* St. Gregory of Nyssa, quoted in *Catechism of the Catholic Church,* 2nd ed. (Vatican City: Libreria Editrice Vaticana, 1997), no. 457.

8 *born of a woman* Galatians 4:4.

9 *Mary's obedience* St. Irenaeus, quoted in Pope John Paul II, *Encyclical Letter on the Blessed Virgin Mary in the Life of the Pilgrim Church (Redemptoris Mater)* (March 25, 1987), no. 19, in J. Michael Miller, ed., *The Encyclicals of John Paul II* (Huntington, IN: Our Sunday Visitor, 2001).

9 *mother of reconciliation* St. Ambrose of Milan, quoted by Pope John Paul II, General Audience of September 17, 1997, in Pope John Paul II, *Theotókos: Woman, Mother, Disciple: A Catechesis on Mary, Mother of God* (Boston: Pauline Books and Media, 2000).

9 *last Adam* Romans 5:12–14; **1 Corinthians 15:45**–49.

10 *conceive the divine Word* St. Bernard, quoted in *The Liturgy of the Hours: According to the Roman Rite* (New York: Catholic Book Publishing Company, 1975), 1:345–46.

10 *God's plan from all eternity* Ephesians 1.

10 *brephos* St. Cyril of Jerusalem, quoted in John Saward, *Redeemer in the Womb: Jesus Living in Mary* (San Francisco: Ignatius Press, 1993), 45–46.

10 *a little child* St. Romanus, quoted in Christoph von Schönborn, *The Mystery of the Incarnation,* trans. Graham Harrison (San Francisco: Ignatius Press, 1992), 29.

11 *Byzantine Christmas hymn* Saward, *Redeemer in the Womb,* 6.

11 *God's Son came* St. Bernard, quoted in the *The Liturgy of the Hours,* 1:446–48.

12 *a little lower than God* **Psalm 8:5.**

12 *God wished* St. Hippolytus, quoted in the *The Liturgy of the Hours,* 1:459–61.

13 *son of Mary* **Mark 6:3.**

13 *God became man* St. Athanasius, quoted in *Catechism,* no. 460.

14 *Angelus's poem* Angelus (Johannes Scheffler), quoted in Schönborn, *The Mystery of the Incarnation,* 51.

14 *nothing little* Columba Marmion, *Christ in His Mysteries,* 8th ed. (St. Louis: Herder, 1931), 7.

14 *Jesus as the ideal of human life* **Matthew 11:29; 19:21; John 13:15.**

14 *Caro quasi vox* St. Augustine, sermon 185. This is sometimes translated "The Word of God without words uttered the flesh as its voice." See http://www.vatican.va/spirit/documents/spirit_20001222_agostino_en.html; St. Augustine, *Sermons for Christmas and Epiphany,* trans. Thomas Comerford Lawler (Westminster, MD: Newman Press, 1952); Saward, *Redeemer in the Womb,* 148.

15 *Foucauld's hidden life* Foucauld, *Spiritual Autobiography,* 82–83.

16 *Love one another* **John 15:12.**

17 *become love* St. Catherine of Siena, letter no. 165; emphasis mine. The letter can be read at http://www.vatican.va/spirit/documents/spirit_20010814_caterina-siena_en.html.

17 *Even the insults* William of Saint-Thierry, quoted in Saward, *Redeemer in the Womb,* 148.

17 *greater love* **John 15:13.**

18 *gave himself for me* **Galatians 2:20.**

18 *Who am I, O Lord?* St. Bonaventure, quoted in St. Alphonsus de' Liguori, *The Passion and the Death of Jesus Christ,* ed. Eugene Grimm (Brooklyn: Redemptorist Fathers, 1927), 364.

19 *foreknowledge of God* **Acts 2:23.**

19 *Which of you* **John 8:46.**

19 *not my will* **Luke 22:42.**

19 *suffering servant* **Isaiah 53:3, 5, 10.**

20 *reflections on the Crucifixion* William Congdon and Joseph Ratzinger, *The Sabbath of History* (Milan: William Congdon Foundation, 2001), 98.

20 *hoax* Angela of Foligno, *Complete Works,* trans. Paul Lachance (New York: Paulist Press, 1993), 280.

20 *foolishness* **1 Corinthians 1:18.**

21 *Jesus and the Eucharist* John 1:29.

21 *from the side of Christ* See *Catechism,* nos. 766, 1225.

22 *who does not know* St. Gregory, quoted in Jean Daniélou, *From Shadows to Reality: Studies in the Biblical Typology of the Fathers* (Westminster, MD: Newman Press, 1960), 55–56.

22 *Here is your mother* **John 19:26–27.**

23 *blood of God* St. John Chrysostom, quoted in Hans Urs von Balthasar, *Mysterium Paschale (The Mystery of Easter),* trans. Aidan Nichols (San Francisco: Ignatius Press, 2000), 30.

23 *Jesus among the dead* Ephesians 4:8–10; 1 Peter 3:18–19; 4:6; John 5:25. See also *Catechism,* nos. 632–35.

24 *Jesus meeting Adam* Epiphanius, quoted in the *The Liturgy of the Hours,* 2:496–98.

24 *alive in Christ* Romans 5:12–21; **1 Corinthians 15:22.**

24 *After his resurrection* Matthew 27:52–**53.**

25 *man of heaven* **1 Corinthians 15:49.**

25 *firstborn from the dead* **Colossians 1:18.**

26 *King of kings* **Revelation 19:16.**

27 *life of Nazareth* Foucauld, *Spiritual Autobiography,* 167.

Chapter 2: God, the Hound of Heaven

29 *Dorothy Day and Eugene O'Neill* See Dorothy Day, *Meditations,* comp. Stanley Vishnewski (Springfield, IL: Templegate, 1997), 9; William D. Miller, *Dorothy Day: A Biography* (San Francisco: Harper and Row, 1982), 103–18; William D. Miller, *All Is Grace: The Spirituality of Dorothy Day* (Garden City, NY: Doubleday, 1987), 9–19; Edward L. Shaughnessy, *Down the Nights and Down the Days: Eugene O'Neill's Catholic Sensibility* (Notre Dame, IN: University of Notre Dame Press, 1996).

30 *The Hound of Heaven* Francis Thompson, *The Complete Poetical Works of Francis Thompson* (New York: Modern Library, 1913), 88–93; among many available editions of the poem, see Francis Thompson, *The Hound of Heaven* (New York: Morehouse, 1986).

32 *See what love* **1 John 3:1.**

33 *daughter of God* Dorothy Day, *On Pilgrimage* (Grand Rapids, MI: W. B. Eerdmans, 1999), 197.

33 *world is like a book* Hugh of Saint-Victor, quoted in Henri de Lubac, *The Discovery of God,* trans. Alexander Dru (Grand Rapids, MI: W. B. Eerdmans, 1996), 89.

34 *Paternal Abyss* Origen, quoted in Ibid., 136.

34 *in the silence* Pseudo-Dionysius, quoted by Pope John Paul II, General Audience of January 19, 2000, in Pope John Paul II, *The Trinity's Embrace: God's Saving Plan: A Catechesis on Salvation History* (Boston: Pauline Books and Media, 2002).

34 *baby talk* Origen, quoted in Stephen D. Benin, *The Footprints of God: Divine Accommodation in Jewish and Christian Thought* (Albany: State University of New York Press, 1993), 12.

34 *tender mother* St. Gregory of Nazianzus, quoted in Ibid., 52.

35 *the Beloved* **Luke 3:22.**

35 *the Father and I* **John 10:30.**

35 *Spirit of truth* **John 14:17.**

35 *mission to baptize* **Matthew 28:19.**

35 *God is love* **1 John 4:8;** emphasis mine.

35 *to see the Trinity* St. Augustine, quoted in Theological-Historical Commission for the Great Jubilee of the Year 2000, *The Holy Spirit, Lord and Giver of Life,* trans. Agostino Bono (New York: Crossroad, 1997), 17.

36 *emptied himself* **Philippians 2:**7–8.

37 *A single font* Synesius of Cyrene, quoted by Pope John Paul II, General Audience of April 5, 2000, in Pope John Paul II, *The Trinity's Embrace.*

37 *Trinity in creation* **Genesis 1:**1–3, **26** (emphasis mine); Psalm 33:6.

38 *Trinity is one God* St. Gregory of Nazianzus, quoted in Pope John Paul II, *Bull of Indiction of the Great Jubilee of the Year 2000 (Incarnationis Mysterium)* (November 29, 1998), no. 3 (Boston: Pauline Books and Media, 1998).

39 *omnipotence of the Creator* Franz Joseph Haydn, quoted in Patrick Kavanaugh, *Spiritual Lives of the Great Composers,* rev. ed. (Grand Rapids, MI: Zondervan, 1996), 40–41.

39 *grandeur of God* Gerard Manley Hopkins, *Poems and Prose* (New York: Penguin, 1953), 27.

39 *Scattering a thousand graces* St. John of the Cross, "Spiritual Canticle," stanza 5, in *The Collected Works of St. John of the Cross,* trans. Kieran Kavanaugh and Otilio Rodriguez (Washington, DC: ICS Publications, 1979).

39 *the universe cries out* St. Augustine, quoted in Mike Aquilina, comp., *The Way of the Fathers: Praying with the Early Christians* (Huntington, IN: Our Sunday Visitor, 2000), 21.

39 *God's plan in creation* Ephesians 1:3–10; **3:9.**

40 *filial relationship with God* Exodus 25:8; 29:45; Leviticus 26:12; Isaiah 43:6; Jeremiah 31:1; Ezekiel 37:27; Hosea 1:10; **2 Corinthians 6:16, 18.**

40 *my Father and your Father* **John 20:17;** emphasis mine.

40 *Abba* Romans 8:15–16; Galatians 4:4–6.

41 *family prayer* St. Cyprian, quoted in *Encyclopedia of Catholic Doctrine,* ed. Russell Shaw, s.v. "Fatherhood of God" (Huntington, IN: Our Sunday Visitor, 1997), 238–39.

41 *God is not a man* **Genesis 1:27;** Isaiah 49:13, 15; 66:13; **John 4:24.**

41 *call none other thy mother* St. Mechtild of Hackeborn, quoted in Patrick Grant, ed., *A Dazzling Darkness: An Anthology of Western Mysticism* (London: Collins, 1985), 147.

42 *my Father's house* **Luke 2:49.**

42 *God our Father* **Matthew 5:**44–**45, 48;** 21:28–22:14; 26:39; **Luke 23:46; 24:49; John 5:18; 20:21.**

43 *They remind me* Charles Péguy, quoted in John Saward, *The Way of the Lamb: The Spirit of Childhood and the End of the Age* (San Francisco: Ignatius Press, 1999), 70.

43 *the Father's loving gaze* See Matthew 6:26–30; 10:29–30; 18:10, 14.

43 *My daughter* Angela of Foligno, quoted in Ronda Chervin, *Prayers of the Women Mystics* (Ann Arbor, MI: Servant, 1992), 35.

44 *Everything comes from love* St. Catherine of Siena, quoted in *Catechism of the Catholic Church,* 2nd ed. (Vatican City: Libreria Editrice Vaticana, 1997), no. 313.

44 *His whole life* Dorothy Day, quoted in Miller, *Dorothy Day: A Biography,* 117–18.

44 *God's silence* Shusaku Endo, *Silence,* trans. William Johnston (New York: Taplinger, 1979), 168.

44 *whence evil comes* St. Augustine, quoted in *Catechism,* no. 385.

45 *devil in Scripture* John 12:31; 14:30; 16:11; 2 Corinthians 4:4; 1 Peter 5:8; 2 Peter 2:4; **1 John 3:8;** 4:3; 5:19; Jude 6.

46 *our poor people* Blessed Mother Teresa of Calcutta, quoted in David Scott, *A Revolution of Love: The Meaning of Mother Teresa* (Chicago: Loyola Press, 2005), 145.

46 *Paul on suffering* **Romans 8:18, 28.**

46 *all shall be well* Julian of Norwich, quoted in *Catechism,* no. 313.

46 *pangs of birth* St. Ignatius of Antioch, quoted in Maxwell Staniforth, trans., *Early Christian Writings: The Apostolic Fathers* (New York: Penguin, 1987), 105. See also Pope John Paul II, *Encyclical Letter Regarding Certain Fundamental Questions of the Church's Moral Teaching (Veritatis Splendor)* (August 6, 1993), no. 92, in J. Michael Miller, ed., *The Encyclicals of John Paul II* (Huntington, IN: Our Sunday Visitor, 2001).

46 *Come to the Father* St. Ignatius of Antioch, quoted in Mike Aquilina, *The Fathers of the Church: An Introduction to the First Christian Teachers* (Huntington, IN: Our Sunday Visitor, 1999), 67.

48 *the Carmelite martyrs* See Terrye Newkirk, *The Mantle of Elijah: The Martyrs of Compiègne as Prophets of the Modern Age* (Washington, DC: ICS Publications, 1995), 42; William Bush, *To Quell the Terror: The Mystery of the Vocation of the Sixteen Carmelites of Compiègne Guillotined July 17, 1794* (Washington, DC: ICS Publications, 1999).

48 *Your Father is merciful* **Luke 6:36.**

48 *the Magnificat* Luke 1:46–55.

49 *mother of mercy* St. Maximus, quoted in Theological-Historical Commission for the Great Jubilee of the Year 2000, *God, the Father of Mercy,* trans. Robert R. Barr (New York: Crossroad, 1998), 72.

49 *rich in mercy* 2 Corinthians 1:3; **Ephesians 2:4.**

49 *the prodigal son* Luke 15:11–32.

50 *baptism and our re-creation* John 14:18; **Galatians 6:15;** Ephesians 4:24; **2 Peter 1:4; 1 John 3:1.**

50 *generator of souls* St. Paulinus of Nola, quoted by Pope John Paul II, General Audience of April 12, 2000, in Pope John Paul II, *The Trinity's Embrace.*

50 *Holy Spirit in us* Romans 8:15–16; 1 Corinthians 2:12–14; 12:3; **Galatians 4:6.**

51 *becoming like God* **Romans 8:29; 2 Corinthians 3:18; 4:4;** Ephesians 4:24.

51 *sanctae trinitatis domicilium* Pope John Paul II, Angelus Address of May 25, 1997, http://www.vatican.va/holy_father/john_paul_ii/angelus/1997/documents/hf_jp-ii_ang_19970525_en.html.

51 *I in you* **John 14:20.**

51 *gift made in love* St. Augustine, quoted by Pope John Paul II, General Audience of November 14, 1990, in Pope John Paul II, *The Spirit, Giver of Life and Love: A Catechesis on the Creed* (Boston: Pauline Books and Media, 1996).

51 *Crimson Dove* Catherine de Hueck Doherty, *Sobornost: Eastern Unity of Mind and Heart for Western Man* (Notre Dame, IN: Ave Maria Press, 1977), 16.

52 *an anticipated Heaven* Blessed Elizabeth of the Trinity, *I Have Found God: Complete Works,* trans. Anne Englund Nash (Washington, DC: ICS Publications, 1984), 2:354–55.

52 *adorable intimacy* Ibid., 271.

Chapter 3: Living as the Image of God

56 *Harry Wu's story* Harry Wu and Carolyn Wakeman, *Bitter Winds: A Memoir of My Years in China's Gulag* (New York: J. Wiley, 1994), 86–87.

57 *Jesus on the devil* **John 8:44.**

57 *like God* **Genesis 3:5.**

57 *Masolino's and Masaccio's paintings* Andrew Ladis, *The Brancacci Chapel, Florence* (New York: George Braziller, 1993).

57 *mother of all living* **Genesis 3:20.**

57 *under the power of sin* **Romans 3:9.**

58 *contempt of God* St. Augustine, quoted in *Catechism of the Catholic Church,* 2nd ed. (Vatican City: Libreria Editrice Vaticana, 1997), no. 1850; emphasis mine.

58 *Dear Sirs* G. K. Chesteron, *Orthodoxy* (Wheaton, IL: Harold Shaw Publishers, 1994), xi.

59 *a little lower than God* **Psalm 8:5.**

59 *able of being divine* St. Gregory of Nazianzus, quoted in Theological-Historical Commission of the Great Jubilee of the Year 2000, *The Holy Spirit, Lord and Giver of Life,* trans. Agostino Bono (New York: Crossroad, 1997), 46.

59 *Before I formed you* **Jeremiah 1:5.**

60 *Jesus and children* Matthew 18:5.

60 *You shall not kill* *Didache,* quoted in *Catechism,* no. 2271.

60 *the very fetus* Athenagoras, quoted in Rodney Stark, *The Rise of Christianity: How the Obscure, Marginal Jesus Movement Became the Dominant Religious Force in the Western World in a Few Centuries* (San Francisco: HarperSanFrancisco, 1997), 124–25.

60 *sacrament of our brothers and sisters* St. John Chrysostom, quoted in Olivier Clément, *The Roots of Christian Mysticism: Text and Commentary* (New York: New City Press, 1995), 121.

61 *Do not pay him homage* St. John Chrysostom, quoted in Pope John Paul II, *Apostolic Letter on Keeping the Lord's Day Holy (Dies Domini)* (Boston: Pauline Books and Media, 1998), no. 71.

61 *all bear the stamp* St. Gregory of Nyssa, quoted in Henri de Lubac, *Catholicism: A Study of Dogma in Relation to the Corporate Destiny of Mankind* (San Francisco: Ignatius Press, 1988), 373.

62 *of our own accord* Lactantius, quoted in Darrell Amundsen, "The Significance of Inaccurate History in Legal Considerations of Physician-Assisted Suicide," in *Physician-Assisted Suicide: Ethics, Medical Practice and Public Policy,* ed. Robert F. Weir (Bloomington: Indiana University Press, 1997).

62 *I owe him* François Fénelon, quoted in Henri de Lubac, *The Mystery of the Supernatural,* trans. Rosemary Sheed (New York: Crossroad, 1998), 77–78.

62 *live to God* St. Augustine, quoted in Gerhart B. Ladner, *The Idea of Reform: Its Impact on Christian Thought and Action in the Age of the Fathers,* rev. ed. (New York: Harper and Row, 1967).

63 *Heedless of danger* Dionysius, quoted in Stark, *The Rise of Christianity,* 73–94.

64 *made for humankind* **Mark 2:27.**

64 *a shadow* **Colossians 2:17.**

65 *our heart is restless* St. Augustine, *Confessions of St. Augustine,* trans. Frank J. Sheed (New York: Sheed and Ward, 1943), 1.1.

65 *Conscience is like God's herald* St. Bonaventure, quoted in Pope John Paul II, *Encyclical Letter Regarding Certain Fundamental Questions of the Church's Moral Teaching (Veritatis Splendor)* (August 6, 1993), no. 58, in J. Michael Miller, ed., *The Encyclicals of John Paul II* (Huntington, IN: Our Sunday Visitor, 2001).

65 *conscience in Scripture* Jeremiah 31:31–33; Romans 2:15; 2 Corinthians 3:3.

66 *inward sense* John Henry Newman, quoted in Jules M. Brady, ed., *Newman for Everyman: 101 Questions Answered Imaginatively by Newman* (New York: Alba House, 1996), 2–3.

66 *O Adam* Giovanni Pico della Mirandola, quoted in Christoph von Schönborn, *From Death to Life: The Christian Journey* (San Francisco: Ignatius Press, 1995), 43–44.

67 *animals turning* St. Gregory of Nyssa, quoted in Panayiotis Nellas, *Deification in Christ: Orthodox Perspectives on the Nature of the Human Person,* trans. Norman Russell (Crestwood, NY: St. Vladimir's Seminary Press, 1987), 87.

67 *Jesus on human freedom* Mark 12:31; **John 8:32.**

67 *she who believed* **Luke 1:45.**

67 *Adam's mortal body and immortal soul* Genesis 2:7.

68 *God's hand in creating each of us* Psalm 139:13; Isaiah 44:2, 24.

68 *hinge of salvation* Tertullian, quoted in Mary Timothy Prokes, *Toward a Theology of the Body* (London: T and T Clark, 1996), 44; *Catechism,* no. 1015.

69 *body as temple of God* John 14:23; 1 Corinthians 3:16; **6:19–20.**

69 *Leonides's story* Eusebius of Caesarea, *The History of the Church from Christ to Constantine,* trans. G. A. Williamson, rev. ed. (New York: Penguin, 1989), 241.

70 *Ex Nihilo* Michael Novak, *Frederick Hart: Changing Tides* (New York: Hudson Hills Press, 2005); Tom Wolfe, *Frederick Hart: Sculptor* (New York: Hudson Hills Press, 1994).

71 *no longer male and female* **Galatians 3:28.**

71 *one life* St. Edith Stein, *The Collected Works of Edith Stein, Sister Teresa Benedicta of the Cross, Discalced Carmelite* (Washington, DC: ICS Publications, 1986), 2:65; emphasis mine.

71 *one flesh* **Genesis 2:24.**

71 *human love in God's plan* Pope John Paul II, General Audience of January 9, 1990, in Pope John Paul II, *The Theology of the Body: Human Love in the Divine Plan* (Boston: Pauline Books and Media, 1997), 60–62.

72 *to love human love* Pope John Paul II, *Crossing the Threshold of Hope,* ed. Vittorio Messori, trans. Jenny McPhee and Martha McPhee (New York: Knopf, 1994), 122–23.

73 *Behold your heart* Dante Alighieri, *Vita Nuova,* trans. Dino S. Cervigni and Edward Vasta (Notre Dame, IN: University of Notre Dame Press, 1995), 48–51.

73 *Jesus and marriage* Genesis 2:24; Matthew 19:5–**6;** Mark 10:8.

74 *With this ring* John Grabowski, "Covenantal Sexuality," *Église et Théologie* 27 (1996): 229–52.

74 *begetter of humanity* Amphilochius of Iconium, quoted in Pope John Paul II, *Encyclical Letter on the Value and Inviolability of Human Life (Evangelium Vitae)* (March 25, 1995), no. 43, in Miller, ed., *The Encyclicals of John Paul II.*

75 *sacrament of the invisible community* Hugh of Saint-Victor, quoted in Dominique Poirel, "Love of God, Human Love: Hugh of St. Victor and the Sacrament of Marriage," *Communio* 24 (Spring 1997): 99–109.

76 *the bridegroom* Matthew 9:14–15; 25:1–13; Mark 2:18–20; Luke 5:34–35; John 2:1–12; 2 Corinthians 11:2; **Ephesians 5:21–33;** Revelation 19:6–**9;** 21:2.

76 *In the baptismal pool* Didymus the Blind, quoted in Jean Daniélou, *The Bible and the Liturgy* (Notre Dame, IN: University of Notre Dame Press, 1956), 192.

77 *one undivided spirit* St. Bernard of Clairvaux, sermon 83 on the Canticle of Canticles, quoted in Pope Pius XII, *Encyclical Letter on St. Bernard of Clairvaux, the Last of the Fathers (Doctor Mellifluus)* (May 24, 1953), no. 11, http://www.vatican.va/holy_father/pius_xii/encyclicals/documents/hf_p-xii_enc_24051953_doctor-mellifluus_en.html. Bernard quotes 1 Corinthians 6:17.

77 *no eye has seen* Isaiah 64:4; **1 Corinthians 2:9.**

Chapter 4: Why the Catholic Church?

80 *Domine Quo Vadis* See "The Acts of Peter," in Willis Barnstone, ed., *The Other Bible* (San Francisco: Harper and Row, 1984), 426–44; Rodney Stark, *The Rise of Christianity: How the Obscure, Marginal Jesus Movement Became the Dominant Religious Force in the Western World in a Few Centuries* (San Francisco:

HarperSanFrancisco, 1997), 186–87; *Knopf Guide: Rome* (New York: Knopf, 1994), 324.

82 *for her sake* Hermas, quoted in Henri de Lubac, *The Splendor of the Church,* trans. Michael Mason (New York: Sheed and Ward, 1956), 38.

82 *my church* **Matthew 16:18;** emphasis mine.

82 *the new Israel* Galatians 6:16.

82 *a chosen race* **1 Peter 2:9**–10.

82 *Lord will become king* **Zechariah 14:9.**

82 *the church as the kingdom* St. Augustine, quoted in Henri de Lubac, *Catholicism: A Study of Dogma in Relation to the Corporate Destiny of Mankind* (San Francisco: Ignatius Press, 1988), 72; Christoph von Schönborn, *From Death to Life: The Christian Journey* (San Francisco: Ignatius Press, 1995), 77.

83 *sacrament of man's salvation* St. Leo the Great, quoted in de Lubac, *The Splendor of the Church,* 37.

83 *Holy Spirit at Pentecost* **Acts 2:3, 8, 11.**

83 *Wherever the Church is* St. Irenaeus, quoted by Pope John Paul II, General Audience of June 17, 1998, in Pope John Paul II, *The Church: Mystery, Sacrament, Community: Catechesis on the Creed* (Boston: Pauline Books and Media, 1998).

84 *Christ is all in all* St. Maximus, quoted in de Lubac, *Catholicism,* 53–54.

84 *Where there is Christ Jesus* St. Ignatius of Antioch, quoted in *Catechism of the Catholic Church,* 2nd ed. (Vatican City: Libreria Editrice Vaticana, 1997), no. 830.

85 *Church is called Catholic* St. Cyril of Jerusalem, quoted in Johann Auer, *The Church: The Universal Sacrament of Salvation,* trans. Michael Waldstein (Washington, DC: Catholic University of America Press, 1993), 423–24; emphasis mine.

85 *a people made one* St. Cyprian, quoted in Second Vatican Council, *Dogmatic Constitution on the Church (Lumen Gentium)* (November 21, 1964), no. 4, in Austin Flannery, ed., *Vatican Council II: The Conciliar and Post Conciliar Document* (Collegeville, MN: Liturgical Press, 1987).

85 *they may all be one* **John 17:21–23.**

86 *addressing churches* **Acts 13:1; 1 Corinthians 1:2.**

86 *one bread* **1 Corinthians 10:17.**

86 *the whole Christ* St. Augustine, quoted in Frederik van der Meer, *Augustine the Bishop: Religion and Society at the Dawn of the Middle Ages* (New York: Harper and Row, 1965), 377–78; *Catechism,* nos. 795–96.

86 *I am Jesus* **Acts 9:**1–**5.**

86 *Jesus as one with the church* Ephesians 5:21–33.

87 *Adam sleeps* St. Augustine, quoted in Claude Chavasse, *The Bride of Christ: An Enquiry into the Nuptial Element in Early Christianity* (London: Faber and Faber, 1940), 159–60. See also Tertullian: "Adam's sleep represented the death of Christ, who had to die the sleep of death so that the Church, true mother of the living, could come from the wound in his side." Quoted in Henri de Lubac, *The Motherhood of the Church,* trans. Sergia Englund (San Francisco: Ignatius Press, 1982), 54.

87 *Here is your mother* **John 19:27.**

87 *the elect lady* **2 John 1:1.**

88 *holy and without blemish* **1 Peter 1:19.**

89 *I have children of God* Papylus, quoted in Yves Congar, *Tradition and Traditions: An Historical and a Theological Essay* (New York: Macmillan, 1967), 328.

89 *apostle and high priest* **Hebrews 3:1.**

89 *mission of the apostles* Matthew 10:40; Luke 10:16; **John 13:20; 20:21.**

89 *on thrones judging* Luke 22:28–**30.**

89 *apart from me* John 5:19, 30; 1**5:5.**

90 *I am with you always* **Matthew 28:20;** John 15:18–23.

90 *the Twelve arranged* Early ordinations through the "laying on of hands" can be seen in Acts 6:6; 1 Timothy 4:14; 2 Timothy 1:6.

91 *succeed them in their office* St. Clement of Rome, quoted in Louis Bouyer, *Liturgical Piety* (Notre Dame, IN: University of Notre Dame Press, 1955), 33–34; Maxwell Staniforth, trans., *Early Christian Writings: The Apostolic Fathers* (New York: Penguin, 1987), 46; Mike Aquilina, *The Fathers of the Church: An Introduction to the First Christian Teachers* (Huntington, IN: Our Sunday Visitor, 1999), 57; Auer, *The Church,* 200, 209–210.

91 *power to forgive sins* St. Cyprian, quoted in Auer, *The Church,* 210–11.

91 *in the place of God* St. Ignatius of Antioch, quoted in Thomas M. Kocik, *Apostolic Succession in an Ecumenical Context* (New York: Alba House, 1996), xvii; *Catechism,* no. 896.

91 *the first is an office* St. Augustine, quoted in Second Vatican Council, *Dogmatic Constitution on the Church,* no. 32.

91 *Blessed Ignatius Maloyan* For a brief biography and account of his martyrdom, see http://www.vatican.va/news_services/liturgy/saints/ns_lit_doc_20011007_beat-maloyan_en.html.

92 *those masters* St. Clement of Alexandria, quoted in Congar, *Tradition and Traditions,* 27–28.

92 *You are Peter* **Matthew 16:18.**

93 *keys of the kingdom* **Matthew 16:19.**

93 *key of the house of David* **Isaiah 22:22.**

93 *Peter's authority* **Matthew 16:19.**

94 *origin of the Church's unity* St. Cyprian, quoted in Congregation for the Doctrine of the Faith, "The Primacy of the Successor of Peter in the Mystery of the Church," *L'Osservatore Romano,* November 18, 1998, 5; Auer, *The Church,* 249.

94 *bearing the Father's name* St. Ignatius, quoted in Charles Journet, *The Primacy of Peter from the Protestant and from the Catholic Point of View,* trans. John Chapin (Westminster, MD: Newman Press, 1954), 123.

95 *If any disobey* Pope St. Clement, quoted in J. Michael Miller, *The Shepherd and the Rock: Origins, Development, and Mission of the Papacy* (Huntington, IN: Our Sunday Visitor, 1995), 73–74.

95 *Peter has spoken* Bishops of the Council of Chalcedon, quoted in Josef Neuner and Jacques Dupuis, eds., *The Christian Faith in the Doctrinal Documents of the Catholic Church,* rev. ed. (New York: Alba House, 1982), 202.

96 *the Spirit of truth* Matthew 28:19–20; John 14:26; 16:12–**13.**

97 *our concern* St. Vincent of Lérins, quoted in Auer, *The Church,* 299–300.

98 *Good trip, happy crossing* Pedro Calderón de la Barca, quoted in Ricardo Arias, *The Spanish Sacramental Plays* (Boston: Twayne, 1980), 135–36.

98 *It is as possible* St. Cyprian, quoted in Jean Daniélou, *From Shadows to Reality: Studies in the Biblical Typology of the Fathers* (Westminster, MD: Newman Press, 1960), 98; Charles Journet, *The Church of the Word Incarnate: An Essay in Speculative Theology* (New York: Sheed and Ward, 1955), 32.

98 *what Jesus taught about salvation* John 3:3–8; 6:53–54; 14:6.

98 *ineffable forethought of God* St. Augustine, quoted in de Lubac, *The Splendor of the Church,* 155.

99 *salvation in no one else* **Acts 4:12.**

99 *God our Savior* **1 Timothy 2:3–4.**

99 *rewards* **Hebrews 11:6.**

99 *anyone who fears him* Acts 10:34–**35.**

99 *raise it up* **John 6:39**–40.

100 *Nothing is more useless* St. John Chrysostom, quoted in Yves Congar, *Lay People in the Church: A Study for a Theology of Laity,* trans. Donald Attwater, 2nd ed. (Westminster, MD: Newman Press, 1965), 341.

100 *Mission means* Madeleine Delbrêl, *We, the Ordinary People of the Streets,* trans. David Louis Schindler and Charles F. Mann (Grand Rapids, MI: W. B. Eerdmans, 2000), 97.

100 *promises to Israel* John 4:22; **Romans 11:26; 28–29.**

101 *Has Christ been divided?* **1 Corinthians 1:13.**

101 *where there are sins* Origen, quoted in *Catechism,* no. 817.

101 *completely one* John 17:11, 20–**23.**

101 *God's holy gifts* *Catechism,* no. 946.

102 *assembly of saints* Nicetas, quoted in Christoph von Schönborn, *Loving the Church: Spiritual Exercises Preached in the Presence of Pope John Paul II,* trans. John Saward (San Francisco: Ignatius Press, 1998), 185.

102 *in spite of everything* St. Josemaría Escrivá, quoted in Alvaro del Portillo, *Immersed in God: Blessed Josemaría Escrivá, Founder of Opus Dei, as Seen by His Successor, Bishop Alvaro del Portillo,* trans. Gerald Malsbary (Princeton, NJ: Scepter, 1996), 3–4; emphasis mine.

103 *worst kind of sinners* Barnabas, quoted in W. A. Jurgens, trans., *The Faith of the Early Fathers: A Source-Book of Theological and Historical Passages from the Christian Writings of the Pre-Nicene and Nicene Eras* (Collegeville, MN: Liturgical Press, 1970), 14.

103 *Jesus' teaching about sinners in the church* Matthew 10:35–36; 13:24–30, 36–43; 16:18.

103 *house of ill-repute* St. Bridget of Sweden, quoted in José Ignacio González Faus, *Where the Spirit Breathes: Prophetic Dissent in the Church,* trans. Robert R. Barr (Maryknoll, NY: Orbis Books, 1989), 15–16.

104 *betrayers in the Church* St. Cyprian, quoted in de Lubac, *The Motherhood of the Church,* 28–29.

104 *in the saints* St. Ambrose, quoted in Ibid., 79.

105 *Jesus and Peter* John 21.

Chapter 5: The Signs and Wonders of the Sacramental Life

108 *A sacrament is physical* Andre Dubus, *Meditations from a Movable Chair* (New York: Vintage Books, 1998), 85–99.

109 *coming into the light* Jean Daniélou, *The Bible and the Liturgy* (Notre Dame, IN: University of Notre Dame Press, 1956), 19.

110 *the mystery hidden* **Ephesians 3:9;** Colossians 1:26.

110 *book of life* **Philippians 4:3; Revelation 3:5; 13:8; 17:8; 20:12,15; 21:27.**

111 *Christ washes away* Quoted in Daniélou, *The Bible and the Liturgy,* 36.

111 *slavery* Theodore of Mopsuestia, quoted in Ibid., 20–21.

111 *sign of that shining world* Theodore of Mopsuestia, quoted in Ibid., 50.

112 *baptized into his death* **Romans 6:**3–**4;** Colossians 2:12.

112 *reality of salvation* St. Cyril of Jerusalem, quoted in Daniélou, *The Bible and the Liturgy,* 44–45.

112 *creatures newly formed* Quoted in the *The Liturgy of the Hours: According to the Roman Rite* (New York: Catholic Book Publishing Company, 1975), 2:582–83.

113 *We have become Christ* St. Augustine, quoted in Pope John Paul II, *Post-Synodal Apostolic Exhortation on the Vocation and the Mission of the Lay Faithful in the Church and in the World (Christifideles Laici)* (December 30, 1988), no. 17, in J. Michael Miller, ed., *The Post-Synodal Apostolic Exhortations of John Paul II* (Huntington, IN: Our Sunday Visitor, 1998).

113 *anointed as Jesus was* Acts 10:38.

113 *spiritual sacrifices* **1 Peter 2:5,** 9.

113 *being by grace* Columba Marmion, *Christ in His Mysteries,* 8th ed. (St. Louis: Herder, 1931), 54–55; emphasis mine.

114 *a people of divine strain* Pope Sixtus III, quoted in Henri de Lubac, *Catholicism: A Study of Dogma in Relation to the Corporate Destiny of Mankind* (San Francisco: Ignatius Press, 1988), 86.

114 *You are gods* **Psalm 82:6**–7.

114 *womb of the Church* St. Leo the Great, quoted in Juan González Arintero, *The Mystical Evolution in the Development and Vitality of the Church* (Rockford, IL: TAN Books and Publishers, 1978), 1:51.

115 *Each one alone* François Mauriac, *What I Believe,* trans. Wallace Fowlie (New York: Farrar, Straus, 1963), 20–21.

115 *I in them* **John 6:56.**

115 *transformed into me* St. Augustine, quoted in Columba Marmion, *Christ the Life of the Soul,* 10th ed. (St. Louis: Herder, 1925), 265.

115 *no longer I* **Galatians 2:20.**

115 *truth of the sacraments* St. Yves of Chartres, quoted in Henri de Lubac, *Theological Fragments,* trans. Rebecca Howell Balinski (San Francisco: Ignatius Press, 1989), 24.

115 *living sacrifice* **Romans 12:1;** 1 Corinthians 1:2; 2 Corinthians 1:1; Ephesians 1:1; Colossians 1:2.

116 *offering of your free will* St. Peter Chrysologus, quoted in *The Liturgy of the Hours: According to the Roman Rite* (New York: Catholic Book Publishing Company, 1975), 2:770–72.

116 *capable of God* St. Thomas Aquinas, quoted in de Lubac, *Theological Fragments,* 30.

116 *gives birth to death* **James 1:15.**

117 *ministry of reconciliation* **2 Corinthians 5:18.**

117 *If you forgive* Matthew 16:19; 18:18; John 20:22–**23.**

117 *everything I have ever done* **John 4:29.**

118 *he prepares a banquet* St. Ambrose, quoted in Francis Fernandez, *In Conversation with God: Meditations for Each Day of the Year* (Princeton, NJ: Scepter, 2000), 2:211–12.

118 *kiss of Christ* Catherine de Hueck Doherty, *Kiss of Christ: Reflections on the Sacrament of Penance and Reconciliation* (Combermere, ON: Madonna House Publications, 1998), 7.

118 *only five minutes old* G. K. Chesterton, quoted in John Saward, *The Way of the Lamb: The Spirit of Childhood and the End of the Age* (San Francisco: Ignatius Press, 1999), 36.

119 *marriage supper of the Lamb* Matthew 19:6; Revelation 19:7, **9.**

120 *Marriage is* St. Gregory of Nazianzus, quoted in Louis Bouyer and others, *A History of Christian Spirituality* (London: Burns and Oates, 1969), 1:346–47.

121 *Ye are gods* Coventry Patmore, "Love Transfigured," in *The World's Greatest Catholic Literature,* ed. George N. Shuster (Garden City, NY: Halcyon House, 1947), 230. He is quoting Psalm 82:6; emphasis mine. See also Coventry Patmore, *Mystical Poems of Nuptial Love,* ed. Terence L. Connolly (Boston: Bruce Humphries, 1938).

122 *so great a good* Dorothy Day, *Thérèse,* 2d ed, (Springfield, IL: Templegate, 1979), v–vi.

122 *spiritual childhood* Matthew 18:3; Mark 10:15; Luke 18:17; **John 3:3;** 1 Peter 2:2; 1 John 3:1.

122 *takes its name* **Ephesians 3:14–15;** *Catechism of the Catholic Church,* 2nd ed. (Vatican City: Libreria Editrice Vaticana, 1997), no. 1656.

123 *father through the gospel* **1 Corinthians 4:14–15.**

123 *to make intercession* **Hebrews 7:25–26.**

123 *Whoever welcomes you* **Matthew 10:40.**

124 *The apostles begot you* St. Augustine, quoted in Henri de Lubac, *The Motherhood of the Church,* trans. Sergia Englund (San Francisco: Ignatius Press, 1982), 90.

124 *priesthood and the early church* Acts 1:21–22; 6:3–6.

124 *affairs of the Lord* **1 Corinthians 7:32.**

125 *perfect continence* Quoted in Christian Cochini, *Apostolic Origins of Priestly Celibacy,* trans. Nelly Marans (San Francisco: Ignatius Press, 1990), 5, 7.

125 *sake of the kingdom* **Matthew 19:12.**

125 *work of divine and spiritual generation* Eusebius of Caesarea, quoted in de Lubac, *The Motherhood of the Church,* 129.

125 *his invisible soul* St. Gregory of Nyssa, quoted in Joseph Lécuyer, *What Is a Priest?* trans. Lancelot C. Sheppard (New York: Hawthorn Books, 1959), 15.

126 *as Christ Jesus* 2 Corinthians 5:18–20; **Galatians 4:14.**

126 *in the place of Christ* St. Cyprian, quoted in Congregation for the Doctrine of the Faith, *Declaration on the Admission of Women to the Ministerial Priesthood (Inter Insigniores)* (October 15, 1976), 5, 41, in *From "Inter Insigniores" to "Ordinatio Sacerdotalis": Documents and Commentaries* (Vatican City: Libreria Editrice Vaticana, 1996). At the altar, the priest "bears in himself at this moment the image of Our Lord Jesus," according to a mid-fifth-century homily. Quoted in A. G. Martimort, "The Value of a Theological Formula 'In persona Christi,'" *L'Osservatore Romano,* March 10, 1977, 6–7.

126 *his invisible power* St. John Chrysostom, quoted in Bernard Piault, *What Is a Sacrament?* trans. A. Manson (New York: Hawthorn Books, 1963), 136–37.

126 *A drunkard* St. Augustine, quoted in Ibid.

126 *Apart from me* **John 15:5.**

127 *is divinized and divinizes* St. Gregory of Nazianzus, quoted in *Catechism,* no. 1589.

127 *anointing in the New Testament* Mark 6:12–14; 16:17–18; James 5:14–15.

127 *completing what is lacking* **Colossians 1:24.**

128 *in Paradise* **Luke 23:43.**

128 *everything is grace* St. Thérèse of Lisieux, *St. Thérèse of Lisieux: Her Last Conversations,* trans. John Clarke (Washington, DC: ICS Publications, 1977), 57.

128 *recognizing your nothingness* Ibid., 139.

128 *the eyes of babes* Matthew 11:25.

129 *The eye of the Christian* Paul Claudel, *I Believe in God: A Meditation on the Apostles' Creed,* ed. Agnès du Sarment, trans. Helen Weaver (New York: Holt, Rinehart and Winston, 1963), 218.

130 *Living in the world* Andre Dubus, "A Woman in April," in *Broken Vessels* (Boston: D. R. Godine, 1991), 143.

Chapter 6: The Word of Life

133 *uncertainty vanished away* St. Augustine, quoted in Romano Guardini, *The Conversion of Augustine,* trans. Elinor Briefs (Westminster, MD: Newman Press, 1960), 238–49.

134 *Jesus and the Scriptures* Matthew 12:1–8, 39–40; Mark 2:23–28; Luke 4:17–18; 6:1–5; 24:27, 44–45; John 1:51; 2:19; 3:14.

134 *Jesus and his church* Matthew 28:19–20; **Mark 16:15;** John 14:26; **16:13;** Acts 2.

134 *preaching of the early church* Psalm 33:9; Acts 3:17–26; 4:11, 23–28; **6:2**–4; Hebrews 1:1–2.

135 *word of life* **Philippians 2:16; 1 John 1:1.**

135 *born anew* **1 Peter 1:23.**

135 *word of Jesus* Luke 10:16.

135 *cut to the core* Luke 24:32; Acts 2:37; Hebrews 4:12.

135 *welcomed his message* **Acts 2:37–38, 41–42.**

137 *Paul's letters* 1 Corinthians 11:2, **23;** Philippians 4:9; 2 Thessalonians 2:14–**15.**

137 *John's Gospel* John 20:30; 21:25.

137 *adapted his teaching* Papias, quoted in Frank Sadowski, *The Church Fathers on the Bible* (New York: Alba House, 1987), 10–11.

137 *ignorance of Christ* St. Jerome, *Commentary on Isaiah,* in Pope John Paul II, *Apostolic Letter at the Close of the Great Jubilee of the Year 2000 (Novo Millennio Ineunte)* (Boston: Pauline Books and Media, 2001), no. 17.

138 *life in his name* **John 20:31.**

138 *in accordance* **Titus 1:9.**

139 *not suitable for gall* Muratorian Canon, quoted in Sadowski, *The Church Fathers on the Bible,* 26.

139 *inspired by God* **2 Timothy 3:16**–17.

140 *Not all that the Lord did* St. Cyril of Alexandria, quoted in Yves Congar, *Tradition and Traditions: An Historical and a Theological Essay* (New York: Macmillan, 1967), 509.

141 *incarnate and living* St. Bernard of Clairvaux, quoted in *Catechism of the Catholic Church,* 2nd ed. (Vatican City: Libreria Editrice Vaticana, 1997), no. 108.

141 *the ministry of the word* Tertullian, quoted in Cheslyn Jones, Geoffrey Wainwright, and Edward Yarnold, eds., *The Study of Liturgy* (New York: Oxford University Press, 1978), 181–83.

141 *these good things* St. Justin, quoted in W. A. Jurgens, trans., *The Faith of the Early Fathers: A Source-Book of Theological and Historical Passages from the Christian Writings of the Pre-Nicene and Nicene Eras* (Collegeville, MN: Liturgical Press, 1970), 56; Mike Aquilina, *The Mass of the Early Christians* (Huntington, IN: Our Sunday Visitor, 2001), 86.

142 *Wisdom* Wisdom 8:4; 9:9–10; 18:14–15; see also Pope John Paul II, General Audience of September 2, 1987, in Pope John Paul II, *Jesus, Son and Savior: A Catechesis on the Creed* (Boston: Pauline Books and Media, 1996).

142 *St. Anthony's response to the word* Anne Jackson Fremantle, *A Treasury of Early Christianity* (New York: Viking, 1953), 475–88. The passage that changed his life is Matthew 19:16–21.

143 *The Devil himself* St. Jerome, quoted in Congar, *Tradition and Traditions,* 383; see Matthew 4:6.

143 *Philip and the Ethiopian* **Acts 8:26–39.**

143 *No prophecy of scripture* **2 Peter 1:20.**

143 *mind of Christ* **1 Corinthians 2:16.**

143 *teaching authority* St. Irenaeus, quoted in Second Vatican Council, *Dogmatic Constitution on Divine Revelation (Dei Verbum)* (November 18, 1965), no. 7, in Dean P. Béchard, ed. and trans., *The Scripture Documents: An Anthology of Official Catholic Teachings* (Collegeville, MN: Liturgical Press, 2002).

144 *the interpretation* St. Clement of Alexandria, quoted in Yves Congar, *Meaning of Tradition,* trans. A. N. Woodrow (New York: Hawthorn, 1964), 93.

144 *vital sustenance* St. Ambrose, quoted in Raniero Cantalamessa, *The Mystery of God's Word,* trans. Alan Neame (Collegeville, MN: Liturgical Press, 1994), 19.

144 *a letter from God Almighty* St. Gregory the Great, quoted in Ibid., 71.

144 *ponder your Creator's words* St. Gregory the Great, quoted in Yves Congar, *Lay People in the Church: A Study for a Theology of Laity,* trans. Donald Attwater, 2nd ed. (Westminster, MD: Newman Press, 1965), 298–99.

145 *the Holy Books* Quoted in Ibid.

145 *not as a human word* **1 Thessalonians 2:13.**

146 *fulfilled in Christ* Hugh of Saint-Victor, quoted in Henri de Lubac, *Medieval Exegesis* (Grand Rapids, MI: W. B. Eerdmans, 1998), 1:237.

147 *Jesus' first actions* **Luke 24:27, 30, 35, 44**–45.

148 *the ultimate author* St. Thomas Aquinas, *The Summa Theologica,* trans. Fathers of the English Dominican Province, Complete English ed. (Westminster, MD: Christian Classics, 1981), I.1.10.

148 *written on the inside* Ezekiel 2:9–10; **Revelation 5:1.**

148 *take up deadly snakes* Mark 16:18.

148 *not how the heavens go* Caesar Baronius, quoted in Dava Sobel, *Galileo's Daughter: A Historical Memoir of Science, Faith, and Love* (New York: Walker and Company, 1999), 65. See also St. Augustine, "On the Literal Interpretation of Genesis": the "Spirit of God . . . did not wish to teach men . . . facts that would be of no avail

for their salvation." Quoted in Stanley L. Jaki, *Genesis 1 through the Ages* (London: Thomas More Press, 1992), 93.

149 *point to chase down* St. Augustine, quoted in de Lubac, *Medieval Exegesis* 2:44.

149 *the countless things* St. Augustine, quoted in Guardini, *The Conversion of Augustine,* 190–91.

150 *understanding of the spirit* St. Gregory of Nyssa, quoted in de Lubac, *Medieval Exegesis* 2:86–87; see also St. Jerome: "After the truth of history, everything should be perceived spiritually." Quoted in Ibid., 1:262.

151 *a new Moses* The Hebrew prophets foretell a new creation in Isaiah 4:5; 65:17; 66:22; Jeremiah 31:35–36; Ezekiel 36:8–11; a new exodus in Isaiah 51:9–11; Jeremiah 16:14–15; Ezekiel 29:3–5; and a new kingdom in Isaiah 9:2–7; Jeremiah 23:5–6; Ezekiel 34:23–24.

151 *similar typological interpretations* Especially in Matthew's Gospel, Jesus is portrayed as a "new Moses" who, like the first Moses, was rescued as an infant from an order that all male Hebrew children be killed (compare Exodus 1:15–16 and Matthew 2:16–18). Also like Moses, he gave God's chosen people a new Passover, the Eucharist, and led a new exodus, a deliverance from sin, by his cross and resurrection, opening up the promised land of heaven. He is described as the new "paschal lamb" in **1 Corinthians 5:7.** His death and resurrection is called an "exodus" in Luke 9:31 (the Greek word, *exodos* is often translated "departure"). Paul compares the Christian life to the Exodus in 1 Corinthians 10:1–4. The Passover, creation, and kingdom symbolism in Revelation is pervasive. For a few examples, see Revelation 1:7 (new creation); Revelation 5:6, 12–13 (new Passover/exodus); and Revelation 11:15; 21:9–10, 22–24 (new kingdom).

151 *The letter teaches* Quoted in William R. Farmer and others, eds., *The International Bible Commentary: A Catholic and Ecumenical Commentary for the Twenty-First Century* (Collegeville, MN: Liturgical Press, 1998), 50; see also *Catechism,* no. 118: "The letter speaks of deeds; allegory to faith; the moral how to act; anagogy to our destiny."

152 *allegorical sense* Matthew 12:39–40; John 6:31–32; 1 Corinthians 10:2; 1 Peter 3:20–21.

152 *moral sense* Matthew 19:4–6; 1 Corinthians 10:1–14.

153 *anagogic sense* **Isaiah 25:1–9;** 1 Corinthians 15:54.

153 *take what is mine* John 16:12–15.

153 *what the Spirit gives* Origen, quoted in Cantalamessa, *The Mystery of God's Word,* 90.

153 *perfect me and reveal* St. Augustine, *The Confessions of St. Augustine,* trans. Frank J. Sheed (New York: Sheed and Ward, 1943), 11.2.2–4.

154 *her holy hands* Joan M. Petersen, ed. and trans., *Handmaids of the Lord: Holy Women in Late Antiquity and the Early Middle Ages* (Kalamazoo, MI: Cistercian Publications, 1996), 326.

154 *Love to occupy* St. Jerome, quoted in Ibid., 229.

154 *Every time I open* Julian Green, *Diary, 1928–1957,* sel. Kurt Wolff, trans. Anne Green (New York: Carroll & Graf, 1985), 76, 202.

154 *The Word increases* St. Ambrose, quoted in Mario Masini, *Lectio Divina: An Ancient Prayer That Is Ever New,* trans. Edmund C. Lane (New York: Alba House, 1998), 22.

154 *Mary and the word* Luke 1:34, **38;** 2:19, 51; **11:28.**

155 *I will put my law* **Jeremiah 31:31–34.**

155 *a letter of Christ* **2 Corinthians 3:3.**

155 *no longer be in darkness* St. Augustine, *Tractates on the Gospel of John, 28–54,* trans. John W. Rettig (Washington, DC: Catholic University of America Press, 1993), 35.9.

Chapter 7: The Possibility of Prayer

157 *From silly devotions* St. Teresa of Ávila, quoted in Phyllis McGinley, *Saint-Watching* (New York: Crossroad, 1982), 111.

158 *an intimate friendship* St. Teresa of Ávila, *The Life of St. Teresa of Ávila,* trans. David Lewis (Westminster, MD: Newman Press, 1962), 8.

158 *Prayer is conversation* St. Clement of Alexandria, *Stromateis: Books One to Three,* trans. John Ferguson (Washington, DC: Catholic University of America Press, 1991), 7.

159 *soul without prayer* St. John Chrysostom, quoted in St. Alphonsus de' Liguori, *The Great Means of Salvation and of Perfection* (Brooklyn, NY: Redemptorist Fathers, 1927), 9.

160 *perfection of the Christian life* Pope John XXIII, quoted in David Scott, comp., *Praying in the Presence of Our Lord with Dorothy Day* (Huntington, IN: Our Sunday Visitor, 2002), 72.

161 *praying for others* Acts 12:5; Philippians 1:3–4; James 5:16.

161 *If it please God* St. Philip Neri, *If God Be with Us: The Maxims of St. Philip Neri,* ed. F. W. Faber (Leominster, UK: Fowler Wright Books, 1995), 21.

161 *Lay this body* St. Monica, quoted in St. Augustine, *The Confessions of St. Augustine,* trans. Frank J. Sheed (New York: Sheed and Ward, 1943), 9.11.27.

161 *prayers of the saints* **Revelation 5:8.**

161 *Gallicanus the Christian* Quoted in Danilo Mazzoleni, "Ancient Graffiti in Roman Catacombs," *L'Osservatore Romano,* February 9, 2000, 6, English edition.

162 *O holy Mother* Quoted by Pope John Paul II, General Audience of November 27, 1996, in Pope John Paul II, *Theotókos: Woman, Mother, Disciple: A Catechesis on Mary, Mother of God* (Boston: Pauline Books and Media, 2000), 151.

162 *my Father and your Father* **John 20:17.**

162 *Because you are children* **Galatians 4:6.**

162 *their mother's womb* St. Basil, quoted in William Lane, *Praying with the Saints: Saints Lives and Prayers* (Dublin: Veritas Publications, 1989), 23.

162 *He is not far* **Acts 17:27–28.**

162 *the ladder* St. Isaac of Nineveh, quoted in *The Way of a Pilgrim, and The Pilgrim Continues His Way,* trans. Helen Bacovcin (Garden City, NY: Image Books, 1978), 182.

163 *the union* St. Gregory of Nazianzus, quoted in *Catechism of the Catholic Church,* 2nd ed. (Vatican City: Libreria Editrice Vaticana, 1997), no. 2565.

163 *poustinia of the heart* Catherine de Hueck Doherty, *Poustinia: Christian Spirituality of the East for Western Man* (Notre Dame, IN: Ave Maria Press, 1975), 74.

164 *Luttrell Psalter* Michael Camille, *Mirror in Parchment: The Luttrell Psalter and the Making of Medieval England* (Chicago: University of Chicago Press, 1998).

164 *I will sanctify* **Ezekiel 36:23.**

164 *Jesus' name* John 20:31; Acts 4:12.

165 *no need of much speaking* Macarius, quoted in Helen Waddell, trans., *The Desert Fathers* (Ann Arbor: University of Michigan Press, 1994), 113.

165 *"Lord Jesus" prayer* Bernard McGinn and John Meyendorff, eds., *Christian Spirituality: Origins to the Twelfth Century,* with Jean Leclerq (New York: Crossroad, 1989), 407ff.

165 *pray always* **Luke 18:1; 1 Thessalonians 5:17.**

165 *Jesus* St. Joan of Arc, quoted in *Catechism,* no. 435.

165 *It is this name* St. Peter Chrysologus, quoted in Ibid., no. 2814.

166 *Maranatha* **1 Corinthians 16:22; Revelation 22:20.**

167 *will of God* Matthew 7:21; 12:50; **26:39;** Mark 3:35; **Luke 1:38;** Hebrews 10:7 (see Psalm 40:7).

167 *your sanctification* **Ephesians 1:9; 1 Thessalonians 4:3;** 1 Timothy 2:3–4.

167 *love one another* **John 13:34.**

167 *In the ways of God* Brother Lawrence of the Resurrection, *Writings and Conversations on the Practice of the Presence of God* ed., Conrad De Meester, trans. Salvatore Sciurba (Washington, DC: ICS Publications, 1994), 116.

168 *Speak to God* St. John Vianney, quoted in Raoul Plus, *How to Pray Well* (Westminster, MD: Newman Press, 1948), 108.

168 *to bang on the Father's door* Luke 11:5–9.

168 *finds his delight* St. Alphonsus de' Liguori, *How to Converse Continually and Familiarly with God,* trans. L. X. Aubin (Boston: St. Paul Editions, 1963), 22–23.

169 *famine in the land* St. Bernard of Clairvaux, quoted in Ghislaine Salvail, *At the Crossroads of Scriptures: An Introduction to Lectio Divina,* trans. Paul C. Duggan (Boston: Pauline Books and Media, 1996), 69.

169 *teach me to eat* Guigo II, quoted in Ibid., 28, 47; see also Psalm 119:103; Ezekiel 3:3; Revelation 10:9.

170 *food from heaven* St. Peter Chrysologus, quoted in *Catechism,* no. 2837.

170 *super-essential* William F. Arndt, F. Wilbur Gingrich, and Walter Bauer, *A Greek-English Lexicon of the New Testament and Other Early Christian Literature,* 2nd ed. (Chicago: University of Chicago Press, 1979), 296–97.

170 *without the Lord's body* Quoted in Josef A. Jungmann, *Christian Prayer through the Centuries,* trans. John Coyne (New York: Paulist Press, 1978), 16, 24; see also Josef A. Jungmann, *The Early Liturgy, to the Time of Gregory the Great,* trans. Francis A. Brunner (Notre Dame, IN: University of Notre Dame Press, 1959); A. G. Hamman, *The Mass: Ancient Liturgies and Patristic Texts* (New York: Alba House, 1967).

170 *Go away from me* **Luke 5:8.**

170 *so much from me* St. Teresa of Ávila, *The Prayers of St. Teresa of Ávila,* comp. Thomas Alvarez (Brooklyn, NY: New City Press, 1990), 118.

171 *do not sin again* **John 8:11.**

171 *seventy-seven times* **Matthew 18:22.**

171 *love and lies* 1 John 4:20.

171 *wicked servant* Matthew 18:23–35.

172 *Maria Goretti's story* Ann Ball, *Modern Saints: Their Lives and Faces* (Rockford, IL: TAN Books and Publishers, 1983), 1:163–71.

172 *the devil tempts* St. Teresa of Ávila, *The Complete Works of St. Teresa of Ávila,* trans. Kieran Kavanaugh and Otilio Rodriguez (Washington, DC: ICS Publications, 1980), 2:191.

173 *snare of the Devil* Columba Marmion, *Union with God,* trans. Raymond Thibaut (St. Louis: Herder, 1949), 178.

174 *ruler of this world* **John 14:30.**

174 *conquered the world* **John 16:33.**

175 *wiser in this science* St. Teresa of Ávila, *Life,* 34.12, in *The Complete Works of St. Teresa of Ávila,* trans. Kieran Kavanaugh and Otilio Rodriguez (Washington, DC: ICS Publications, 1980).

Chapter 8: The Miracle and Meaning of the Mass

178 *Olivier Messiaen's life and works* Olivier Messiaen, *Music and Color: Conversations with Claude Samuel,* trans. E. Thomas Glasow (Portland, OR: Amadeus Press, 1994), 28; Paul Griffiths, "The Man Who Brought the Organ into Modernity," *New York Times,* February 7, 1999; Paul Griffiths, *Olivier Messiaen and the Music of Time* (Ithaca, NY: Cornell University Press, 1985).

179 *We live according* St. Ignatius, quoted in Joseph Cardinal Ratzinger, *A New Song for the Lord: Faith in Christ and Liturgy Today,* trans. Martha M. Matesich (New York: Crossroad, 1996), 60.

179 *a pledge* Quoted in *Catechism of the Catholic Church,* 2nd ed. (Vatican City: Libreria Editrice Vaticana, 1997), no. 1402.

179 *in remembrance* **Luke 22:19.**

180 *not one single race* St. Justin, quoted in Mike Aquilina, *The Mass of the Early Christians* (Huntington, IN: Our Sunday Visitor, 2001), 24.

180 *Eucharist as thanksgiving* Matthew 26:27; Mark 14:23; Luke 22:17; 1 Corinthians 11:24.

180 *Leave everything* *Didascalia,* quoted in Pope John Paul II, *Apostolic Letter on Keeping the Lord's Day Holy (Dies Domini)* (Boston: Pauline Books and Media, 1998), no. 46.

180 *Jesus' post-resurrection meals* **Luke 24:27, 30, 35.**

181 *day of the sun* St. Justin, quoted in *Catechism,* no. 1345: "On the day we call the day of the sun, all who dwell in the city or country gather in the same place. / The memoirs of the apostles and the writings of the prophets are read, as much as time permits. When the reader has finished, he who presides over those gathered admonishes and challenges them to imitate these beautiful things. / Then we all rise together and offer prayers for ourselves . . . and for all others, wherever they may be, so that we may be found righteous by our life and actions, and faithful to the commandments, so as to obtain eternal salvation. / When the prayers are concluded we exchange the kiss. / Then someone brings bread and a cup of water and wine mixed

together to him who presides over the brethren. He takes them and offers praise and glory to the Father of the universe, through the name of the Son and of the Holy Spirit and for a considerable time he gives thanks (in Greek: eucharistian) that we have been judged worthy of these gifts. / When he has concluded the prayers and thanksgivings, all present give voice to an acclamation by saying: 'Amen.' / When he who presides has given thanks and the people have responded, those whom we call deacons give to those present the 'eucharisted' bread, wine and water and take them to those who are absent."

181 *on their foreheads* **Revelation 14:1.**

182 *liturgy in heaven and on earth* Revelation 1:13; **2:17;** 4:4, **8;** 5:1, 6, 8; 7:3; 8:3; 12:1–6; 13:8; 14:1; 15:7; 16; **19:4;** 21:9; 22:4. Citations in Scott Hahn, *The Lamb's Supper: The Mass as Heaven on Earth* (New York: Doubleday, 1999), 66–67, 119–20.

182 *a table before me* St. Ambrose, quoted in Jean Daniélou, *The Lord of History: Reflections on the Inner Meaning of History,* trans. Nigel Abercrombie (Chicago: H. Regnery, 1958), 228–29; see Psalm 23:5.

183 *greetings of the Mass* **Ruth 2:4; 2 Corinthians 13:13.**

183 *Jesus promises to be with us* Matthew 18:20.

183 *the law of friendship* St. Thomas Aquinas, *The Summa Theologica,* trans. Fathers of the English Dominican Province, Complete English ed. (Westminster, MD: Christian Classics, 1981), III.75.1. See also U.S. Conference of Catholic Bishops, "The Real Presence of Jesus Christ in the Sacrament of the Eucharist: Basic Questions and Answers," *Origins* 31, no. 7 (June 28, 2001).

183 *On the Lord's Day* *Didache,* quoted in Aquilina, *The Mass of the Early Christians,* 70.

184 *prayers of intercession at Mass* Acts 10:3–4, 30–31; 1 Thessalonians 5:25; James 5:16; Revelation 8:3.

184 *the Gloria in Scripture* Luke 1:32; 2:13–14; 4:34; John 14:26; Revelation 15:4.

184 *songs of the Mass* Matthew 26:30; Mark 14:26; 1 Corinthians 14:25–26; Ephesians 1:14–16; 5:18–20; Philippians 2:5–11; Colossians 3:16; 2 Timothy 2:11–13.

184 *To sing* St. Augustine, quoted in Sacred Congregation for Divine Worship, *The General Instruction of the Roman Missal,* 4th ed. (March 27, 1975), no. 19, in James Socías, ed., *Daily Roman Missal* (Chicago: Scepter Publishers, 1993), xlix.

185 *praise of his glory* **Ephesians 1:11–12,** 14.

185 *Alleluia* Psalm 146–50; Revelation 19:1, 3–4, 6.

186 *Drink Christ* St. Ambrose, quoted in Raniero Cantalamessa, *The Mystery of God's Word,* trans. Alan Neame (Collegeville, MN: Liturgical Press, 1994), 10.

186 *response to God's word* Exodus 24:3; Luke 1:26–**38.**

186 *slaughtered* **Revelation 6:9.**

187 *Thy dear sanctuary* Blessed Miguel Pro, quoted in Ann Ball, *Blessed Miguel Pro: Martyr for Christ the King* (Rockford, IL: TAN Books and Publishers, 1996), 105–8.

187 *Blessed be God* **Psalm 68:35.**

187 *God passed into man* quoted in Pope John Paul II, *Apostolic Letter to Mark the Centenary of* Orientalium Dignitas *of Pope Leo XIII (Orientale Lumen)* (Boston: Pauline Books and Media, 1995), no. 6.

188 *children of the bridal chamber* St. Cyril of Jerusalem, quoted in Jean Daniélou, *The Bible and the Liturgy* (Notre Dame, IN: University of Notre Dame Press, 1956), 220.

188 *Eucharist as wedding banquet* Isaiah 54:5–8; Hosea 2:19–20; Matthew 9:14–15; 25:1–13; Mark 2:18–20; Luke 5:33–35; 14:7–14, 24; John 2:1–11.

188 *promised in marriage* **2 Corinthians 11:2.**

188 *a great mystery* **Ephesians 5:32.**

188 *Christ's Bride* St. Augustine, quoted in Claude Chavasse, *The Bride of Christ: An Enquiry into the Nuptial Element in Early Christianity* (London: Faber and Faber, 1940), 147.

188 *spiritual worship* **Romans 12:1.**

188 *Lift up your hearts* Lamentations 3:41.

189 *must be of stone* St. John Chrysostom, quoted in Jerome Gassner, *The Canon of the Mass: Its History, Theology, and Art* (St. Louis: Herder, 1949), 106; Jean Daniélou, *The Angels and Their Mission, according to the Fathers of the Church,* trans. David Heimann (Westminster, MD: Newman Press, 1957), 62.

189 *Jesus' prayer at the Last Supper* John 13–17.

189 *Holy, holy, holy* Isaiah 6:3; Revelation 4:8.

189 *Blessed is he* Psalm 118:25–26; Matthew 21:9.

190 *Fill us also* Quoted in Gassner, *The Canon of the Mass,* 25.

190 *Byzantine liturgy* Quoted in Yves Congar, *I Believe in the Holy Spirit,* trans. David Smith (New York: Crossroad Publishing, 1999), 3:231; see Luke 1:35.

191 *Passover* Exodus 12:1–23.

191 *out of Egypt* Pesahim 10.5; Oscar Cullmann and F. J. Leenhardt, *Essays on the Lord's Supper,* trans. J. G. Davies (London: Lutterworth, 1958), 40.

191 *from slavery to freedom* Quoted in Sofia Cavaletti, "The Jewish Roots of Christian Liturgy," in *The Jewish Roots of Christian Liturgy,* ed. Eugene J. Fisher (New York: Paulist Press, 1990), 17; emphasis mine. From the *Zohar:* "Whoever speaks of the

Exodus from Egypt with rejoicing and gladness will assuredly rejoice with the Shechinah (Divine Presence) in the world to come. The Holy One, blessed be he, also rejoices at this story. God, the Holy One . . . gathers around him his heavenly hosts and . . . all of them assemble together and join themselves with the Jewish people and listen to their tale of praise and happiness at the redemption brought about by God." Quoted in Eliyahu Ki Tov, *The Book of Our Heritage: The Jewish Year and Its Days of Significance,* trans. Nachman Bulman (New York: Feldheim, 1978), 2:259.

192 *the Last Supper* Matthew 26:17–19, **26–29;** Mark 14:12–16, **22–25; Luke 22:7–20;** 1 Corinthians 11:23–26.

192 *Jesus' "hour"* John 2:4, 7:30, 12:23, 13:1, 17:1.

193 *Jesus' body and blood* **John 6:35, 41, 51, 54–55, 57.**

193 *spirit and life* **John 6:52, 63,** 66, **68.**

193 *Thomas's cry* **John 20:28.**

193 *I sing the gift* Olivier Messiaen, quoted in Griffiths, *Music of Time,* 24.

194 *the Eucharist and the apostles* **Exodus 24:11;** Luke 24:30, **35;** Acts 1:4; **10:41.**

194 *the Eucharist and the early church* Acts 2:46; 5:42; 20:7, Titus 1:5–9.

195 *foretelling the Eucharist* See Luke 9:11–17 and Luke 22:19; 24:30. See also John 6:1–15.

195 *Paul transmits the Eucharistic teaching* **1 Corinthians 11:23–26** (emphasis mine); 15:3; Galatians 1:14, 18–19; 2:2, 9; cf. Roch Kereszty, "The Eucharist in the New Testament," in *The International Bible Commentary: A Catholic and Ecumenical Commentary for the Twenty-First Century,* ed. William R. Farmer and others (Collegeville, MN: Liturgical Press, 1998), 215–38; Yves Congar, *Tradition and Traditions: An Historical and a Theological Essay* (New York: Macmillan, 1967), 8–13; John Koenig, *The Feast of the World's Redemption: Eucharistic Origins and Christian Mission* (Harrisburg, PA: Trinity Press, 2000).

196 *We do not receive* St. Justin, quoted in Congar, *I Believe in the Holy Spirit,* 3:244–45.

196 *real sharing* 1 Corinthians 10:16; 11:20, 27–31; Revelation 3:20.

196 *a kingdom and priests* 1 Peter 2:4–5, 9; **Revelation 1:6;** 5:10; see also Pope John Paul II, *Post-Synodal Apostolic Exhortation on the Vocation and the Mission of the Lay Faithful in the Church and in the World (Christifideles Laici)* (December 30, 1988), no. 17, in J. Michael Miller, ed., *The Post-Synodal Apostolic Exhortations of John Paul II* (Huntington, IN: Our Sunday Visitor, 1998).

196 *priest's role* 1 Timothy 4:14; 2 Timothy 1:6.

197 *You are the angels* St. Hildegard of Bingen, quoted in Gassner, *The Canon of the Mass,* 312.

197 *mystery of the faith* **1 Timothy 3:9.**

197 *entire mystery* St. Thomas Aquinas, quoted in Gassner, *The Canon of the Mass,* 318.

198 *pure bread of Christ* St. Ignatius, quoted in Mike Aquilina, *The Fathers of the Church: An Introduction to the First Christian Teachers* (Huntington, IN: Our Sunday Visitor, 1999), 62–65.

198 *eulogy for Tarsicius* Pope Damasus I, quoted in Antonio Baruffa, *The Catacombs of St. Callixtus: History, Art, Faith* (Vatican City: Libreria Editrice Vaticana, 2000), 30–31.

198 *one bread* **1 Corinthians 10:17.**

198 *a real human body* St. Irenaeus, quoted in the *The Liturgy of the Hours: According to the Roman Rite* (New York: Catholic Book Publishing Company, 1975) 2:727–28.

199 *Blessed are the dead* **Revelation 14:12–13.**

199 *Through him* Romans 11:36.

199 *Amen* **2 Corinthians 1:19–20;** Revelation 3:14.

200 *Remember, O Lord Didache,* quoted in W. A. Jurgens, trans., *The Faith of the Early Fathers: A Source-Book of Theological and Historical Passages from the Christian Writings of the Pre-Nicene and Nicene Eras* (Collegeville, MN: Liturgical Press, 1970), 1:3.

200 *sign of peace* Matthew 5:23–25; John 14:27; **Ephesians 2:14,** 18.

200 *unites souls* St. Cyril of Jerusalem, quoted in Daniélou, *The Bible and the Liturgy,* 133.

201 *This is the Lamb* John 1:29; Revelation 19:9.

201 *Our paschal lamb* Exodus 12:22; John 19:14, 29, 36; **1 Corinthians 5:7.**

201 *covenant blood* **Exodus 24:8; 1 Corinthians 11:25.**

202 *blood of Abel* **Hebrews 12:22–24.**

202 *do not deserve to be* 1 Corinthians 11:27–30.

202 *I am not worthy* Matthew 8:8.

202 *banquet of Wisdom* Proverbs 9:1–6; Isaiah 6:6–7.

202 *to become gods* St. John of Damascus, quoted in Gassner, *The Canon of the Mass,* 314.

203 *from earthly to visible things* St. Ambrose, quoted in; Daniélou, *The Bible and the Liturgy,* 158.

203 *until he comes* **1 Corinthians 11:26.**

203 *Maranatha* **1 Corinthians 16:22; Revelation 22:20.**

203 *day of the Lord* **Joel 2:31;** Acts 2:20; 2 Timothy 1:12, 18; 4:8; 2 Peter 3:12–13.

203 *time will be no more* Revelation 10:6.

204 *I was dead* **Revelation 1:18;** 21:5.

Chapter 9: The Life of the World to Come

205 *Blessed is she* **Luke 1:45.**

206 *whatever he tells you* **John 2:5.**

206 *inseparable* St. Germanus I, quoted in *On the Dormition of Mary: Early Patristic Homilies,* trans. Brian J. Daley (Crestwood, NY: St. Vladimir's Seminary Press, 1998).

206 *flamelike choirs* Quoted in Henri de Lubac, *The Splendor of the Church,* trans. Michael Mason (San Francisco: Ignatius Press, 1999), 261–62.

206 *our formation* St. Andrew of Crete, quoted in *On the Dormition of Mary: Early Patristic Homilies,* 114; emphasis mine.

207 *Paul in Athens* Acts 17:16–34.

207 *Jesus as the gateway* John 6:54; 11:25.

207 *medicine of immortality* St. Ignatius of Antioch, quoted in *Catechism of the Catholic Church,* 2nd ed. (Vatican City: Libreria Editrice Vaticana, 1997), no. 1405.

207 *My desire* **Philippians 1:23.**

208 *then shall I be* St. Ignatius, quoted in *Catechism,* no. 1010.

208 *Lazarus and the angels* Luke 16:22.

208 *liturgy for the dead* Jean Daniélou, *The Angels and Their Mission, according to the Fathers of the Church,* trans. David Heimann (Westminster, MD: Newman Press, 1957), 95; *Catechism,* no. 335.

208 *After that the judgment* **Hebrews 9:27.**

209 *the least of these* **Matthew 25:40.**

209 *Those who do not love* **1 John 4:20.**

209 *I do not judge* **John 12:47–48.**

209 *Jesus on hell* **Matthew 7:23; 13:41**–42; **25:30, 41; Mark 9:43; Luke 16:19–31.**

210 *Hell is not to love* Georges Bernanos, *The Diary of a Country Priest,* trans. Pamela Morris (New York: Image Books, 1954), 127, 133; emphasis mine.

210 *the love and the merits* St. Bonaventure, quoted in Hans Urs von Balthasar, *Dare We Hope: "That All Men Be Saved"?* trans. David Kipp and Lothar Krauth (San Francisco: Ignatius Press, 1988), 88.

211 *all become Yours* St. Catherine of Siena, quoted in Ibid., 214–15.

211 *all to come to repentance* **2 Peter 3:9.**

211 *God our Savior* **1 Timothy 2:3–4.**

212 *St. John Bosco's story* Réginald Garrigou-Lagrange, *Life Everlasting,* trans. Patrick Cummins (Rockford, IL: TAN Books and Publishers, 1991), 42.

213 *my heart is mercy* St. Faustina Kowalska, *Diary: Divine Mercy in My Soul,* 3rd ed. (Stockbridge, MA: Marian of the Immaculate Conception, 2000), no. 1777.

213 *but not yet* St. Augustine, *Confessions* 8.7. See also Romano Guardini, *The Conversion of Augustine,* trans. Elinor Briefs (Westminster, MD: Newman Press, 1960), 231, 234.

213 *the work of conversion* John 9:4.

214 *We are clay* St. Clement I, quoted in Simon Tugwell, *Human Immortality and the Redemption of Death* (Springfield, IL: Templegate Publishers, 1990), 73–74.

214 *my Father's house* **John 14:2–3.**

214 *right hand of God* **Romans 8:34.**

214 *see him as he is* **1 John 3:2.**

214 *face to face* **1 Corinthians 13:12.**

215 *see Thee in heaven* John Henry Newman, quoted in Carol Zaleski and Philip Zaleski, eds., *The Book of Heaven: An Anthology of Writings from Ancient to Modern Times* (New York: Oxford University Press, 2000), 197–98.

215 *kingdom of immortality* St. Cyprian, quoted in Garrigou-Lagrange, *Life Everlasting,* 210. For another translation, see *Catechism,* no. 1028.

216 *parable of the talents* Matthew 25:14–30.

216 *our intercession* Revelation 8:3–5.

216 *solicitude for our regard* St. Cyprian, quoted in Garrigou-Lagrange, *Life Everlasting,* 229.

216 *doing good on earth* St. Thérèse of Lisieux, *St. Thérèse of Lisieux: Her Last Conversations,* trans. John Clarke (Washington, DC: ICS Publications, 1977), 102.

217 *the Father's throne* St. Edith Stein, *The Collected Works of Edith Stein, Sister Teresa Benedicta of the Cross, Discalced Carmelite* (Washington, DC: ICS Publications, 1986), 4:135.

218 *holiness without which* **Hebrews 12:14.**

218 *judgment and purification* Proverbs 24:16; Matthew 12:31–32; 1 Corinthians 3:10–15; 1 Peter 1:7.

218 *God as fire* Deuteronomy 4:24; Isaiah 66:15–16; **Hebrews 12:29;** Revelation 1:14; 2:18.

218 *test of fire* **1 Corinthians 3:10–15.**

219 *Our God is called* Origen, quoted in Balthasar, *Dare We Hope,* 243–44.

219 *the divine inflowing* St. Catherine of Genoa, *Fire of Love!: Understanding Purgatory* (Manchester, NH: Sophia Institute Press, 1996), 23.

219 *ordained by the apostles* St. John Chrysostom, quoted in James Gibbons, *The Faith of Our Fathers: Being a Plain Exposition and Vindication of the Church Founded by Our Lord Jesus Christ,* 11th ed. (Baltimore: John Murphy & Company, 1881), 254.

219 *holy and tremendous Victim* St. Cyril of Jerusalem, quoted in *Catechism,* no. 1371.

220 *The faithful wife* Tertullian, quoted in Gibbons, *The Faith of Our Fathers,* 252.

220 *Calemira and Hilaria* Quoted in Garrigou-Lagrange, *Life Everlasting,* 153.

220 *Judas the Maccabee's prayers* **2 Maccabees 12:38–45.**

220 *Paul on the Body of Christ* **Romans 14:7; 1 Corinthians 12:25–26; Galatians 6:2; Colossians 1:24.**

221 *translated from his pains* St. Perpetua, quoted in Yves Congar, *The Wide World My Parish: Salvation and Its Problems,* trans. Donald Attwater (Baltimore: Helicon Press, 1961), 65–66.

221 *About that day* **Mark 13:32.**

222 *redemption of our bodies* **Romans 8:23.**

223 *the hope of resurrection* St. Irenaeus, quoted in *Catechism,* no. 1000.

223 *in the end* Matthew 5:18; Mark 13:31; 1 Corinthians 7:31; 15:24, 28; **2 Peter 3:13;** Revelation 20:11; 21:1, 4–5.

223 *marriage of the church to the lamb* Revelation 19:7, 9

224 *every nation and race* Revelation 7:9–12.

224 *paradise of God* **Revelation 2:7.**

224 *tree of life* Revelation 22:2, 14, 19.

Afterword

225 *the evening of life* St. John of the Cross, *The Collected Works of St. John of the Cross,* trans. Kieran Kavanaugh and Otilio Rodriguez, rev. ed. (Washington, DC: ICS Publications, 1991), 672; *Catechism,* no. 597.

226 *passion of love* Origen, *Commentary on Ezekiel,* 6.6, in Jean-Pierre Batut, "Does the Father Suffer?" *Communio* 30 (Fall 2003): 387.

226 *whole concern of doctrine* *Catechism,* no. 25.

ABOUT THE AUTHOR

David Scott is a writer and editor with a special interest in religion and culture. In a career that spans more than two decades, he has published hundreds of articles in journals and periodicals in the United States and abroad. His essays and reporting have appeared in the Vatican newspaper, *L'Osservatore Romano,* as well as in *National Review, Commonweal, Crisis, Inside the Vatican, National Catholic Register, Washington Report on Middle East Affairs,* Beliefnet.com, and elsewhere.

His books include *A Revolution of Love: The Meaning of Mother Teresa* (Loyola Press, 2005), *Praying in the Presence of the Lord with Dorothy Day* (Our Sunday Visitor, 2002), and *Weapons of the Spirit: The Selected Writings of Father John Hugo* (Our Sunday Visitor, 1997), cowritten with Mike Aquilina.

Scott holds an advanced degree in Religion and the Bible and is formerly editor of *Our Sunday Visitor,* the nation's largest circulation independent Catholic newspaper. Currently he serves as editorial director of The St. Paul Center for Biblical Theology and as contributing editor of Godspy.com. He lives in Pittsburgh with his wife Sarah and their five children.

You can contact him at David@DavidScottWritings.com or visit his Web site www.DavidScottWritings.com.

Washington National Cathedral, Washington, DC
Entrance with *Ex Nihilo* and *Adam*, Indiana limestone

♆

ABOUT THE COVER

I believe that art has a moral responsibility, that it must pursue something higher than itself. It must be an enriching, ennobling, and vital partner in the public pursuit of civilization. It should be a majestic presence in everyday life just as it was in the past.

—Frederick Hart

Frederick Hart, creator of *Ex Nihilo*, a detail of which appears on the cover, gained international stature for his *The Creation Sculptures* on the west facade of Washington National Cathedral, which include three typana, *Ex Nihilo* (Out of Nothing), *Creation of Day*, and *Creation of Night*, and three trumeau figures, *St. Peter*, *St. Paul*, and *Adam* carved in Indiana limestone. The cathedral, located in Washington, DC, is the sixth largest Gothic cathedral in the world. The works were commissioned in 1974, and dedicated between 1978 and 1984. Hart, who died in 1999, was in 2004 awarded posthumously the National Medal of Arts, the highest honor given to an artist by the United States government. The picture at left shows *Ex Nihilo* within its architectural context. For more information on Frederick Hart and his work, visit the website www.frederickhart.com.

❖

A SPECIAL INVITATION

Would you like to help yourself and the greater Catholic community by simply talking about Catholic life and faith? Would you like to help Loyola Press improve our publications? Would you be willing to share your thoughts and opinions with us in return for rewards and prizes? If so, please consider becoming one of our ***special Loyola Press Advisors.***

Loyola Press Advisors is a unique online community of people willing to share with us their perspectives about Catholic life, spirituality, and faith. From time to time, registered advisors are invited to participate in brief online surveys and discussion groups. As a show of our gratitude for their service, we recognize advisors' time and efforts with ***gift certificates, cash, and other prizes.*** Membership is free and easy. We invite you, and readers like yourself, to join us by registering at ***www.SpiritedTalk.org***.

Your personal information gathered by SpiritedTalk.org is stored in a protected, ***confidential*** database. Your information will never be sold to or shared with another third party! And

SpiritedTalk.org is for research purposes only; at no time will we use the Web site or your membership to try to sell you anything.

Once you have registered at SpiritedTalk.org, every now and then you will be invited to participate in surveys—most take less than ten minutes to complete. Survey topics include your thoughts and ideas regarding the products and services you use in relation to Catholic life and spiritual growth. You may also have the opportunity to evaluate new Loyola Press products and services before they are released for sale. For each survey you complete, you will earn gift certificates, points, or prizes! Membership is voluntary; you may opt out at any time.

Please consider this opportunity to help Loyola Press improve our products and better serve you and the greater Catholic community. We invite you to visit ***www.SpiritedTalk.org***, take a look, and register today!

—The Loyola Press Advisory Team

Other books by the Author

A REVOLUTION OF LOVE: THE MEANING OF MOTHER TERESA

In countless photos and unforgettable television images, Mother Teresa appeared unflappable in her single-minded advocacy for the poor, but she was actually a complex figure. David Scott's discovery of the full meaning of Mother Teresa shows her to be a saint exquisitely matched for our times—a global figure who wanted to knit the world together in a "revolution of love."

ISBN 0-8294-2031-2
5 3/4" x 7 3/4" Hardcover
160 pages • $18.95

To order, call **800.621.1008** or visit **www.LoyolaBooks.org.**